MARKETS IN WEST AFRICA

Studies of markets and trade among the
Yoruba and Ibo

by

B. W. HODDER, M.A., B.Litt. (Oxon.), Ph.D. (Lond.)

Reader in Geography, Queen Mary College,
University of London

and

U. I. UKWU, B.A., (Lond.), Ph.D. (Cantab.)

Lecturer in Geography,
University of Ibadan

IBADAN UNIVERSITY PRESS
1969

© B. W. Hodder and U. I. Ukwu 1969

PRINTED BY THE CAXTON PRESS (WEST AFRICA) LIMITED IBADAN

Contents

List of Illustrations   v

Preface   vii

Introduction   ix

PART I — MARKETS IN YORUBALAND
by B. W. Hodder

1. The Yorubaland Scene   3
2. Origins of Trade and Markets   24
3. The European Impact on Trade and Markets   ...   33
4. Social and Political Elements   50
5. The Market Network Today   58
6. Economic Functions of Periodic and Daily Markets ...   71
7. The Markets of Ibadan   94

PART II — MARKETS IN IBOLAND
by U. I. Ukwu

8. The Iboland Setting   113
9. The Development of Trade and Marketing   126
10. The Marketing Landscape   152
11. Patterns of Trade   173
12. Case Studies: Rural Markets   200
13. Case Studies: Urban Centres and Market Institutions   227

Additional Bibliography   251

Index   253

List of Illustrations

		Page
1	The boundaries of Yorubaland	5
2	Natural divisions of Yorubaland	5
3	Rainfall	8
4	Yoruba-speaking groups	11
5	Distribution of population	14
6	Some elements in Yoruba agriculture	18
7	Some elements in Yoruba cottage industry	21
8	Ikereku village	39
9	Market changes in South-west Nigeria	45
10	Distribution of periodic markets in Yorubaland ...	61
11	Akinyele market ring	65
12	Commercial core of Ibadan	98
13	Ibo-speaking groups	114
14	Old Ibo trading system	131
15	Cycle of trade at Uburu and Uzuakoli	137
16	Density of beer-selling centres	162
17	Ibo marketing landscape	166
18	Official ports of evacuation	189

19 Movement to market at Umumakanu and Ugwueke
    na Ezeukwu   218

20 Distances travelled to market in selected parts of
    Iboland, 1962   223

21 Mean distances travelled to market   225

22 Umuahia-Ibeku   229

23 Onitsha   233

24 Onitsha: commercial complex   239

25 Onitsha: main market   243

PREFACE

THIS volume owes much to the Department of Geography in the University of Ibadan, which provided the time, means and opportunity to work along these lines. In the case of the Yoruba study, acknowledgement must also be made to many people in the official ministries in Nigeria and Dahomey, and more especially to the Chief Trade Officer, Ministry of Trade and Industry, Western Region of Nigeria. Thanks are also due to Professor R. J. Harrison Church for his guidance and encouragement; to Professor Mabogunje and Dr P. C. Lloyd; and to the Director of the National Archives at Ibadan for providing access to a number of relevant files. The author's greatest debt, however, is certainly to successive years of undergraduates and graduates at Ibadan, many of whom travelled with him in their own home areas in Yorubaland and on numerous occasions acted as interpreters and field assistants. These undergraduates and graduates are too numerous to mention here by name, but specific acknowledgement has occasionally been made in appropriate places.

The data presented in the Ibo study are derived mainly from field work and have been supplemented by the author's experience of a childhood and youth spent in Iboland as well as by his intuitions—for what they are worth—as an Ibo-speaking person. The author is deeply grateful for the kindness with which he was received and helped everywhere during his fieldwork. Of the school headmasters, teachers and pupils who so enthusiastically co-operated in carrying out surveys in markets and villages, four deserve special mention: Messrs C. Idima and G. Uwa of Ugwueke, and Messrs C. Olugbue and G. Ukaegbu of Umunakanu. Special thanks are also due to His Highness the Eze Aro and Council, His Highness the Amayanagbo of Bonny, Mr T. Fombe of Bonny, and to Messrs O. Iheukumere of Uzuakali and S. Okoria of Uburu for much of the historical data. For guidance and encouragement the author is indebted to his co-author whose work on Yoruba markets first stimulated his interest in the subject; to his supervisors at Cambridge, Mr A. T. Grove and Mr P. Haggett; and to Mr G. I. Jones, also of Cambridge, who has contributed from his deep knowledge of Iboland to the author's understanding of his own society. The Nigerian Archives at Ibadan and a number of Departments in the Federal and Regional Governments gave ready access to much unpublished material, while the University of Cambridge provided room, facilities and a warm and stimulating environment.

B. W. H. and U. I. U.
July, 1967.

Note: The political divisions referred to in these pages are those that existed at the time of writing, that is in the early 1960s.

Introduction

THE two studies that make up this book were originally presented in rather different forms as doctoral theses at the Universities of London and Cambridge respectively. Though both studies have been written by geographers and refer to market institutions in contiguous parts of West Africa, they illustrate widely differing approaches. While the Yoruba study is chiefly concerned with the analysis of markets as institutions, the Ibo study pays particular attention to markets as central-places and analyses the characteristics and processes of marketing and trade associated with these institutions. Nevertheless, it is hoped that it will be found convenient to have under one cover these two studies of phenomena which have only recently begun to receive serious attention in academic discussion and research.

These two studies, however, must only be regarded as preliminary attempts to analyse the market institutions of two neighbouring parts of West Africa. Apart from the limitations imposed by the large size of the areas covered, a disproportionate amount of time had necessarily to be spent simply in collecting such basic data as the names, locations and types of markets. Furthermore, the lack of any adequate comparative material elsewhere made the formulation of ideas and general hypotheses peculiarly difficult. To some extent this difficulty was lessened by concentrating attention on Yoruba markets as they interest the economic geographer, and on Ibo markets as they are relevant to central-place theory. This, however, has meant that a host of issues and problems have been ignored or at best given only cursory attention; and in this sense these studies provide only a body of basic information and a few ideas, some of them admittedly very tentative, upon which further more detailed research can now be built.

The Yoruba study, written from the point of view of an economic geographer, describes and analyses market institutions in Yorubaland and demonstrates their practical and theoretical significance for the understanding of the social and economic life of the Yoruba. The evolution of the present network of markets is examined in the light of the natural, social and economic environments of the area. Though some markets may conceivably have arisen out of the needs

of local or neighbourhood exchange, traditional markets in Yorubaland seem to be clearly associated genetically with long-distance
trading contacts. The European impact over the last one hundred
years has brought about changes, both in the network of markets
and in their operations and functions; but the traditional social and
political elements and functions of markets have by no means been
destroyed.

A distinction between periodic and daily markets in Yorubaland
is made as a necessary preliminary step in the analysis of market
types, distribution and economic functions. This distinction facilitates discussion on the relative importance of wholesale and retail
trading in the various types of markets; allows comparisons to be
drawn with the markets of Europe since medieval times; suggests
certain conclusions about the relationship between periodism and
the size of market areas; and, finally, illuminates the notion that
shops are simply the end-products of the change from periodic to
continuous marketing. It is contended, indeed, that markets in
Yorubaland illustrate a number of intermediate stages in the development of an exchange economy; and to the extent that these stages
have already occurred in many western countries, it is true that
economic behaviour among the Yoruba is both normal and predictable. Finally, the notions and ideas put forward in this study are
illustrated and their validity tested in an analysis of the markets of
Ibadan City.

The Ibo study traces the origins, distribution and development of
markets in Iboland, considers their present-day importance in the
commercial exchange system relative to other institutions, and
examines the functional areal relationships resulting from marketing
activity. Market-places, traditionally the chief institution of Ibo
trade, are declining in importance as new permanent institutions of
the central-place type grow in number, size and functions. The study
shows that the pattern of development can be explained in the context
of relations and processes—social, economic and technical—which
occur universally. Data from case studies of markets and marketing
activity make it possible to describe in some detail the spatial patterns
of the internal trade, an aspect of the economic geography of the area
on which, hitherto, very little work has been done. Analysis of areal
relationships focuses on the implications of marketing periodicity.
The conventional techniques of distinguishing nodes and delimiting
their hinterlands are shown to be inadequate, since they ignore the
temporal element in the competition between periodic centres. The
multiple orientation of rural communities to markets is demonstrated
by case studies and the usefulness of the concept of the marketing

ring is examined. An attempt is made to correlate the distances travelled to market with the various factors affecting them.

While these two studies reveal a number of important differences—not only in points of detail but also in interpretation—the similarities between Yoruba and Ibo markets are most striking; and this appears true of any comparative analysis of West African markets, in so far as this is yet possible. Above all, however, two general conclusions or comments seem to arise from the following chapters. In the first place, the importance of market studies to a full understanding of life and work in southern Nigeria and similar areas of the world can hardly be exaggerated. The analysis of the economies of tropical underdeveloped countries normally concentrates on the productive sectors or upon large-scale internal and external exchange: there is in the literature on the geography of the tropics very little, for instance, on market institutions associated with local exchange. Yet for most of the population it is through such markets that most agricultural and cottage industrial products first enter the exchange economy; and it is through these same markets that imported goods finally reach the consumer. Certainly in both Yorubaland and Iboland the market provides a vital link in the chain of distribution. Moreover, it involves very large daily movements of people and goods and fulfils an important social function for Yoruba and Ibo people. Admittedly, however, marketing processes are individually on a very small scale; and it is only their great number and frequent repetition that gives them such significance. Furthermore, they are often very difficult to describe in any general way, let alone to understand, and they are not susceptible to analysis except after laborious field investigations which may demand the application of knowledge and techniques more commonly associated with the social anthropologist than with the geographer. The principles and methods of marketing geography as it is understood and being developed in the more advanced societies appear to have limited relevance to market studies in tropical underdeveloped lands. Though undoubtedly present in some form or another in many countries, markets differ widely in form and function according to the natural, social and economic environments in which they occur. Nevertheless, to attempt any geographical analysis of economic life in these areas without reference to markets and local exchange is to ignore those institutions and processes of most immediate and vital concern to the bulk of the population. The practical uses of this kind of knowledge—to town and country planning, to plans for commercial and business expansion, and to economic development generally—are not difficult to envisage.

Secondly, it is clearly important to try to construct some general conceptual framework within which to consider the highly varied, complex phenomena of market institutions. Without some such framework, the study of markets can never develop beyond the presentation of a series of discrete descriptions. Yet to develop this framework is by no means an easy task at the present stage of geographical knowledge about market institutions in underdeveloped societies. The ideas formulated in both of the following studies suggest that all types and operations of markets in southern Nigeria, and probably throughout West Africa, may be seen as intermediate stages on a single, albeit many-stranded continuum from the most elementary to the most complicated economies. Simply and diagrammatically stated the argument can be represented as follows:

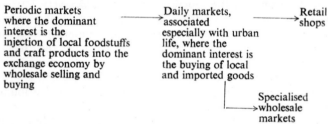

This notion, tracing the development of markets from the simplest periodic markets through to the retail shops and large specialised markets in the larger towns, appears to fit in with the facts as they are presented in both these studies, and is further strengthened by a number of analogies drawn between African markets and those of Europe from medieval times to the present day. Though in detail the institutional manifestations of the processes of distribution and exchange differ from society to society, these differences arise chiefly from the different historical, natural, economic, social, psychological and technological factors operating in one society as distinct from another. The problems, trends and end-products, however, remain fundamentally the same in all societies.

Part I
Markets in Yorubaland

Chapter One

The Yorubaland Scene

YORUBALAND, defined here as that continuous area where Yoruba-speaking peoples predominate, covers a large part of the Western Region of Nigeria but also extends northwards into the Northern Region and westwards across the international boundary into Dahomey (Fig. 1). Reaching to the sea in the south, Yorubaland is broadly contained between the Weme-Okpara rivers in the west, the line of the Moshi River in the north, the Niger River in the north-east, and the Osse River in the east (Fig. 2). Defined in this way, Yorubaland is a compact area of some 45,000 square miles, stretching inland from the coast for up to two hundred miles to just north of the 9° parallel, and at its widest point extending from east to west for about three hundred miles.

The Country

Though occasionally rising to over 2,000 feet and containing some rather striking rock domes, most of Yorubaland consists of gently undulating countryside, reaching northwards from the coast to beyond the watershed between the coastal and Niger drainage systems. None of the major rivers—either those, like the Weme, Yewa, Ogun, Oshun, Shasha, Oni and Oluwa, which flow southwards into the coastal lagoon and creek system, or those smaller streams flowing northwards and eastwards into the Niger—are very conspicuous features of the landscape, their valleys being for the most part wide and shallow. Moreover, the ubiquitous bush[1] masks much of the detail of the landscape and makes it difficult to find good vantage points from which to view any considerable part of the Yoruba countryside. Thus the nature of both the topography and the vegetation gives the visitor to the country an impression of monotony. Closer acquaintance, however, reveals that the landscape varies widely from one part of Yorubaland to another: from tropical rain forest and mangrove swamps to light tree and grass savanna; from broad lagoons and wide rivers to narrow hill streams; and from low marshy plains to impressive rock outcrops.

Four major natural divisions of the Yoruba countryside may be

3

distinguished (Fig. 2). In the extreme south the coastal lagoon and swamp forest country, extending inland for up to forty miles and rarely rising to over twenty feet above sea level, lies behind a straight or gently curving but steep sandy beach against which the Atlantic surf beats incessantly. A remarkable continuous natural waterway, lying parallel to the coast, stretches from Lake Nokué in southern Dahomey eastwards to beyond the eastern limits of Yorubaland. Only at Cotonou and Lagos, and in the creek entrances in the extreme east, are there any permanent break-throughs to the sea.[2] This whole countryside, indeed, is one of stretches of water—lagoons and strips of swamp edged with mangrove and other swamp forest vegetation—separated by sand spits covered either with light bush and scrub, or planted with trees, especially the coconut.

To the north, the coastal lagoon and swamp forest country is bounded fairly sharply by a rise to the coastal plateau which extends northwards for up to seventy-five miles from the coast. The Tertiary clays, shales and sandstones of this region, together with a narrow outcrop of Secondary, mostly Cretaceous, material in the extreme north-east, have been weathered into a softly undulating topography, rarely rising to as much as 600 feet above sea level, though in this part of Yorubaland the major rivers have in a number of places entrenched themselves quite deeply into the sedimentaries. Much of this region is covered with a thick, dry forest vegetation—now mostly secondary forest and dominated by the larger relict trees such as the iroko (*Chlorophera excelsa*) and the cottonwood (*Ceiba pentandra*)—mixed frequently with the oil palm *bush*.

These two most southerly natural divisions include the area of heaviest rainfall—normally over 75 inches a year—in the extreme south-east of the Yoruba country. Westwards and northwards, however, mean annual rainfall drops to under 50 inches. Lasting generally from late March to late October, the rains have two maximum periods separated by a short or 'little' dry period of four or five weeks during which relatively little rain falls (Fig. 3).[3] Mean monthly minimum and maximum temperatures are normally about 70° F. and 90° F. respectively, the latter dropping to about 80° F. in the July-August period. Relative humidities at midday rarely fall below 60%; so that the climate of this southerly section of Yorubaland is generally regarded as distinctly oppressive. Though the rainfall and temperature conditions are adequate for the growth of most West African crops, other environmental conditions are less favourable: on the sedimentaries of the coastal plateau, for instance, groundwater conditions are frequently poor and soils are generally considered to be acidic and impoverished, having been

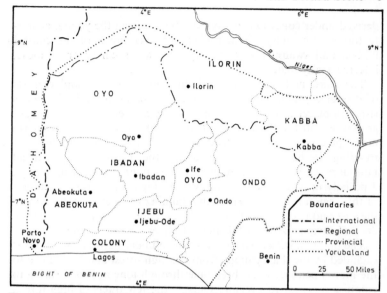

Fig. 1   *The Boundaries of Yorubaland.*

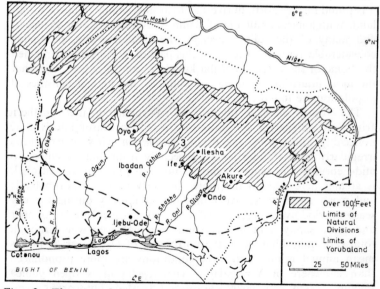

Fig. 2   *The natural divisions of Yorubaland*
1. Coastal lagoon and swamp forest country; 2. Coastal plateau; 3. Dissected Yoruba uplands; 4. The northern fringe.

derived under conditions of coarse leaching from the young, coarse-textured sedimentary parent rocks; and over much of the coastal lagoon and swamp forest country soils are swampy or of loose, infertile sandy material.

The third and largest natural division of Yorubaland consists of dissected granite and other crystalline basement complex rocks rising in places to over 2,000 feet above sea level. Though the topography is still for the most part only gently rolling, it is broken in many places by long quartzite ridges, notably in the north-south trending Ilesha hills running along the Oyo-Ondo provincial boundary, and even more frequently by striking domes or inselbergs, especially in parts of Ondo and western Oyo. The forest vegetation of this region is now preserved in a number of reserves, especially in the east and south-east of the dry forest zone, but only rarely in the derived savanna zone of this part of Nigeria and Dahomey.

The oil palm (*Elaeis guineensis*), which under natural conditions is excluded by the thick canopy from the high forest and is confined to the more open areas, has been able through long ages of clearing to colonise much of this region. Outside the few tracts of high forest, the oil palm is now almost ubiquitous, both in farmlands and in the *bush*, as far north as a line extending through Akure and Oyo, though it is found farther north in riverine areas and among tracts of woodland. With a mean annual rainfall almost everywhere over 45 inches, and many of the soils, especially the Ibadan group, possessing considerable reserves of fertility, this part of Yorubaland contained the home of the earliest Yoruba kingdom; and it is here, too, that the most flourishing farming communities and highest densities of population are found today.

The fourth natural division of Yorubaland—the northern fringe—has a sharper and more protracted dry season and is more noticeably affected by the drying *harmattan* wind which blows irregularly from the north-east, especially from mid-December to mid-February. The range of temperatures, both diurnal and seasonal, is greater here than in the more southerly parts of Yorubaland; and mean monthly relative humidities at midday during the dry season period average below 40%. Moreover, soils here are thinner and more sandy than farther south; so that even where rainfall totals are quite high, as in the north-west of Oyo (over 50 inches mean annual rainfall), drought conditions are more pronounced than elsewhere in Yorubaland. The vegetation is open guinea savanna, often with coarse grass and twisted, fire-scarred trees, and large areas are now taken up by reserves. Altogether, these northern parts of Yorubaland, more especially in the north-eastern

and north-western corners, hold few attractions for the farmer today
and constitute, in fact, part of West Africa's so-called 'Middle Belt'
of what is today sparsely populated, backward and 'difficult' country,
however well settled it may have been in the past.[4]

The People

Yorubaland is commonly thought of as a cultural region, though
as defined for the purposes of this study it refers more to a language
group than to a true cultural or racial group. It is true that there
are differences in dialect among the Yoruba,[5] but these are now
considerably less than the differences between the Yoruba language
and the languages of the neighbouring Fon, Bini (Edo), Nupe or
Igbirra peoples. Certain parts of the country—notably Ibadan, Oyo,
Ilorin and Kabba divisions—are more dominantly Yoruba-speaking
than other parts: these four divisions, for instance, had at least 90%
of their total populations returned as Yoruba-speaking in 1952.[6]
Over a still larger area—the six western provinces of the Western
Region together with Ilorin and Kabba divisions in the Northern
Region of Nigeria—the population averaged over 70% Yoruba-
speaking in 1952; and it is this larger area that Ojo distinguishes
as the 'core region' of Yorubaland, where Yoruba culture is most
typically to be found.[7]

There is for the most part a clear consensus of opinion in the
field about where Yoruba country ends and where, for instance, Fon,
Nupe, Igbirra or Bini country begins. Three reservations, however,
may be made on this point. First, there are places where the density
of population is so low as to make any decision difficult to reach;
and this is particularly true of the northern and north-western limits
where some authorities would extend the boundary to include the
Sabe Yoruba.[8] The main reason for not including them here is that
the Sabe Yoruba are physically well separated from their neighbours
by a wide belt of virtually uninhabited country running northwards
from Meko. The Sabe Yoruba, together with the other important
Yoruba enclaves to be found elsewhere in Dahomey and Togo, are
excluded from Yorubaland as it is defined here because they are not
contiguous with the main Yoruba-speaking area of West Africa.
Secondly, there is a certain amount of overlapping of peoples around
the edges of Yorubaland, especially in the north where the Yoruba
are geographically mixed with the Fulani and Nupe over considerable
areas. Finally, there are important numbers of non-Yoruba within
Yorubaland, forming an especially large group in the more cosmo-
politan Colony province (30% of the total population there in 1952).

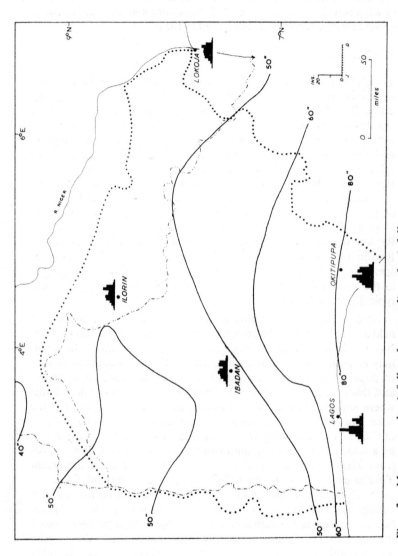

Fig. 3   *Mean annual rainfall and seasonality of rainfall.*

The most important numerically are the Ibo and Hausa in the towns, and the Igbirra and Urhobo in the rural areas.

Historically, the boundaries of Yorubaland have expanded and retracted with the growth and decline of the various Yoruba kingdoms. Oyo, the earliest and greatest of these, at its peak probably covered a greater area and encompassed more people than did Benin, Dahomey, or Ashanti.[9] Certainly its power, originating from the political and military role of the Alafin of Oyo (now Old Oyo), though subject in spiritual matters to the Oni of Ife in the traditional home of the Yoruba, at one time extended from Old Oyo westwards to beyond Ketu, Dassa, Sabe and Kitibo into what is now Dahomey and Togo, northwards to the banks of the Niger, and eastwards to the frontiers of the kingdom of Benin.[10] Yet only relatively recently can Yorubaland be considered to have extended to the sea. Oyo territory proper never reached to the sea, external trade being conducted through coastal towns like Porto Novo, Badagry and Benin, which were under Oyo influence and where there were Yoruba colonies.[11] Whatever the reason for this late expansion to the coast,[12] it does help to account for there being such meagre information about the Yoruba kingdoms compared, for instance, with the Ashanti and Dahomey kingdoms which, though also originally inland, made direct and important contacts with the coast during the eighteenth century. As a result, European traders frequenting the Slave Coast during the eighteenth and nineteenth centuries were not brought into contact with the Yoruba in the way they were with with the Ashanti and Dahomey.[13] Though Yorubaland began to be penetrated by European missionary and trading elements from the middle of the nineteenth century, it long remained a dominantly inland territory: in 1888 it was defined as an area, 'the four corners of which are and have been from time immemorial, known as Egba, Ketu, Ijebu and Oyo'.[14] After the drawing of the modern political state boundaries, and more especially after the drawing of the Anglo-French boundary in 1889, the British concept of Yorubaland retracted in the west and expanded in the east; and in 1939 Yorubaland was officially defined by the Nigerian colonial government as being composed of the four provinces of Oyo (then including the present Ibadan province), Abeokuta, Ijebu and Ondo. Their total area was just over 29,000 square miles, and their population just over $2\frac{1}{4}$ million. By now, however, Yoruba-speaking peoples were dominant along parts of the coast, especially in the area centring on Lagos; and the large groups of Yoruba in the adjacent portions of south-eastern Dahomey and the Northern Region of Nigeria were clearly consolidated as parts of the major Yoruba-speaking region of West Africa.

It has been observed that Yoruba culture is remarkably uniform for a people so numerous and inhabiting such a large area.[15] To some extent this uniformity is understandable if we accept, as most authorities now do, the idea that Yoruba culture and people originated from a common dispersal centre at Ife (Ile Ife). But this same common point of origin can also explain many of the important differences between various parts of Yorubaland today. Each kingdom of the Yoruba has presumably been the result of long historical processes of migrations and conquests. There have been several waves of migrations into what is now termed Yorubaland, each new group of people pushing the indigenes further south into the forest zone.[16] During the nineteenth century, too, and especially from the fourth decade onwards, slave-raidings and constant war-rings with Dahomey as well as between a number of rival factions within the Yoruba people themselves led to internal disintegration. When Old Oyo (Katunga) was sacked in 1837, the greater part of northern Yorubaland passed into Fulani hands. On the south-east and east, the Benin kingdom also asserted its sovereignty. From all these conflicts and pressures Yorubaland emerged during the general peace established finally by the British in 1893, not as a homogenous cultural or political unit, but as a number of independent or virtually independent kingdoms. It is against this background that the different groups and sub-groups of the Yoruba must be viewed. In a number of areas, notably Ekiti, small parochial units demonstrate fierce local patriotisms which often seem to upset completely any conception of the basic cultural uniformity of the Yoruba-speaking peoples.

Fadipe divides the Yoruba-speaking peoples of today into two main cultural groups: (i) the Ife-Ilesha-Ekiti group, which comprises the descendants of the original migrants from Ife; and (ii) the Oyo and Egba Yoruba, descendants of a second wave of migrants from the same centre.[17] It has been demonstrated that these two groups differ in a number of ways, notably in customs concerning marriage and burial, in political organisation and in dialect. For the purposes of the present study, however, this simple two-fold classification tends to mask significant differences between smaller groups; the Yoruba-speaking peoples, consequently, are here divided into a number of groups of which the Yoruba Proper, Egba, Ekiti and Ijebu are the most important numerically. Each of these groups can be further sub-divided into many sub-groups (Fig. 4).

Rivers commonly form the effective boundary between many of the groups or sub-groups; and in a number of cases provincial boundaries have some meaning as divisions between one group and another. But the general distribution of Yoruba groups shows little coincidence at all with the two major political boundaries. The international boundary between Dahomey and Nigeria cuts off numbers of the Ketu, Awori and Nago from their kinsmen in Nigeria; and the regional boundary between the Western and Northern Regions of Nigeria similarly divides the Oyo Yoruba, though further east the regional boundary is roughly coincident with the boundary between the Kabba and Ekiti Yoruba.[18] These extensions of contiguous groups across political boundaries are common enough phenomena in West Africa and here indicate something of the former extent of the Yoruba empire of Old Oyo in its hey-day.

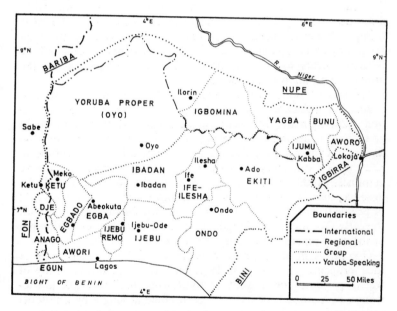

Fig. 4 Yoruba-speaking groups.
The names underlined refer to non-Yoruba peoples.

The population of Yorubaland today, based on the 1952 census figures, corrected proportionately on the basis of estimated increases,[19] is probably rather under six million, of which about five million live in the Western Region of Nigeria, about 600,000 in the Northern Region of Nigeria, and the remainder in south-eastern Dahomey. The heaviest population densities, however, are found in a crescent-shaped area stretching along both sides of an axis running from Lagos through Ibadan and Ilesha to Owo (Fig. 5). Within this crescent, densities frequently exceed 200 persons to the square mile. Any explanatory description of this pattern of population distribution within Yorubaland must be made with caution. It is possible to point out the coincidence of the heaviest population densities with the main cocoa and oil-palm belt, outside the forest reserve areas. The densely populated crescent, too, lies on the better drained and generally most fertile soils of the dry forest belt on the basement rocks where, moreover, rainfall is neither too high nor too seriously reduced in its effectiveness by the drying *harmattan* winds and sandy soils of the more northern districts. But such remarks do not establish any simple causal relationships between the natural environment, economic activities and population distribution. Many other variables must also be considered, and it is impossible at the present stage of knowledge about the historical geography of Yorubaland to assess the relative significance of all the possible factors which must have operated in bringing about the present distribution of population.

There is no doubt, for instance, that the now 'empty' parts of northern Yorubaland at one time supported a considerable population including many large settlements. Some writers, indeed, would go so far as to attribute no importance at all to natural environmental factors in explaining the distribution of population in Yorubaland, and this is particularly relevant to any explanation of the relative emptiness of the more northerly parts of the country. Lloyd, for instance, distinguishes only historical factors: the early movements of people from the dispersal centre of Ife, the fluctuating fortunes of the early Oyo and Benin kingdoms, and the disturbances arising out of the early nineteenth century tribal wars and slave-raiding.[20]

One of the most striking characteristics of the Yoruba people is their propensity for living in large nucleated settlements, many of which pre-date the advent of the European. The whole phenomenon of Yoruba urbanism has been noted at length by a number of writers,[21] and it is clearly associated with the relatively advanced social and political development of the Yoruba compared with most African peoples. But what matters most for the purposes of the present study is the fact of these extraordinary nucleated settlements. Whether or not many of these settlements can really be termed 'towns' or 'urban settlements' is largely a matter of definition and is not really relevant here, but it has been found convenient in the pages that follow to use these terms to apply to settlements with populations of 5,000 or more inhabitants.

Whatever criteria of urbanism are adopted, the Yoruba are probably the most urbanised people in Africa. By 1952 one town (Ibadan) had almost half a million inhabitants, another (Lagos) had over a quarter of a million, four others over 100,000, another six over 40,000, and twenty others had over 20,000. In their distribution, the larger towns of Yorubaland reflect the high density of population in the crescent-shaped area already referred to: indeed, the number and size of these towns is often very largely responsible for the total densities of population being so high. The only anomalous area in this respect is northern Oyo where there is a disproportionate number of towns, suggesting the former importance and subsequent depopulation of the area: in Oyo Province as a whole, 65% of the total population in 1952 lived in towns of 5,000 or more inhabitants, compared with about 50% for the whole of Yorubaland.

In their characteristics, Yoruba towns vary from area to area. In northern Yorubaland, for instance, the town is usually just an untidy agglomeration of large compounds, whereas in Ijebu the individual buildings and compounds are smaller and often arranged along streets in a crude grid pattern.[22] Moreover, there are important regional differences in the local detail of patterns of settlement—especially as between towns and rural settlements. In this connection, Lloyd has suggested the existence of at least three settlement patterns. In the Ado-Ekiti area the metropolitan town stands in the centre of a number of subordinate towns, but between the metropolitan town and subordinate towns there is a ring of hamlet-size settlements. In the Ibadan and Abeokuta areas, however, the metropolitan town is simply surrounded by hamlet settlements, there being a notable lack of any subordinate towns. Finally, in Ijebu, the metropolitan town is surrounded by village-size settlements. On the whole, these variations in settlement pattern are believed to be due chiefly to sociological and historical factors, though to the north of Ijebu-Ode physical features are clearly important in explaining the dispersed village settlement type on the sedimentary escarpment where perennial streams are infrequent.[23]

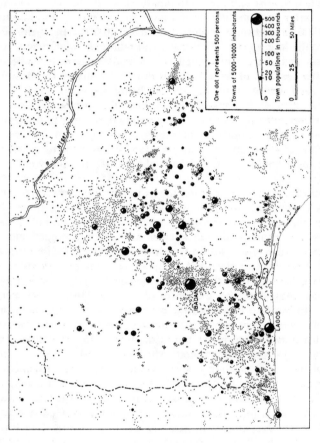

Fig. 5   The   Distribution   of   population   in   Yorubaland (after Morgan and Prothero).

Economic Life

Yorubaland is certainly one of the most prosperous of the main cultural regions of West Africa today; and the social and economic evidences of prosperity, such as schools, hospitals and roads, are more highly developed here than anywhere else in Nigeria or Dahomey. Yet the Yoruba are at the same time a predominantly agricultural people, and this is true even of the majority of those living in towns, with the exception of Lagos, the federal capital and chief port. Elsewhere, even in the largest towns like Ibadan, many people include some farming in their pattern of activities, frequently being part-time or seasonal farmers as well as dwellers in the towns. It is this very fact that limits the usefulness of functional criteria in determining urbanisation in Yorubaland. Goddard has examined this phenomenon in some detail for Oyo where he illustrates the town-farm relationships, showing a clear distinction between the *oko etile* ('near farms') and *oko egun* ('distant farms').[24] In Irun, a much smaller town in Ekiti, it is estimated that over 90% of the men and 75% of the women attend the farms extending for a radius of over seven miles from the town. Farms less than three miles from the town are attended daily from about 7 a.m. to 3 p.m., while those three to five miles away are normally visited daily from about 5.30 a.m. to 7.30 p.m. In the case of farms over five miles from the town, however, semi-permanent settlements are to be found where farmers and their families may stay for months, sending their produce to town every market day and coming into town for visits, perhaps at weekends, but more commonly only during festivals.[25]

Three separate elements can be distinguished in the agricultural economy of Yorubaland: (i) the export production economy, centering on cocoa and oil palm kernels; (ii) the local and internal exchange economy involving surplus foodstuffs, palm oil, palm wine, cotton and kola nuts; and (iii) the dominantly subsistence economy, which is most common in parts of the north-western and north-eastern corners of the country. It is with the second of these three types that this study is most directly concerned; but it is not always possible to separate one type from another, especially in any analysis of the areal distribution of economic activities. In any one area the pattern of land use is always complicated and constantly changing: 'it is impossible to generalise about the types of mixtures to be expected even within a fairly homogeneous area'.[26] Moreover, all three types have their effect on the economic life of most people in Yorubaland, probably the large majority of farmers having at least some element of each of these three types in their pattern of farming activities. Small, highly diversified farms are one of the chief characteristics of Yoruba farming.

One of the reasons for the relatively high level of social and economic development in Yorubaland today compared with other parts of Nigeria and Dahomey is undoubtedly the fact that it contains the great cocoa belt of Nigeria (Fig. 6). This is an important element in the economic geography of Yorubaland and will be shown to have important repercussions on prosperity and the pattern of spending throughout the year; but though considerable, the significance of cocoa production for market studies is indirect. The same may be said of oil-palm kernel production though not of the production of palm oil, palm wine and cotton, all of which enter directly into the local and internal exchange sectors of the economy. Of the greatest importance for the purposes of the present study, however, is the production not of external exchange or export crops, but of staple food crops such as yams, maize, cassava, rice, cocoyams, citrus fruits, beans, groundnuts, bananas, plantains, coconuts, peppers, millets, guinea corn and the kola nut.

Over most of the Yoruba country, the indigenous system of cultivation involves some form of bush fallowing: one or two year's cultivation followed by several years of rest, and involving the cutting and burning of the bush. As the density of population increases, however, the length of the fallow period tends to decline, often with very serious effects on soil fertility and crop yields. Because yams, the traditional staple crop, is so demanding of the soil and cannot yield continuously throughout the year, a common tendency is for yams to be displaced by other root crops such as cassava and cocoyams. On the whole, however, the farming calendar of the Yoruba is changing only very slowly; and the rhythm of agricultural activities throughout the farming year is important in explaining both the variations in prosperity of the population and the variations in the amount and kinds of goods entering the trading network. Like the variations from year to year, the rhythm of agricultural activities throughout the year is often determined by the incidence of rainfall, and both the seasonal and annual rhythms deeply affect the life and economic prosperity of the people.

The non-agricultural sector of the Yoruba economy is relatively advanced by African standards, and this is especially true of cotton spinning, weaving, indigo dyeing, basketry, pottery, calabash and leather working (Fig. 7). The Yoruba, in fact, have 'one of the most diversified economies of West Africa; and even before the arrival of the British their craft industries had reached a high level'.[27] In 1823 Adams noted the well developed local industries of Porto Novo, especially in cotton and iron workings,[28] and commented on the greater development of such industries among the Yoruba (Hio or Oyo) people to whose king the Porto Novans were then paying tribute: 'the Hios are a fine race of people and are well skilled both in agriculture and in manufacturing articles for domestic purposes . . . The cloth manufactured in Hio is superior, both for variety of pattern, colour and dimensions, to any made in the neighbouring states; and some of the articles wrought by them in iron exhibit much skill and ingenuity'.[29] In every traditional Yoruba settlement there was and to some extent still is a specialisation of industries by compounds, there being, for instance, *ile onisasa* ('woodworking compound') or *ile iporin* ('iron-smelting compound').

Yorubaland, especially in Lagos and Ibadan, also has by West African standards a highly developed network of factory industries: food-processing, drink, textiles, cement and furniture among many others. But on the whole the bulk of manufactured goods entering into local and internal exchange in Yorubaland are the products of local craft industries or have been imported from abroad.

Both in agriculture and in the craft industries, the division of labour between the sexes is very marked. Yoruba women here play very little part in the actual work on a farm—though they do take part in some of the harvesting operations—but they are dominant in certain craft industries, such as dyeing, pottery and vertical loom weaving. They also engage in a number of food-processing industries, such as the making of palm oil and the preparation of *gari* from cassava. Much more of a Yoruba woman's time, however, is normally devoted to trading, and Yoruba women traders are to be found in markets all over West Africa. Although a few goods and manufactures are dealt with by men, the greater part of the petty trading in Yoruba markets is in the hands of women.

* * *

Local and internal exchange in Yorubaland to a large extent reflects the variety of environments—natural, social and economic— found within this considerable portion of the Guinea coastlands. Though traditionally the Yoruba compound and, still more so, the village community as a whole is largely self-sufficient in food supplies and most other household needs, probably few, if any, compounds or village units were ever completely so; and certainly nowadays self-sufficiency in this sense is unknown. The exchange of goods on a very local scale and internal exchange between different parts of Yorubaland have for long been characteristic features of the economy.

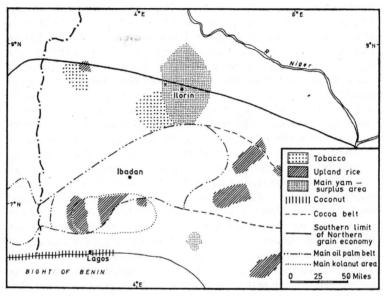

Fig. 6   Some elements in Yoruba agriculture.

As a corollary to the movement of goods from one part of Yoruba country to another there is some considerable local specialisation of production—both in crops and in craft industries. Some divisions, such as Ibadan, Oshun, Ondo, Ife, Egbado, Ilesha and parts of Ijebu and Oyo, have specialised mainly in the production of cocoa; and in many parts of these areas, as well as in the many large towns, the population must increasingly depend on the production of surplus food in other areas. A number of surplus food-producing areas can be distinguished: Ilorin (for beans), Okitipupa and Ijebu (for *gari* and palm oil), Ekiti and Oyo (for yams and maize), Badagry and Epe (for fresh and dried fish), and Ilorin and Yagba districts (for yams). For instance, in Ilorin and Kabba provinces respectively, it was officially estimated in 1957 that after allowing for seed require-ments, food consumption, losses and wastage, 22,000 and 62,000 tons of yams were still left as surpluses for export.[30] Similarly, certain areas have become known for certain types of craft industries, such as the weaving of Ekiti and south-eastern Ilorin (vertical loom weaving by women), and of Ondo, Oshogbo, Ibadan, Oyo, Iseyin and Ilorin (horizontal loom weaving by men); the pottery of Ekiti, Akoko, Ondo, Oyo and Ilorin; the mats of Ekiti and south-western Yorubaland; the leather and calabash work of Oyo; and the dyeing of Oshogbo, southern Ilorin, Ondo, Ogbomosho, Oyo, Shaki and Iseyin.

Apart from this movement of goods and local specialisation of production within Yorubaland, there is also a considerable movement of goods between Yorubaland and other parts of Nigeria and Dahomey. Thus while the Western Region supplies the Northern and Eastern Regions with palm oil, *gari*, kola nut, and fresh fruits, it depends on these same regions, particularly on the Northern Region, for maize, rice, beans, onions, cattle and dried fish to supplement those produced at home.[31]

This specialisation of production between different parts of Yorubaland and neighbouring regions inevitably calls for, and in turn, stimulates the growth of an extensive system of trading and markets; and it is more especially within this context of local and internal exchange of commodities that the following chapters discuss the market institutions of Yorubaland.

The word *market* has of course a great number of meanings, referring to many things and ideas; and the same can be said of the Yoruba word *ǫja*. The sense in which *market* or *ǫja* is used here, however, is strictly that of an institutionalised activity occurring at a definite place and involving the meeting of people there at a particular time. A market in this sense has been defined as 'an authorised public concourse of buyers and sellers of commodities meeting at a place more or less strictly limited or defined, at an appointed time'.[32] This excludes those innumerable small places of *ad hoc* trading involving a handful of women meeting at street corners, in front of compounds, or on building sites. More important still, this definition also excludes the theoretical concept of a market as, for instance, 'the whole of any region in which buyers and sellers are in such free intercourse with one another that the prices of the same goods tend to equality easily and quickly'.[33] This study, indeed, does not include any discussion of 'markets' in the wider, more purely economic or theoretical sense; nor does it include any examination of such phenomena as the various Marketing Boards.

Yoruba markets, as defined here, are clearly important elements of the social and economic landscape; and it is impossible to travel far within Yoruba country without coming across a gathering of perhaps three to four thousand women engaged in the buying and selling of goods from local districts, from other parts of Yorubaland, from other parts of Nigeria and Dahomey, and from overseas. Markets are thus vital links in the distributive chain. Yet their characteristics and functions embrace far more than this simple statement would suggest. Markets in Yorubaland are very much more than economic institutions; and their analysis involves the consideration of a large number of non-economic variables. The next chapter indicates the genesis of this complexity by examining the various origins of markets and the economic-historical context within which they have developed.

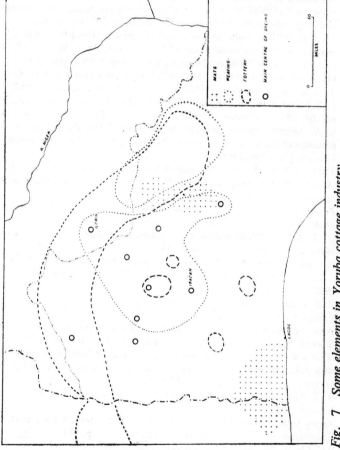

Fig. 7 *Some elements in Yoruba cottage industry.*

NOTES

1. The term *bush* locally connotes anything from low scrub to secondary forest growth.
2. On the characteristics of the western sector of this sand spit country see J. C. Pugh, 'The Porto Novo - Badagry sand ridge complex', *Research Notes (Ibadan)*, No. 3, 1953, pp. 3-14.
3. As Ireland points out, the 'little dry' season is most marked in the extreme south-west of Nigeria. It decreases in intensity eastwards and northwards and may conveniently be bounded to the east by 5°E. longitude and to the north by 9°N. latitude. In some form or another, then, the 'little dry' is characteristic of the western half of Yorubaland. See A. W. Ireland, 'The little-dry season of southern Nigeria', *N.G.J.*, Vol. 5, 1962, pp. 7-20.
4. On the whole question of the 'Middle Belt' see H. Bramner and H. O. Walker, 'Climatic definition of the middle belt', appendix to *Document L* (60), 127, *CCTA/CSA*, 1960; R. A. Pullan, 'The concept of the middle belt in Nigeria— an attempt at a climatic definition', *N.G.J.*, Vol. 5, 1962, pp. 39-52; and S. A. Agboola, 'Some geographical influences upon the population and economy of the middle belt west of the Niger'. M.A. Thesis, University of London, 1962 (unpublished).
5. The term 'Yoruba' is used throughout these pages as being synonymous with 'Yoruba-speaking peoples'. See C. D. Forde, *The Yoruba-speaking peoples of south-western Nigeria*. London, 1951.
6. *Population census of the Western Region of Nigeria*, 1952; *Population census of the Northern Region of Nigeria*, 1952.
7. G. J. A. Ojo, 'Yoruba culture: a geographical analysis.' Ph.D. Thesis, National University of Ireland, Dublin, 1963 (unpublished), p. 31.
8. See, for instance, A. L. Mabogunje, *Yoruba towns*, Ibadan, 1962, Fig. 2.
9. J. D. Fage, *An introduction to the history of West Africa*. Cambridge, 1959 (2nd edition), p. 88.
10. Ibid., p. 88; also Mabogunje, op. cit., p. 5.
11. Fage, op. cit., p. 90.
12. According to a number of writers, the sea was traditionally *fetish* to the Yoruba. See, for instance, Dalzel's comments: 'the Fetische of the Eyeos (Oyos) was the sea . . . and themselves, and their king, were threatened with death, by the priests, if they ever dared to look on it'. A. Dalzel, *The history of Dahomey*. London, 1793, p. 15.
13. A. B. Ellis, *The Yoruba-speaking peoples of the slave coast of West Africa*. London, 1894, p. 8.
14. Treaty signed between the Alafin of Oyo and Britain, 23 July, 1888. See S. Johnson, *The history of the Yorubas*. Lagos, 1937, p. 574
15. P.C. Lloyd, *Yoruba land law*. London, 1962, p. 30.
16. Ibid., p. 31.
17. N. A. Fadipe, 'The sociology of the Yoruba.' Ph.D. Thesis, University of London, 1939 (unpublished).
18. J. R. V. Prescott, 'Nigeria's regional boundary problems', *G.R.*, Vol. 49, 1959, p. 493.

19. It was hoped to be able to use at least some of the results of the more recent census material, but this has yet to be published.
20. Lloyd, op. cit., p. 51.
21. See, for instance, P. C. Lloyd, 'The Yoruba town today'., *Sociological Review*, new series, Vol. 7, 1959, pp. 45-63; also Mabogunje, op. cit.
22. Lloyd, op. cit. (1962), p. 56.
23. Ibid., pp. 54-58.
24. S. Goddard, 'Town-farm relationships in Yorubaland: A case study from Oyo', *Africa*, Vol. 35, 1965, pp. 1 - 14.
25. Information kindly supplied in the field by Mr M. A. Ogunyesi.
26. P. Rees, 'The agricultural census of Nigeria, 1950', *W.A.I.S.E.R. Conference Proceedings*. Ibadan, 1953, p. 148.
27. P. C. Lloyd, 'Craft organisation in Yoruba towns', *Africa*, Vol. 23, 1953, p. 30
28. Captain John Adams, *Remarks on the country extending from Cape Palmas to the River Congo*. London, 1823, pp. 80-81.
29. Ibid., p. 94.
30. Agboola, op. cit., p. 98.
31. A. Adedeji, *A survey of highway development in the Western Region of Nigeria*. Ibadan, 1960, pp. 7-9.
32. *Final Report, U.K. Commission on Market Rights and Tolls*. London, H.M.S.O., 1889, p. 2.
33. A. Marshall, *Principles of economics*. London, 1930 (8th Edition), pp. 324-325.

CHAPTER TWO

Origins of Trade and Markets

MARKETS were important institutions in Yorubaland well before the arrival of the European administrations, so that the precise origin of many indigenous markets can only be traced, if at all, through oral evidence. The earliest literary material is provided by the first European observers in Yoruba country—notably Clapperton, Lander and the first Christian missionaries.[1] From these and other contemporary accounts it is possible to reconstruct something of the background to trade and markets in the area during the first half of the nineteenth century.

Insecurity

The general conditions of physical insecurity which prevailed in Yorubaland until well into the latter half of the nineteenth century were responsible for a number of market characteristics, many of which have continued through to the present day. The predominance of women traders in Yoruba markets—already traditional by the early nineteenth century—probably resulted originally from the need to adapt marketing and trading to the dangers of movement through the countryside. Even during the earliest tribal wars, the mutual need to hold markets seems normally to have been recognised sufficiently to allow transactions to be safely carried out on neutral territory: the women would go to the market, the opposing warriors remaining at a distance on either side. It has also been suggested that the predominance of women in Yoruba markets may date back to times when it was unsafe for men to move away from their farms while women enjoyed relative immunity from attacks.[2] The earliest European observers frequently commented on this predominance of women in markets: at Egga (Egua), 'the principal market-town in this part of Africa', observed Lander, for instance, 'women were the chief if not the only traders'.[3] On the other hand, some of the early travellers noted significant numbers of men in the markets: in 1847, Townsend described 'parties of women going to buy farm produce, and parties of men and boys bringing it to sell'.[4] It is probable, in fact, that local temporary easings of the general picture of insecurity

24

allowed movements of a much wider and more general character than were normally possible.

Within the market site, the generally insecure conditions throughout the countryside were reflected in the seating of women. Women sat in sections, by tribal or by lineage groups, with their backs to the path leading from the market place to their own home territory. In this way no woman would find it necessary to traverse the market place in order to flee homewards in case of a disturbance. This phenomenon has been noted in other parts of West Africa,[5] and in origin was undoubtedly a logical adaptation to the need for security.

Insecurity was also reflected in the exact location of many early markets, a number of which were outside settlements. Clearly, neutral ground between warring factions was unlikely to be within a town; and should a fight break out in a market the damage was certain to be less in farm or bush country than in compound land. Even where a market was held in a town, its precise location still reflected the need for security. Many of the Yoruba towns were walled and markets were usually held just outside the gates: at Ketu, for instance, the *Oja'nla* (Great Market) was held just outside the Idena gate to prevent enemies disguised as traders from entering the town.[6] Finally, insecurity often explains why the earliest markets were so often associated with the names of certain men: strong, capable men of influence who could keep the peace, ensure safe conduct to travellers, and protect those who came to trade.

Traditional markets, then, reflected in a number of ways certain adaptations to the prevailing conditions of insecurity within the Yoruba country. Given the need for exchange of products, even on the most local scale, market places, where reciprocal arrangements to maintain the peace between warring factions could be most easily effected, were vitally important institutions. Recognised market places made local exchange possible and, moreover, encouraged and facilitated the perpetuation of social relationships and public order. In this sense, market institutions evolved as necessary elements in a countryside torn by strife.

Slaving and Legitimate Trade

Slaving was a notable feature of some markets until well into the nineteenth century; and Lander found that 'the commerce of this country is almost entirely confined to slaves'.[7] At Jannah (Ijana) market, he found the people preparing to go on a slaving expedition because a brig had recently arrived at Badagry for slaves.[8] Farther north the travellers came across a caravan of slaves where 'women bore burdens on their heads that would tire a mule, and children not more than 5 or 6 years old trudged after them, with loads that would give a full-grown person in Europe the brain fever'.[9]

On the other hand, there was already a great deal of legitimate trading taking place by the very early nineteenth century, and it is probable that slaving and legitimate trade had existed side by side for a very long time. Contemporary accounts suggest that the beginnings of an exchange economy in Yoruba country date back at least to several decades before European contacts. In Porto Novo at the end of the eighteenth century, Adams found an abundance of European goods—cloth, tobacco, iron, corals, cowries and beads alongside African cloth from Oyo and Ijebu, hides and potash, soap and livestock'.[10] Clapperton commented that 'a considerable quantity of cloth is made, and bartered with the people of the coast for rum, tobacco, European cloth, and other articles'.[11] At Katunga (Old Oyo), moreover, there was noted an immense range of goods—both local and imported: 'three or four different kinds of corn; beans, peas and vegetables in abundance; the micadenia butter; ground or guinea nuts, country cotton cloths, indigo, red clay, salt and different varieties of pepper; besides *trona*, snuff, tobacco, barbs, hooks and needles, the latter of the rudest native manufacture. There were, also, finger rings of tin and lead; iron bracelets and armlets; old shells, old bones, and other venerable things, which European antiquaries would gaze on with rapture; besides native soap, little cakes of cheese and butter; or English common blue plate, a great variety of beads, both of native and European manufacture, among the former of which we recognised the famous Aggra bead, which at Cape Castle, Accra and other places, is sold for its weight in gold, and which has vainly been attempted to be imitated by the Italians and our countrymen. Provisions also were offered for sale in abundance; and besides beef and mutton, which was made up into little round balls, weighing about an ounce and three-quarters each, and presented not the most delicate or tempting appearance, we observed an immense quantity of rats, mice, and lizards, dressed and un-dressed, all having their skins on, and arranged in rows'.[12] Similarly, Lander and Clapperton met 'many hundreds of people of both sexes and all ages, with vast quantities of bullocks, sheep and goats, together with fowls and pigeons, which were carried on the head in neat wicker baskets. Several of the travellers were loaded with packages of country cloth, and indigo in large round balls. They are all slaves and were proceeding to the coast, from the interior, to sell the goods and animals under their charge'.[13] There was also exchange with the areas north of Yorubaland: at Wow, for instance, the market was 'supplied abundantly with Indian corn, palm oil . . . together with *trona* and other articles brought thither from the borders of the desert of Zaarha, through the medium of the wandering Arabs'.[14]

This coexistence of slaving and legitimate trade was logical enough in a situation where headloading was virtually the only means of transporting goods on land. Even in the drier, more open northern parts of Yorubaland, animals were only occasionally used for carrying goods; at Jaguta, for instance, Lander met a party of traders with asses carrying *trona* for the Gonja markets: 'these asses were the first beasts we had observed employed in carrying burdens, for hitherto people of both sexes and of all ages, especially women and female children, have performed these laborious duties'.[15] Taxes were usually imposed on those travelling along the roads: 'turnpikes are as common from Badagry to this place (Bidjie) as on any public road in England. Instead of horses, carriages, etc., people carrying burdens alone are taxed.'[16] The only exceptions to this were the wives of the various kings. Thus the king of Katunga's ladies 'arrived here lately with loads of *trona* and country cloth, which they barter for salt, and various articles of European manufacture, particularly beads; with these they return home, and expose them for sale in the market, and afterwards the profits are taken to their husbands. These royal ladies are distinguished from their countrywomen only by a peculiar species of cloth, which is wrapped round their goods, and which no one dares to imitate, on pain of perpetual slavery. This severe punishment is often inflicted, for, as the king's wives pay no tribute or turnpike dues whatever, and must besides be entertained by the chiefs of every town through which they pass, strong inducements are offered for others to attempt to deceive by using forbidden cloth'.[17]

Markets and Long-Distance Trade

Slaving and legitimate trade clearly showed in their characteristics a strong association with long distance trade; and trading between towns, often over very great distances, was a notable feature of the Yoruba country well before the arrival of the European administration.

In so far as it is possible to reconstruct the distribution of markets in the countryside through which the early European observers passed, it is clear that they were often on or very near the chief trade routes of the day. These trade routes commonly followed junction zones, there being, for instance, a line of old market towns—

from Ilaro through Eruwa and Ogbomosho and Ilorin—lying along the contact zone between forest and savanna where the products of each could be most easily exchanged. Similarly, the markets along the coastal lagoons and creeks were important contact points between agriculturalists and fishermen. Other markets were found at the junction of different peoples: Ketu market, for instance, was regarded as an important link between the Yoruba and Dahomey peoples; Ajara market depended for its development upon its position at the edge of the Porto Novo kingdom, this being the farthest that traders could safely go from the capital; Iperu market was a contact point between the Egba and Ijebu groups of the Yoruba; and Mamu market was traditionally a frontier market between the Ijebu and Ibadan Yoruba. Many long-distance trade routes, too, followed the dominantly north-south trends of the watersheds of the main rivers, while the rivers themselves were often important channels of trade along which important markets like Egua and Mokoloki were located.

Along the land trade routes passed long-distance caravans, most of them connecting the Niger crossings at Kome (Wonjerque) and Rabba (near Jebba) with the coast at Badagry and Porto Novo. The drier northern, western and south-western parts of Yorubaland were found to be comparatively open, and there were certainly fewer obstructions in the way of caravan routes to the coast at Badagry, Porto Novo and Whydah than there were through the wider belt of forest farther to the east. All these routes passed through Yoruba country and normally passed either through Ilorin or Old Oyo (Katunga), but they were by no means always well defined or permanent. In fact, the crossing of the Yoruba country, with its bush and forest inhabited by warring groups, was a hazardous, often dangerous undertaking, and trade 'tended to trickle unobtrusively and furtively along ill-defined tracks'.[18] Thus traders and merchants were forced by physical insecurity to gather together in caravans where they could give each other support in case of attack. In the days before the arrival of the European, the caravans helped to distribute European and other goods—salt, ostrich feathers and glass beads—from the coast to the interior and made possible the reciprocal movement of slaves, gold, ebony and leopard skins from the interior to the coastal traders. As with markets, physical insecurity helps to explain both the existence and some of the characteristics of long-distance trade. The routes along which these caravans passed acted as channels not only of trade but also of culture; and the markets on these highways played a not unimportant role in disseminating and diffusing the cultural influences which accompanied trade. Islam, for instance, penetrated along these trade routes and spread from market centres into different parts of the Yoruba country.

The nature of the relationship between markets and caravans, then, lay in the way in which markets occurred on long-distance trading or caravan routes between the coast and the north. An important origin of many Yoruba markets, indeed, was that of a resting place: the Sapon market at Abeokuta, for instance, took its name (*Se apon li ore*—'do favours to bachelors') from its origin as a place where hospitality—prepared food, soap, native beverages and shelter—could be offered to passing groups of traders.[19] If such a resting place became popular, a market place into which farmers brought their wares for sale soon sprang up; weekly fairs were held; market sheds were built all over the place and it became a sort of 'caravanserai or sleeping place for travellers . . . If the site be on a caravan route, so much the better; the wives of the farmers ever ready to provide refreshments for wearied travellers render the spot in time a recognised halting place'.[20] One of the best known caravanserai in the Egba country was Atadi, a few miles north of Abeokuta. On one occasion in 1856 there was said to gather there a caravan some 4,000 strong; and such was its effect in the village that prices of food soared high during the two days the caravan was there.[21]

These market centres on caravan routes in turn stimulated food production in their immediate neighbourhood: thus Lander describes Bumbum as 'a great thoroughfare for companies of merchants trading from Hausa, Borgoo and other countries to Gonja; and consequently a vast quantity of land is cultivated in its vicinity with corn and yams, to supply them with provisions'.[22]

Both from their commodity structure, which included European and other non-Yoruba goods as well as local produce, and from their location on long-distance trade routes, all the traditional markets described by the early travellers in Yoruba country were clearly related genetically to long-distance trading. Many of these markets, in fact, must have grown out of the demands of this kind of trade.

This is an important point. For orthodox thinking about the rise of markets and trading commonly starts from the individual's propensity to barter—perhaps involving 'silent barter', deduces from this the necessity for local markets as well as division of labour, and infers, finally, the necessity of trade, eventually of foreign trade, including even long-distance trade.[23] But in the light of what is known about traditional markets in Yorubaland as they existed in the early nineteenth century, the sequence of this argument must in many cases be reversed. For many Yoruba markets the true starting point was not 'local trade', but 'long-distance trade'—the result of division of labour and the geographical location of goods. This long-distance trade engendered markets—institutions involving acts of barter and of buying and selling—thus eventually, though by no means necessarily, offering to some individuals an occasion to indulge in their propensity for haggling and bargaining. This, in brief, seems to be the true sequence of events for many traditional markets in Yorubaland, and to this extent supports the argument put forward by Polanyi and others.[24]

This notion is also relevant to the suggestion that Yoruba markets are not indigenous, but introduced phenomena. According to Hambly, for instance, 'the large market places of Nigeria are not a typical Negro trait; they resemble the large bazaars of North African and Egyptian towns. There is nothing in the general style and organisation of the extensive markets at Ibadan and Ilorin to justify their inclusion with the unpretentious trade of typical Negroes ... They are probably derived from a northern Arab culture'.[25] What Hambly means exactly by 'derived' is not clear; but there is no doubt that in their physical origin Yoruba markets are wholly indigenous phenomena. In their location, structure and general characteristics, however, Yoruba markets are admittedly far from parochial institutions; and this fact fits in well with the sequence of events from long-distance trading to the growth of markets outlined here.

On the other hand, to deny completely the possibility of markets arising out of the demands of purely local exchange might seem to be carrying the argument too far.[26] It is unlikely that the sequence of events was in all cases and at all times the same. It must be emphasised, first, that European observers saw the Yoruba country-side chiefly as travellers along the major long-distance trade routes, and so in most cases were unable to comment at first hand on markets lying away from these routes. Lack of evidence to show the origin of markets in the needs of local or neighbourhood exchange is to be expected and cannot reasonably be taken to mean that no markets originated in this way.

In this respect it is tempting to compare Yoruba markets with the markets of medieval Europe, where a distinction could be made between fairs and markets. It can perhaps be argued that many Yoruba markets are *in origin* more like fairs, in the medieval sense of the term. Fairs were almost exclusively associated with long-distance trading, and supplied goods from distant sources, whereas

markets were for a much more restricted local exchange. As one
oft-quoted thirteenth century writer put it, 'fairs deal with the large
things ... and to them come men from afar. Markets are for lesser
things, the daily necessities of life ... and only people from near at
hand come'.[27] Both in size and function, fairs differed from markets:
fairs were larger, served a much wider population, and dealt in goods
from a much larger area, including goods—especially luxury goods—
from other countries.

Yet this distinction is perhaps too sharp to be applied with any
real validity to Yorubaland today. Even the large markets on the
great trade routes passing through Yorubaland were described by
the early travellers as being 'weekly' or 'twice-weekly'. They were
certainly never as infrequent as the medieval fairs. They did not
function solely or even primarily as places where, at long intervals,
foreign goods could be obtained. Though European and other non-
Yoruba goods were to be found in these early nineteenth century
markets, the products of local farming and craft industries were
always well in evidence. At no time and in no case is there any
suggestion that markets did not show the same mixture of commodities from far and near that is so striking a feature of all Yoruba
markets today.

It seems, perhaps, more reasonable to postulate the existence of,
on the one hand, those markets whose origin lay chiefly in their
location on long-distance trading routes, and, on the other, those
markets whose origin lay in the demands of local neighbourhood
food and craft exchange. This whole question has been examined
at some length elsewhere, and it is pointed out that there is as yet
no evidence to support the notion that markets in Yorubaland could
have arisen out of the needs of local exchange.[28] Yet even accepting
the possibility of two different market origins in this way, the markets
to which they gave rise have certainly never shown any difference,
whether in size, commodity structure or organisation.

NOTES

1. H. Clapperton and R. Lander, *Journal of a second expedition into the interior of Africa from the Bight of Benin to Soccattoo*. London, 1829; R. Lander, *Records of Clapperton's last expedition to Africa*. London, 1830, 2 volumes; R. Lander and J. Lander, *Journal of an expedition to explore the course and termination of the Niger*. London, 1832, 3 volumes. Apart from the invaluable

records to be found in the *Church Missionary Intelligencer, Proceedings of the Church Missionary Society*, and *Church Missionary Gleaner*, see S. Tucker, *Abeokuta, or sunrise within the tropics*. London, 1853; T. J. Bowen, *Adventures and missionary labours in several countries in the interior of Africa*. Charleston, 1857; and G. Townsend, *Memoir of the Reverend Henry Townsend*. London, 1887.

2. F. J. Pedler, *Economic geography of West Africa*. London, 1955, p. 139
3. R. Lander and J. Lander, op. cit., Vol. 1, p. 108.
4. H. Townsend, *Church Missionary Society, Journals*, June, 1856, (CA2/085).
5. Bohannan has noted this, for instance, among the Tiv, in his unpublished manuscript: *The Tiv market place*, 1961.
6. G. Parrinder, *The story of Ketu*. Ibadan, 1956, p. 17.
7. Clapperton and Lander, op. cit. p. 57.
8. Ibid., p. 13.
9. R. Lander and J. Lander, op. cit., Vol. 1, p. 123.
10. Adams, op. cit., p. 77.
11. Clapperton and Lander, op. cit., p. 57.
12. R. Lander and J. Lander, op. cit., Vol. 1, pp. 179-180.
13. Ibid. pp. 112-113.
14. Ibid., p. 59.
15. Ibid., p. 153.
16. Ibid., p. 68.
17. Ibid., p. 110.
18. E. W. Bovill, *Caravans of the old Sahara*. London, 1933, p. 254.
19. A. Ajisafe, *History of Abeokuta*. Lagos, 1924, p. 69.
20. Johnson, op. cit., pp. 90-91.
21. Townsend, op. cit., p. 92.
22. R. Lander, and J. Lander, op. cit., Vol. 1, p. 153.
23. Bohannan, op. cit., p. 157.
24. K. Polanyi, C. W. Arensberg and H. W. Pearson, (eds.), *Trade and market in the early empires*. Glencoe 1957. See also N. Pirenne, *Medieval cities*. Princeton, 1925, p. 142: 'Medieval commerce developed from the beginning under the influence not of local, but of export trade'; and M. Weber, *General economic history* (trans. F. H. Knight). London, 1930, p. 195, who contends that trade does not arise within a community; it is an external affair involving different communities.
25. W. D. Hambly, *Culture areas of Nigeria*. Chicago, 1935, p. 462.
26. For a critical discussion of this point see G. E. N. De Ste. Croix, *The Economic History Review*, second series, Vol. 12, No. 3, 1960, pp. 510-511. Though Polanyi's work is important in that it emphasises the significance of long-distance trading in the origin of many markets, this does not mean (argues De Croix) that local food exchange markets could not exist independently of these streams of long-distance trade.
27. Humbert de Romans (1194-1277) quoted in M. W. Thomas, *English economic history*. London, 1957, p. 64.
28. B. W. Hodder, 'Some comments on the origins of traditional markets in Africa south of the Sahara', *T. I. B. G.*, 1965, pp. 47-59.

CHAPTER THREE

The European Impact on Trade and Markets

IT is possible to distinguish five main ways in which the penetration of the European colonial administration into Yorubaland during the latter half of the nineteenth century affected trade and markets: (i) by establishing peaceful conditions; (ii) by building roads and railways; (iii) by encouraging the growth of European trading firms; (iv) by introducing a number of new crops and the whole concept of cash cropping on a large scale; and (v) by introducing a money economy. Clearly these forces varied in their timing and precise effects in different parts of Yorubaland as European influence or control extended inland from the coast, reaching into the northern, north-eastern, and north-western corners of the Yoruba country by the end of the century.

The establishing of peaceful conditions

It has already been noted that caravans passing along the trade routes of Yorubaland had always been liable to attack and normally required armed protection. A trader would always find it dangerous to travel without protection beyond those areas in which he or she had kinsmen or special friends. In the period before peaceful conditions were secured, then, both the extent of trading and the movement of people were restricted by physical insecurity.

The establishment of this general peace, admittedly, was by no means immediate or complete. Even as late as 1897 Johnson could write that 'there is probably no other country on this earth more torn and wasted by internal dissensions, tribal jealousies and fratricidal feuds, a state of things which unhappily continues up to the present time'.[1] Moreover, it is clear that the pre-British rulers had been well aware of the importance of peaceful and orderly conditions to the development of trade between the peoples belonging to different groups and sub-groups of the Yoruba. Thus the Apomu war, which started the final breakdown of the paramountcy of the Alafin of Oyo over the various tribes of Yorubaland, is said to have had as an indirect cause an order issued by the Alafin to the authorities of Apomu to maintain the peace among the Egba, Ife, Ijebu,

33

Oyo and Ijesha who frequented Apomu markets.[2] Indeed, the
subsequent general upheaval among the Yoruba kingdoms was
partly the result of rival attempts—by the Egba, Ibadan and Ijebu
particularly—to control trade routes connecting Lagos and the
lagoon areas with the hinterlands.

During the latter part of the nineteenth century, however,
conditions were certainly more stable and peaceful than they had
been for some time, and this allowed easier movements of people
and an increase in trading activities. The most important migration
of people was southwards, perpetuating—though now for different
reasons—the southwards movement of people initiated earlier in the
century by the Fulani invasions from the north. The early history
of the Yoruba was very largely that of the northern Oyo kingdom,
the other groups and sub-groups of the Yoruba being then only
small and insignificant peripheral units. Clapperton and Lander
in the 1820s had noted the greater importance, cultural development
and density of towns in the northern parts of Yorubaland. But in
later years this situation was reversed. The remaining part of the
nineteenth century saw 'the beginning of a major shift of population
from the higher, healthier grassland environment of the north, to
the lower, humid forest country farther south. The cause of the
shift was the invasion of these northern areas by the Fulani armies
whose movements on horseback were least impeded in this grassy
upland country. As town after town was destroyed, the population
moved farther south into the more forested and better protected
areas. From the middle of the century, the arrival of European
missionaries and traders in Badagry and Lagos, as well as the rise
of export tree crop production, further accentuated these southwards
movements of people. Today, the areas of high density of population
and comparatively great wealth in the Yoruba country are to the
south and east. The north and west have become areas of low
population density . . . But in these same areas are still to be found
some of the largest Yoruba towns such as Ogbomosho, Iseyin and
Shaki. These have survived the vicissitudes of the nineteenth century
on account of remarkable military leadership or strategic locations'.[3]

During the latter half of the nineteenth century, especially, the
southwards movement of people changed the whole pattern and
emphasis of population and settlement distribution in Yorubaland.
In southern Yorubaland trade expanded and the number of markets
increased. The centre of gravity of the trading interests moved
southwards as the European administration slowly extended inland
from its bases along the coast. All these changes, however, stimulated
and were themselves frequently made possible by the building of new

lines of communications to help European administration.

The building of roads and railways

To a large extent the building of roads and railways in Yorubaland by the European administration was a corollary of the new general peace. Many of the earliest lines of communication were built partly to facilitate control over the expanding hinterland of the Lagos Colony and Protectorate. Initially, lagoon and river routes dominated the pattern of transport in the Protectorate; and the markets supply-ing the Colony in 1874, for instance, clearly reflected this dependence upon water transport for the movement of goods and people. Until the 1920s, roads were more often built or improved for military and strategic rather than for economic reasons: an attitude that was wholly understandable in that the chief means of moving goods of all kinds on land was by headloading. From the commercial point of view, therefore, it was necessary only to keep clear a path or track wide enough for a single file of head-porters. Roads, in fact, were at best only hammock tracks. In most early maps, roads were divided into two categories: (i) hammock roads, which were wide enough to allow the use of the hammock; and (ii) bush roads, which were not. Even well into the present century, administrators found the need for only the most elementary of road building: 'in the 20 miles between Ilaro and the next large town going south, which was called Ajilete, I had to dismount, on account of fallen tree trunks and other obstacles, 65 times each journey . . . For my own comfort, therefore, and incidentally [*sic*] for the improvement of communi-cations generally, road-making became one of my chief hobbies'.[4]

One of the most powerful incentives to the building of motor roads was the high cost of head porterage: in the Badagry area it was estimated in 1933 that motor freights cost $4\frac{1}{2}$d. per ton mile against 4/- per effective ton mile for head loads.[5] There was also the great difficulty of getting carriers: in Badagry, for instance, orders to the local White Cap Chiefs to supply carriers seem frequently to have failed. It was also hoped that the building of new roads would assist trade at Badagry, putting the town in touch with a much larger, effective hinterland than could her lagoons, rivers and creeks. An entry of 1929 in the minutes of the Badagry Town Council is typical: 'We beg to ask the District Commissioner to assist us in getting the proposed Badagry-Ado road started. When this is constructed it is hoped that trade will flourish at Badagry'.[6] It was also hoped that road links with the interior would help to increase the quantity of foodstuffs at Badagry market and so reduce costs. Most of the foodstuffs sold at Badagry market were still being brought from Ejinrin market or from Lagos. In 1930 the cost of a pan of *gari* at Abeokuta was 3d. and corn 6d., while at Badagry these same goods cost 6d. and 1/- respectively.

Everywhere, in fact, the building of roads was to have important and eventually decisive effects on the growth of trade and markets in Yorubaland. It may be questioned whether many new routes for goods were formed, even for new goods, but certainly the quantities of goods increased, and those that formerly had been handed along a chain of intermediaries from one market area to the next were now moved much longer distances by professional or semi-professional traders. Internal trade and markets were in this way given an important new fillip.

The importance of roads in maintaining and expanding markets and trading activities was realised by both the British and French governments in their respective territories; and along the border their competitive aims strongly reflected this realisation. Efforts were made by the French to join up the border villages with an 8-feet wide road, running south to north through the main markets to as far as Alagbe near Ketu. At Ifoyin the French constructed a large market which attracted most of the villagers of Ilashe and Ihumbe from the British side. They also opened markets at Gbojo and at Modogan which were centres for the Yoruba on the British side. This encouragement given by the French to new markets at Ifoyin, Gbojo and Modogan had an adverse effect on markets on the British side: those at Idofa, Asa, Ihumbe and Meko were 'rather deserted or overgrown or considerably dwindled in size'.[7] The new 8-feet wide road on the Dahomey side of the border was cited as the principal reason for this diversion of trade to the Porto Novo—Ketu—Sabe routes. In 1913 it was recommended that the Chief Serikei Abassi of Aiyetoro in Badagry District be given a trade jurisdiction over Meko district, and be asked to establish markets in the now neglected border settlements so as to divert trade from French into English channels.[8]

As the impact of the British and French grew in their respective areas of Yorubaland, the international boundary cutting through the Yoruba country came to have more social as well as political meaning. Economically, however, the boundary is only today beginning to function efficiently outside the few customs control posts. Smuggling has always been a problem and has by no means yet been stopped entirely. In the 1930s it was frequently referred to in official documents: 'a great deal of smuggling is at present taking place from Dahomey into Nigeria at a point about 50 miles north of Wasimi and opposite to Shaki, Shaki being the main Motor Road connection to such towns as Iseyin, Oyo, Ibadan, Abeokuta and Ogbomosho. Articles being smuggled are cigarettes, corrugated iron sheets, bags of salt, a large quantity of cloth. The procedure being that a lorry meets the carriers at Shaki, which acts as a distributing centre to the aforementioned towns, especially Abeokuta and Ogbomosho'.[9] Markets were visited to 'feel the pulse' of the people, to get their views, and to observe one of the most important links in the chain of smuggling. This large-scale and long-distance smuggling was believed to be bad for trade on the British side of the boundary, though the more local, small-scale smuggling, rife in the border markets, was often considered to be simply an expression of poor roads and insufficient customs posts along the border: 'I consider it inequitable', wrote one district officer, 'to ask a petty trader to walk some 100 miles to the nearest customs station in order to pay a sum of say 5/- customs duties'.[10]

The construction of the modern road network had a definite effect in increasing the number of markets. In a number of cases this creation of markets involved the shifting of settlements; and the way this occurred can be illustrated from Akinyele (Ibadan). The original site of the parent settlement of Akinyele Aba lay some 500 yards to the west of the present site. After 1905, however, when the present road from Ibadan to Oyo was constructed, most of the inhabitants moved down to the road to establish a market close to the already existing village of Olosun. The original site of the present settlement is nowadays deserted except for two families and over 30 ruined houses. In Oje (Ibadan), also, the two primarily residential sections of the original settlement lay well away from the road where Oje market was established, again in the 1905-6 period. Whereas the houses in the section of the village farthest away from the road are inhabited chiefly by farming families, many of whom have their family compounds in Ibadan, most of the buildings alongside the road are in fact simply stores of one kind or another or are inhabited by non-farming families: carpenters, blacksmiths, tailors, barbers, labourers, and produce buyers for cocoa and palm kernels.

In some cases, too, the building of roads, together with the peaceful conditions being maintained, stimulated the movement of the inhabitants of settlements—some of them considerable in size—away from their former defensive sites, enclosed by rocky hills or on the tops of outcrops, downhill towards sites more suitable for trading on or near the new road.[11] Old Eruwa, for example, gave birth to New Eruwa, some $2\frac{1}{4}$ miles away, in this way; and here, as in the cases of Oke Iho (1917) and Igbetti (1905), this movement of the settlement downhill involved also the movement of the market.

Another effect of the building of roads was to stimulate the building of markets at the nearest point on the road from a town or village. In practice, this often effected at least a partial movement of settlement from the original site to the market place on the main road. One example of this is at Ode on the main Lagos-Ibadan road north of Iperu Remo, where the market was built by the main road in 1954. At Ogbomosho, too, the market was laid out on the main road nearby in 1932. The District Officer of Oyo, on a visit to Ogbomosho, was asked by the *Bale* and chiefs 'to lay out building plots at the juncture of the Iloyi and the main roads, being anxious to start a new market there and has built one small block of stalls . . . The idea would appear to be a good one. The success of this market would result in a considerable decrease in traffic on the town roads, in that it would no longer be necessary for lorries to go into the town, for food. It might also develop into a station for passengers and produce . . . Again, should it prove successful, it is probable the people will wish to build houses round it'.[12] Today, twenty years later, there is a settlement of some thirty houses there. In the case of Ikereku (Ibadan), the construction of a motorable laterite road to the settlement in 1952 encouraged the movement of the market away from the market square in front of the *Bale's* house down to a site by the road where, moreover, an important Hausa kola-packing centre was rapidly developing (Fig. 8).

In some cases, formerly important trading towns on the local caravan trade routes were by-passed by modern lines of communication and declined as trading centres; and this sometimes perpetuated and even accentuated a decline already initiated by the southwards drift of population after the Fulani raids in northern Yorubaland. Thus Shaki once had an important periodic market which was attended by people from the surrounding countryside including Ijaiye, Ilorin and Abeokuta.[13] But this favourable location along the main trade route inland from the coast ended with the building of the modern road network and the railway, both of them concentrating on the Niger crossing at Jebba. The construction of the modern road network also frequently led to a decline in the importance of waterways as lines of movement, though these had never been really significant outside the main rivers and coastal lagoon waterways of southern Yorubaland: thus the Yewa, as an important navigable waterway, had allowed Okeodan to remain a great slave mart until well into the 1860s; and Abeokuta for long depended on the Ogun River as a line of communication with Lagos.

The construction of the railway had fewer direct effects on the growth and location of markets in Yorubaland, though some markets, such as Wasimi and Lalupon, owe their existence entirely to their location at railway stations; other markets, as at Ilaro, were shifted to the railway station. Indirectly, however, its effects were more far-reaching. The construction of the railway inland from Lagos began as early as 1898, the line reaching to Abeokuta in 1900, Ibadan in 1901, and Jebba, on the Niger, in 1909. To some extent the aim in building this line was to secure effective political control of the interior country. But this was bound up with the desire to tap a widening hinterland and to retain as much trade as possible within the control of Lagos Colony.[14] In Dahomey, to the

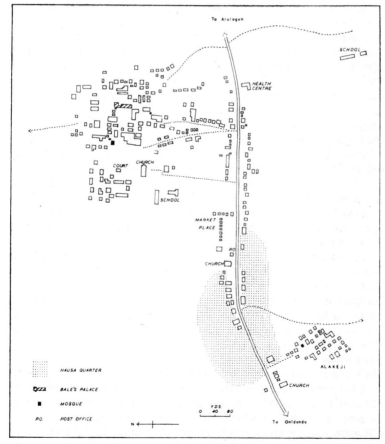

Fig. 8 Ikereku village, Oyo (based on field survey).

west, the French built a parallel line northwards from Cotonou, through Porto Novo, through the middle of the Yoruba area to as far north as Pobe.

This railway system in the Yoruba country was supplemented in the 1920s by a very rapidly improving system of roads as motor transport became more common. The number of markets and the general extent of local and internal trading movements were given a further impetus. Applications for the opening of new markets increased. In the Abeokuta area, for instance, applications were received for the opening of markets at Arikola station (1934) and at Opeji (1935).[15] Applications also came in for the improvement of stalls and sheds in existing markets, as at Itoku market (Abeokuta): 'that your petitioners are hawkers and women of straw financially unable to erect sheds at Itoku market for use. As it has ever been the duty of the Alake to seek after the interest, welfare and good wishes of his people and subjects in all matters, Your petitioners for themselves and on behalf of all others concerned, humbly crave for the unparalleled aid and protection of the Alake, thereby the Administration may erect iron sheds at Itoku market as early as possible for the use of all persons retailing foodstuffs and other ingredients on payment of easy and nominal rent on each shed'.[16]

The way in which the number and location of markets have changed during the present century can be seen from the example of the Badagry area in south-western Nigeria (Fig. 9). Between 1912 and 1940, the main changes were (i) an increase in the number of markets northwards on the higher, better drained land; they followed the construction of motorable roads and, in one case at least, the railway (1929). Associated with this was the northwards shift of the population and a simultaneous decline in the size and number of settlements in the south, below the 50 feet contour line. (ii) the decline of markets along the Dahomey border, especially in the south. (iii) from 1941 to the present day, however, with the building of better roads and a great increase in motorised traffic, there has been a decline in the total number of markets in the more accessible parts of the country, though the southern Ipokia district, relatively isolated as it is from neighbouring areas, still shows a high density of small markets. Otherwise, as between Badagry and Ado, the smaller markets on the new tarred road have disappeared.

A further example of the effects of modern road construction upon the number and location of markets is to be seen in the area north of Ibadan. In the 1908-1913 period there were six markets along the main road, even then motorable, whereas today there are only three. The total number of markets has fallen from 14 to 8, all of which are now accessible by motorable roads.

Thus whereas the establishment of peaceful conditions, the extension of European control and the building of communications resulted initially in the growth of markets, the more recent trend, associated with the construction of tarred roads and a rapid increase in motorised transport, has been a decline in the number of markets, notably in those areas by-passed by the modern road system.

The growth of European trading firms

Another effect was that European trading companies established centres or depots in the main towns of Yorubaland. Initially these centres were concerned chiefly with buying cash crops for export from Nigeria or Dahomey; but soon they also began the 'staking' of African traders with imported goods. One of the difficulties these trading companies had to face, however, was the Yoruba middleman system, which had developed long before during the heyday of slave trading. European observers found this to be restrictive to the development of their trade, Millson, for instance, arguing that 'greed for gain and the profits of their trade with the coast has given rise to a complete and exclusive middleman system, which prevents the entry of European merchants into the interior and seriously curtails the development of commerce'.[17] This difficulty was particularly serious in the Ijebu country. In 1891 Ito Ike and Ode Keta were described as 'landing places and markets in the territory of the Ijebus, a weak branch of the Yorubas, whose geographical position has hitherto enabled them to hold the interior commerce entirely in their own hands, and to prevent the spread of European enterprise and civilisation'.[18] Between 1840 and 1890 there had been intermittent wars between Ibadan and Ijebu arising largely from the control exercised by the Ijebus over one of the two trade routes to Lagos, and from their insistence that all trade within and across Ijebu kingdom should be in the hands of Ijebu people; strangers bought and sold at the frontier markets, such as Ejinrin and Oru. This exclusiveness hindered the easy penetration of Ijebu by European trading firms.[19]

After 1893, however, as a result of the successful conclusion of a number of treaties, penetration began even in Ijebu country. The sale of European goods had formerly been controlled by societies of male traders known in some areas, notably Ijebu-Igbo, as the *Pampa Society*. This society controlled the young men and organised them in time of war; but in peace time they carried out works on fortifications and buildings and were also responsible for trade, trade prices and control of markets, from which they received a revenue in the form of market tolls.[20] These societies, however, disintegrated when their monopoly was broken by the opening of European stores in the inland towns. By the end of the century, European firms were established in most of the large centres of Yorubland. At the same time a growing number of Yoruba were being given the opportunities of employment in government, as well as in the various trading firms.

The direct influence of the Europeans on the normal conditions of trading in market places was negligible. However important the indirect effects of European penetration were, European traders kept out of this stage of the distribution process. Syrian traders, trying to trade competitively in the market place with Yoruba women, were soon forced to desist. Syrians in Ife market, for instance, caused such a disturbance that the Government formed two sets of rules: (i) to prohibit the driving of lorries within the boundaries of established markets and to prevent the obstruction of roads in the neighbourhood; and (ii) to prohibit the selling of goods by non-natives in any market—'No person, being a non-native of Nigeria, shall sell or expose for sale any goods within any market or other open space set aside for the transaction of trade or in any place other than a permanent shop or other building, without the permission in writing of the Native Authority'.[21] Though this ordinance was challenged by the Syrian traders, the legal conclusion was that 'if there is any likelihood of breaches of the peace occurring owing to this Syrian invasion of an ancient right to exclusive trading then my opinion is that an order prohibiting their trading save by license would be valid'.[22]

The introduction of new crops and the development of cash crops

In the early years of the British administration, oil palm, especially for palm oil, was the major export crop grown in Yorubaland; and this was accompanied by an increasing amount of palm kernels after the turn of the century. With this notable exception of the indigenous oil palm, however, most of the cash crops in Yorubaland today, as in much of West Africa, were introduced or developed by Europeans. Leaving aside altogether the question of the introduction of food crops like cassava and maize by the early Portuguese along the coast, a number of new food crops were introduced (like the onion), or developed (like the coconut); and the policy of the British in their sector of introducing new crops and developing them through the native farmers was followed fairly strictly, though with the help of government nurseries.[23] In Dahomey, oil palm cultivation was begun on a large scale in about 1840 when trees were planted by prisoners of the Dahomey (Abomey) and Porto Novo kings; and later in the century both the British and French governments sought to extend oil palm cultivation as the chief source of trade along the coast. Their methods of doing this, however, varied in a number of ways; and the regular, tidy plantations of oil palm, with the undergrowth cleared and controlled, and food crops growing between the trees, found on the Dahomey side today, contrasts strikingly with the untidy oil palm bush so characteristic a feature of the Nigerian Yoruba landscape.

Other tree crops included rubber. Experiments were made in the 1880s in manufacturing rubber from local trees in the Badagry area, one of which — the *Abba* — was found to react favourably to the primitive method of straining with lime juice. But, as one official complained in 1889, 'if we could only induce the natives to get the milk a large trade might be done, but they are intolerably lazy and do not care to attempt a new trade'.[24] Once again, the reluctance of a native peasantry to enter with enthusiasm into the cultivation and harvesting of a commercial tree crop, the ultimate value of which they had to take on trust, was interpreted by officialdom as laziness. Cocoa similarly had little success in the coastal zone. Together with the kola *Gbanja* (*Cola nitida*)[25] introduced from the Gold Coast into Lagos Colony in 1902, cocoa was eventually moved further inland.

In the interior of Yorubaland, the utilisation of land for new cash crops—notably cocoa and kola— had a great impact, not only on the pattern of land use, but also upon the life and prosperity of the Yoruba. It is indeed difficult to think of Yorubaland today, or of its network of market institutions, out of the context of cocoa and kola. The latter is to be found in almost every market; and it dominates in many of the western Yoruba markets. Cocoa itself, though scarcely entering directly into the local exchange economy, nevertheless has deep repercussions on the whole economic life of the Yoruba people. The development of cocoa production was frequently cited after the 1920s as the cause of improvements in general trading prosperity. At Ikerre (Ekiti), for example, it was observed in 1933 that 'the increase in cocoa production hereabouts has stimulated petty trading and it is evident that the occupants of this town are quite well endowed with this world's goods in comparison with the four other districts I have visited'.[26]

Associated with the growth of cash crops, especially cocoa, was the establishment by the administration of 'scale markets', which consisted simply of scales at which goods could be weighed and checked in for collection. These still exist, but they are by no means necessarily in market places or even in settlements; and even where they are in market places they are there only incidentally, so far as the operations of the market itself are concerned. During the 1930s the establishment of scale markets was rigidly controlled: 'I consider', wrote one Resident in 1933, 'that the scale markets should not be placed close together, and that the distance between them on the road should be at least 1½ miles. In most cases a market every 4 miles should be reasonable . . . The greater the number of markets there are the less the control of them'.[27] At this time there were 72 scale markets in Ibadan Division alone.

The introduction of a money economy

Internal trade, based both on regional and craft specialisation, grew under European administrations as a result of the general peace, improved roads and methods of transport, employment with the government, the growth of European trading firms, and the introduction of new cash crops, notably cocoa. But one of the greatest single effects of the European impact during the period at the turn of the century was the introduction of a money which could be used for all purposes, for all commodities and as an interchangeable standard of value. Neither the introduction of cash crops nor of extended trading affected Yoruba market institutions so drastically as did money. General-purpose money made all commodities expressible in terms of a single standard and hence immediately exchangeable.[28] Today the Yoruba is everywhere accustomed to money, not only as a medium of exchange but also as a standard of value.

On the other hand, it must be emphasised that certainly by the time of the earliest European contacts, Yorubaland had already relieved its economic life of the drawbacks of trade by barter. According to a number of writers, barter must have been common at one time, though no solid evidence of this seems to exist. Throughout the nineteenth century, indeed, the main medium of exchange was the cowrie (*Cyprea moneta*) for small transactions, and slaves for larger transactions. Other commodities such as gin, palm oil, manillas (bracelets), brass rods, iron hoes, yams, tobacco, cloth and salt, were occasionally used in some parts of the Guinea coastlands. But Tucker noted in the 1850s that the only currency of the Yorubas was 'the white cowrie (40 to the English penny). Strung in heads of 2,400 (4s. 2d.) so that £2 - £3 worth was about as much as a man could carry, one cannot be surprised at the expense and difficulty of conveying money from Badagry to Abeokuta'.[29] Bowen,

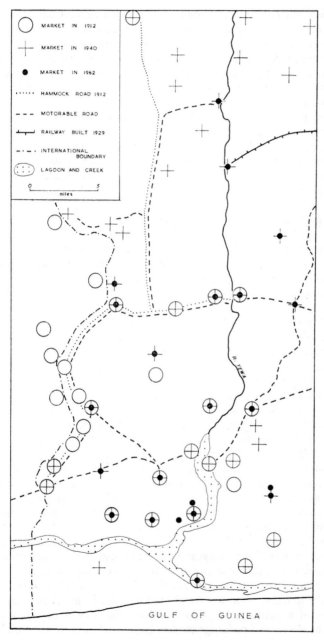

Fig. 9 Some changes in markets in South-west Nigeria.

a few years earlier, had noted of the whole Slave Coast that the currency was 'a little shell called a cowry . . . They are not found in Western Africa, but are brought by Europeans from India and Zanzibar'.[30] At an earlier stage altogether, then, the native system of currency had developed from coastal contacts with Europeans.

The general use of the cowrie had allowed regional specialisation of production to develop well before European penetration in the second half of the nineteenth century. Clapperton's account of the market at Old Oyo (Katunga) makes it clear that the beginnings of an exchange economy and specialisation in agricultural and craft industries must date back to well before European contacts.[31] Along the coastal lagoons, fishing centres — Porto Novo, Badagry, Ajido, Ogudu, Ikorodu, Ejinrin, Epe, Mahin and Atijere — attracted custom from all over southern Yorubaland; Ijebu was noted for its silver and goldsmithing; Shaki, Ogbomosho and Iseyin for dyeing and weaving; Oshogbo for *adire* cloth; and Ilorin for pottery. Only the eastern part of Yorubaland, notably Ondo, seems to have had little specialisation of agricultural or craft industry; and significantly, it was in this part of Yorubaland that European influence was subsequently to be most active in initiating specialisation along these lines.

While the cowrie shell had the great disadvantage for the development of trade that it was cumbersome and difficult to transport — and this disadvantage became more serious as slaves became more difficult to obtain — it had the advantage that it made very small transactions possible. Attempts to introduce British coinage into West Africa in the late nineteenth century were at first unsucessful, for there was no denomination of British money small enough to facilitate the African's small retail transactions. Coins were soon used by the colonial governments, however, who required something of stable value with which to pay the salaries and wages of the European administration, including the Public Works employees; they also required a monetary unit for imposing taxes. However, so long as the coined currency was not adapted to native needs by the provision of suitable coins of small denomination, such as one tenth of a penny, the African preferred to use cowries for most purchases.[32] In 1897 Johnson noted that 'cowries are an absolute necessity at the present stage of the country, and should be used *pari passu* with coins for purchases below one penny'.[33] It was not until March 1908 that the first real attempt to cater for the needs of petty trade was made: the introduction of a new local coinage, consisting of pennies and tenths of a penny (*anini*). At that date, cowries were still widely used as the rate of exchange even in Lagos and as far north as Ilorin.

An Order in Council of that year authorised the issue of nickel (one penny) and aluminium (one tenth penny) coins. It was hoped that 'the introduction of these new coins would do much to develop trade in those districts which were suffering from a scarcity of brass rods, cowries, manillas and wires, the importation of which is now prohibited'.[34] Up to the 1930s, however, cowries were still being used in some places: in the Idere (Oyo) area in 1933, for instance, cowries were still being used, 150 cowries then being worth one penny.[35]

Nowadays, however, the use of coined money as the medium of exchange in markets is universal; and this has had a number of effects, one of which has been that price mechanisms now apply to a far wider range of goods than they ever did before, another being to stimulate the extension of trading into the more remote parts of Yorubaland.

* * *

The European impact on trade and markets has not of course been limited to those items noted in the present chapter, but enough has been said to indicate something of the nature and extent of this impact. It is probable that the development of modern transportation facilities, the introduction of western administrative and trading institutions, and the utilisation of new crops and associated cash cropping, together with a fixed, reliable coinage, had in Yorubaland the effect of reinforcing the economic elements and functions of the market. At the same time the European impact reduced the market's non-economic or socio-political elements. Nevertheless, Yoruba markets are still very much more than simply economic institutions. Consequently it seems advisable, before examining in detail the economic elements of Yoruba markets, to try to isolate those elements of a non-economic character, and to give some indication of their importance in the marketing complex.

NOTES

1. Johnson, op. cit., p. 98.
2. Fadipe, op. cit., pp. 555-556.
3. A. L. Mabogunje, and M. O. Oyawoye, 'The problems of the northern Yoruba towns: the example of Shaki'. *N.G.J.*, Vol. 4, 1961, p. 2.
4. H. L. Ward Price, *Dark subjects*. London, 1916, p. 71.
5. *Miscellaneous Information*. Nigerian Secretariat, Lagos, 1933.
6. *Minutes of Badagri Town Council*, 1929, November 14th.
7. N.R.O., *Government House Archives*, 1913. See also C. W. Newbury, *The western slave coast and its rulers*. Oxford, 1961, pp. 170-171.
8. N.R.O., *Government House Archives*, 1913. Quoted in Newbury, op. cit., p. 171.
9. N.R.O., *Oyo Papers*, 1935.
10. N.R.O., *Oyo Papers*, 1939.
11. See on this point M. B. Gleave, 'Hill settlements and their abandonment in western Yorubaland', *Africa*, Vol. 33, 1963, pp. 243-351.
12. N.R.O., *Oyo Papers*, 1932.
13. Mabogunje and Oyawoye, op. cit., p. 3.
14. B. W. Hodder, 'The growth of trade at Lagos (Nigeria)', *Tidjschrift voor Economische en Sociale Geografie*, Vol. 50, 1959, p. 202.
15. N.R.O., *Abeokuta Papers*, 1934-1935.
16. N.R.O., *Abeokuta Papers*, 1940.
17. A. W. Millson, 'The Yoruba country, West Africa', *Proc. R.G.S.*, Vol. 13 (Second Series), 1891, p. 579.
18. Ibid., p. 578.
19. P. C. Lloyd, op. cit. (1962), p. 141.
20· Forde, op. cit., p. 21.
21. N.R.O., *Ife Papers*, 1938.
22. Ibid.
23. B. W. Hodder, and C. W. Newbury, 'Some geographical changes along the Slave Coast of West Africa', *Tidjschrift voor Economische en Sociale Geografie*, Vol. 52, 1961, p. 82.
24. N.R.O., *Badagri Letter Book*, 1889.
25. The indigenous kola (*Cola acuminata*), is consumed locally by the Yoruba, who value it highly in their culture, few ceremonies being complete without it.
26. N.R.O., *Ekiti Papers*, 1933.
27. N.R.O., *Oyo Papers*, 1933.
28. Bohannan, op. cit., p. 91.
29. Tucker, op. cit., p. 26.
30. Bowen, op. cit., p. 203.
31. Clapperton and Lander, op. cit., p. 12.
32. A. Mcphee, *The economic revolution in British West Africa*. London, 1926, p. 236. See also G. I. Jones, 'Native trade currencies in southern Nigeria during the eighteenth and nineteenth centuries', *Africa*, Vol. 28, 1958, pp. 43-54.

33. Johnson, *op. cit.*, p. 97
34. U.A.C., *Statistical and Economic Review*, No. 8, 1951, pp. 1-2.
35. N.R.O., *Intelligence Report*, S.P. 10746/A, 1934, p. 5.

CHAPTER FOUR

Social and Political Elements

IT has already been observed that women rather than men are concerned with most marketing activities; and this fact lies at the root of many of the non-economic elements of Yoruba markets. Most markets contain no more than a handful of men, though there is some seasonal variation in this respect, more men appearing during the slack period in cocoa farming or when there is stock to buy or sell or much heavy work to do in the packing of kola nuts and cassava flour. On the other hand, certain types of markets contain much greater numbers of men: in the Oyo (Akesan) night market, for instance, the numbers of men and women are about equal, though again it is the women who do most of the trading, the men attending chiefly for social reasons.

This raises the whole question of the place of women in Yoruba society, without which the significance of the market as an important social and economic institution cannot fully be appreciated. Historically, it has been shown that the dominance of women dates back to times of insecurity when women normally met for trading purposes on neutral ground between warring groups. Their importance today in Yoruba society is indicated by the fact that they are recognised as a class under the name 'market women'.[1] In the 1950 Lagos census of population, over 80% of the 39,000 classed as traders and sales workers were women; and politically their role has been recognised as considerable. Unlike their counterparts in Iboland, for instance, Yoruba women rarely work in the fields, except to help with certain of the harvesting operations. Women in Yorubaland enjoy very considerable social and economic independence. They may be trading on their own account, perhaps with money or goods borrowed from their husbands; and their long tradition of independent marketing and petty trading with their own or at least with family capital is thought to provide them with a much stronger basis for adjustment to an emancipated status than is available elsewhere.[2]

Above all, however, marketing, petty trading, or at least attending a market forms part of the Yoruba woman's way of life; and her rewards may lie as much in the social life offered by the markets as in her cash profits. Petty trading in Yorubaland is a skill, a pleasure and a necessity, and to walk through almost any market is to appreciate that 'trading is the essence of social life, from childhood upwards. Here are not only bargains to be made, but gossip and banter and a chance to make assignations'.[3] It is as true of Yoruba women as of most West Africans, that they 'do not regard trade as an occupation . . . and would not refer to it as such'.[4] Certainly not all women in the market are interested in material profit to the same extent. Those who have a 'pin-money' trade, for instance, do not think primarily in terms of making a profit: the point is rather that they have something for sale in the market.

One of the most significant and interesting ways in which markets fulfil an important social function for Yoruba women concerns the use of the market as a meeting place for the perpetuation of lineage rights and obligations. For the women, the neutrality of the market place is most important in the sphere of kinship. Yoruba households being patrilocal, women are separated from most of their kinsmen. In a traditional Yoruba town, each of the family compounds houses a lineage, or part of a lineage, tracing its descent from the same male ancestor. The whole lineage itself is part of a vaguer social grouping, whose members recognise a distant kinship with each other, though the relationship is not traced directly.[5] Thus whereas men are surrounded by their agnates, women must travel to see their agnates or other kinsmen; and, as Bohannan has pointed out among the Tiv, this leads to worries on the part of the husbands about their hold over their spouses should they visit their natal households. Worries of this kind do not arise when women can meet their kinsmen in a market. In the market a woman can get all the news without creating a 'role conflict' in herself or arousing her husband's apprehensions.[6] Moreover, as Marshall has noted, by making use of kinship, residential and associational ties at nearly all points along the distributive network, women today seek to secure their share of the market.[7] The extent to which they have been successful is correlated with the extent to which they have been able to cultivate and exploit various economic and social relationships as well as with the degree of their operational flexibility within the marketing structure. Clearly, many social patterns of Yoruba women may be correlated with, affected by, or even have arisen out of women's participation in trade. Many social relationships, in fact, are facilitated, perpetuated and even caused by the marketing complex in Yoruba country.[8]

Geographically, this is particularly interesting in that it often explains why some women ignore nearby markets and attend more distant markets instead. In such cases the women feel that their social obligations and relationships outweigh the considerations of time, effort, and even of expense.

The religious aspects of markets in Yorubaland may be considered under three headings: fetishes, Christianity and Islam. Most markets have or have had at some time a market fetish, its purpose being chiefly the maintenance of the peace of the market-place. Town spirits are still believed to meet and even to live in trees in or around the market-places. The custom of lopping branches off the market trees whenever the reigning *ọba* dies is still widespread throughout Yorubaland; for this ensures that the market spirits join in mourning the death of the *ọba*. At other times, sacrifices are made to these market spirits for the peace and tranquillity of the town. As recently as December, 1960, the chief (*Ewi*) of Ado-Ekiti, who through diviners and priests forecast disaster for the town, implored the townspeople to keep away from the market for a day during which it was planned to placate the spirits of the market-place. The loss of a day's trade and the distrust of these traditional ceremonies and superstitions by many people in the town led to this warning being ignored. On the day the offering should have been made, a man ran amok, matcheting a girl to death in the market and seriously injuring several other people. All in the market fled, and marketing operations were not resumed until the people had been assured that the necessary offerings to the market spirits had been made.[9]

The material evidences of market fetishes are clearly seen, not only in trees, but in a number of other ways as well. In the centre of Ketu *Oja Kekere*, for instance, is a little mound, said to be the burying place of the founder of the market, the 'Little Mother (*'Ya Kekere*).[10] Three crossed sticks at Idofin (Dahomey) represent the three founders of the market there and mark the association between members of several lineages for the purposes of meeting peacefully for trade at that place. Most Yoruba festivals, too, take place in the market-places: at Ede, for instance, the *Egungun* festival in June involves the movement to the market-place of all the masks.

Just as most Yoruba markets are associated with some fetish or other, so the early Christian and Muslim missionaries quickly recognised the value of the market as a place for the propagation of the gospel. Market-places were found to be 'useful for preaching',[11] in the phrase of many early missionaries, and many of the earlier churches and mosques were to be found there. At Badagry, for instance, the first Christian church was built between the two public markets then in existence.[12] Even today the main church or mosque is normally adjacent to the market-place. On the other hand, neither

Christianity nor Islam has had any effect at all on the periodicity of markets, which still completely ignores the seven-day week of the Christian and Muslim worlds. An effect, however, is felt in so far as the size of the market is concerned. In a place where Christianity is strong, if a market falls on a Sunday it is rather smaller and begins to get into its stride later — that is, after morning service — than usual. Yet when a market falls on a Friday in the strongly Muslim areas — notably in northern Yorubaland — it is normally larger than on other days of the week: in northern Oyo, indeed, a market on Friday is known as 'Honey Friday' market, because of the greater trade done on that day. Similarly, as far as the religious festivals are concerned, Yoruba festivals, such as *Egungun*, the Christian festivals, and the Muslim festivals like *Eid el Fitr*, result in an increase in marketing activity before the festival and a sudden decline at the time of the festival itself.

Apart from their sociological and religious significance, markets can also be looked upon as effective meeting places of urban and rural culture. It is suggested, for instance, that 'by unconscious imitation many urban fashions are copied by the villagers from the frequent contact with townspeople who regularly attend the rural markets and mix with the people. In this sense, then, rural markets play a significant role in bringing social change to dwellers in rural areas'.[13] As the dichotomy between town and country becomes more and more distinct, this characteristic is likely to become more important.

The socio-political elements in the origin of markets can clearly be seen in their precise location, notably by the fact that the chief market of any place is normally in front of the house of the *balẹ*, *ọba* or *emir* of a settlement. In a great number of cases, this main market is called *ọja ọba*, often contracted to *ọja'ba* (king's market), lying in front of the palace of the *ọba* or another chief. As Johnson has traced this, 'as soon as houses begin to spring up and a village or hamlet formed, the necessity for order and control becomes apparent. The men would thereupon assemble at the gate of the principal man who has attracted people to the place and formally recognise him as the *balẹ* (mayor, or 'father of the land') and thenceforth the mayoralty becomes perpetuated in the family. The house of the *balẹ* becomes the official residence, and is thenceforth kept in good repair by the men of the town . . . From this we see how it is that the principal market of the town is always in the centre of the town and in front of the house of the chief ruler. This rule is without exception [*sic*] and hence the term *Ọlọja* (one having a market) is used as a generic term or title of all chief rulers of a town be he King or *Baḷè*.[14] It is to this origin of the central market of many towns that the practice of paying rents or dues to the chief dates back. In Ibadan, for instance, the people of Ọja'ba market — unlike those of the other large markets — pay rent to the local chief or his wives and not to the Town Council.

In general, as Lloyd has noted, the market is nowadays looked upon as a type of public land; and the land is thus vested in the chiefs. At Ondo, for instance, Isele market has been rebuilt within the palace area. Moreover, all new public markets may only be created by the command of the chiefs; and the opening of a new market is traditionally heralded by the performance of certain rituals by the palace servants on behalf of the *ọba*, though other more secular ceremonies are now frequently practised.[15]

One of the most important non-economic functions of Yoruba markets is their use as centres for the dissemination of information relating to local and central government administration. This has been recognised by the government for a long time: 'I have to inform you', wrote one official to the Oyo Resident in 1935, for example, 'that arrangements have been made to issue a statement by bell ringer in all markets in Oyo Province . . . urging all persons to combine to prevent the circulation of counterfeit coins'.[16] Today, at the local government level much is done in this way. The spread of knowledge about health matters, the vaccination of people against smallpox and similar diseases: all these and similar matters can best be spread through a market. Markets are also good places for the dissemination of political information and for the local chiefs to meet their people.

In all these and many other ways, Yoruba markets show marked similarities in their social, religious or political functions and characteristics to the markets of medieval Europe. As in medieval times, where the market was near the manor of the lord, to whom market tolls were given, reciprocal obligations were and are expected in the maintenance of the market-ground and in the order and security of the market in Yoruba country. Moreover, just as today the local chief, *baḷè* or *ọba* is the only one who can grant permission for the establishment of a new market, so it was in medieval England where the notion grew up that a market was a property right and that a new market could only be granted by royalty.[17] Furthermore, the precise location of a market in Yorubaland settlements often shows a response to the same kind of factors of location as existed in medieval England where the market became the focus of the community and 'here too clustered the principal buildings of the town, as well as its church. In settlements of feudal origin the market was held and controlled by the lord abbot or bishop, and the market-place lay directly before the gate of the castle, church, abbey or monastery'.[18] Again, as in medieval Europe, Yoruba markets were especially quickly recognised and are still so recognised as good places to confront debtors in front of witnesses and so to reach settlements out of court.

Market Organisation

The form and extent of market organisation varies widely from market to market; and to some extent this is reflected in the physical layout of the market. An increasing number of markets are neatly laid out with a regular pattern of covered concrete market stalls. The larger markets of this kind may have a market supervisor, or market master. On the other hand, the majority of markets, both large and small, urban and rural, still contain only temporary stalls, usually of thatched roofs held up by wooden poles. Other sellers take advantage of any local shade there is — under a tree, for instance — or sit out in the open.

It is probably true to say that all markets are organised in some way or another today. In the Ijebu area, for instance, the *Pampa* Society still flourishes: at Ajegunle market male members of this society can be seen sitting under a thatched roof on the edge of the market. Originally the *Pampa* Society was composed of young men and organised them in time of war; it carried out works on forti-fications and buildings; and it was also responsible for trade and trade prices, as well as the control of markets, and received a revenue from markets tolls. Today, however, the functions of the society are far more limited. Its members are not normally the younger men and the society may in fact form only a small group of elders who expect to be consulted in any case of argument or disturbance.

In the earlier years of the present century, most groups of com-modities were organised in trade guilds, each of which had some kind of recognised head, herself often subject to a powerful head of all market women in the market. At Ogbomosho, *Iyabọde* is responsible for the four night markets (Igbo, Jagun, Morifon and Ijẹru). As head market woman and market organiser, she collects payment in kind from the market sellers whenever she wishes. At Badagry, a woman with similar functions is known as *Iya Ọja* (Mother of the market). At *Ọja'ba* (Ibadan), the various traders are organised into associations, and these associations have presidents or chairmen who look into the day-to-day running of their associations.[19] Trade associations of this kind, however, are of course a modern phenomenon, and cannot correctly be described as an element of traditional market administration.

On the whole, however, this kind of commodity organisation is lapsing in all but the larger urban markets: at Oje (Ibadan) market, for instance, there has been no market women head since 1946 and no evidence is now to be found of trade guilds organised within the limits of the market there. This is not to say that trade guilds do not exist. At Oke-Igbo (Ondo), for instance, Ọja'ba market contains a number of guilds known as *Ẹgbẹ alatẹ*, *Ẹgbẹ elekuru*, and *Ẹgbẹ alaṣọ*. But they have certainly become less rigid and affect the smaller markets of the countryside only in the sense that most visiting or itinerant traders are members of one guild or another, organised from the larger urban centres.

The organisation of the market from the point of view of order and sanitation is laid down in the Western Region by a bye-law of 1953 which reads for Ejinrin market, for instance, that a person will be committing an offence if he or she 'allows a stall which he has hired to be insanitary or fails to keep it clean', or 'deposits refuse in any place other than in a receptacle provided for the purpose'.[20] In any market today, however, the various elements of market operations are normally organised by different people. Thus at Mamu market, disturbances are dealt with by the Local Government Police, trade disputes by the market elders (*Pampa*), kola marketing by five market supervisors, and sanitation and the general running of the market by a market master.

* * *

Yoruba markets are clearly not merely 'economic' institutions or phenomena, but are multi-functional institutions associated with several non-economic aspects of Yoruba culture. Yoruba markets, in fact, demonstrate those characteristics of social institutions as that term is used by social anthropologists: that is, that markets have social organisation, values, material objects, and event sequences.[21] Of Yoruba markets it can be shown that: (i) each market has a social organisation; (ii) there is a set of notions and ideas, or values, about what a market should be; (iii) centring on each market there is a set of events which follow one another in a regular and predictable pattern; and (iv) material objects—goods of one form or another— are exchanged in the markets. The next chapter concentrates attention on the last two of these characteristics in an analysis of event sequences in the market network of the Yoruba country.

NOTES

1. A. L. Mabogunje, 'Yoruba market women', *Ibadan*, No. 9, 1959, pp. 5-12.
2. P. Marris, *Family and social change in an African city*. Northwestern University, 1961, p. 145.
3. G. Hunter, *The new societies of tropical Africa*. London, 1962, p. 171.
4. P. T. Bauer, *West African trade*. Cambridge, 1954, p. 11.
5. Marris, op. cit., pp. 13-14.
6. Bohannan, op. cit., p. 95.
7. G. Marshall, 'Some patterns of trade among women in Western Nigeria', *N.I.S.E.R. Conference Proceedings*. Ibadan, 1962, pp. 146-164. I am indebted to Miss Marshall for a number of useful discussions on the sociology of Yoruba markets.
8. Ibid.
9. Ojo, op. cit., p. 79.
10. Parrinder, op. cit., p. 70.
11. Bowen, op. cit., p. 296. Note also the tendency for markets in medieval England to be held on Sundays and often in the churchyard, 'the time and place most likely to attract a large concourse of buyers. This practice was not stamped out till after the Reformation'. See A. Birnie, *An economic history of the British Isles*. London, 1935, p. 78.
12. Townsend, op. cit. (1887), p. 49.
13. A. Adediran, *Report on markets in Ibadan Division*. Unpublished, contained in the files of the Ministry of Trade and Industry, Western Region of Nigeria, Ibadan.
14. Johnson, op. cit., p. 98.
15. Lloyd, op. cit. (1962), p. 72.
16. N.R.O., *Oyo Papers*, 1935.
17. F. C. Dietz, *An economic history of England*. New York, 1949, p. 40.
18. R. E. Dickinson, *The West European city*. London, 1951, pp. 323-324.
19. I am grateful to Miss Mechthild Jungwirth for introducing me to several aspects of the organisation of *Oja'ba* market, Ibadan.
20. *The Laws of Nigeria*, Vol. VIII, p. 527.
21. See on this point Bohannan, op. cit., p. 11.

CHAPTER FIVE

The Market Network Today[1]

YORUBA markets include a bewildering variety of types. One possible classification indicates type according to function in the distributional chain. Among the Nigerian Tiv markets, for instance, four such types have been distinguished: (i) the feeder markets, which overlap into subsistence trade in very small amounts; (ii) the bulking centres, which are marked by subsistence trade in which the small amounts bought at feeder markets, or else carried directly to the bulking centres by the producer, are combined into fairly large loads by traders who then take them on to (iii) the major markets, which are marked by the presence of more than the exceptional money trader. Money traders buy the bulked lots of the subsistence trader, and send them by lorry either to (iv) the large-scale trade centres of Nigeria, or else to major markets in other areas, where the produce is distributed along similar market lines.[2] Such a classification, however, can have only very limited value in the absence of far more detailed data on the movements of goods and traders within the area.

A classification based on the division between retail and wholesale trading was also found to have little value here because the majority of Yoruba markets include at least some physical confrontation of producer and consumer. In Yorubaland, as in most other under-developed countries, a clear-cut distinction between retail and wholesale trading is not yet distinguishable. A similarly unworkable classification in the context of Yorubaland focuses attention on the kinds of goods or services provided in the markets: for instance (i) personal service markets, (ii) perishable produce markets, (iii) agricultural staples markets, (iv) manufactured consumer goods markets, and (v) capital goods markets.[3] Most Yoruba markets exhibit important elements of the first four types, inextricably mixed; and commodity specialisation on a market basis is a very rare phenomenon in Yorubaland. Yet another classification has a simple morphological basis, and may distinguish between street (linear) markets, triangular markets, and rectangular markets;[4] but here again, except for strictly limited *ad hoc* purposes, such a classification has little value for the geographer.

The writer has elsewhere suggested a classification based upon (a) location in rural or urban areas, and (b) periodicity.[5] This tentative classification distinguished five main types: (i) the urban daily market, characteristic only of the large towns; (ii) the urban nightly market, commencing at dusk and continuing to about 10 p.m.; (iii) the rural daily market, which is commonly only for fresh meat; (iv) the rural periodic night market; and (v) the rural periodic day market. The observations on which this classification was based, however, referred only to a small part of Yorubaland; and over a wider area several arbitrary elements introduced themselves. The major objection to this classification for the whole of Yorubaland was found to be the basic difficulty of distinguishing urban from rural settlement in the region. As many writers have pointed out, probably in no other considerable area in tropical Africa is this difficulty so important. Though Yorubaland is perhaps the most urbanised part of tropical Africa, the population even in the largest towns outside Lagos is still predominantly rural in its activities.

For the whole of Yorubaland, a basically much simpler classification was found to be the most valid and useful for the purposes of the present study. This classification distinguishes simply between (i) periodic markets, and (ii) daily markets. Within each of these two major classes of markets there are a number of types, all based in some way or another upon timing:

Periodic Markets (Day or Night)	2-day (rare)
	4-day
	8-day
Daily Markets	Day
	Morning
	Night

This classification has the important merit of being objective and based upon a single variable which can immediately be established.

Periodic Markets

Periodic markets take place in Yorubaland over four-day, or divisions or multiples of four-day, periods. Markets may thus occur on the 1st, 5th, 9th of a month — 4-day markets; or on the 1st, 9th, 17th of a month — 8-day markets. It is true that the local Yoruba, when referring to these periods, use the term '5-day', or more commonly '5-5-day' markets (for 4-day markets); similarly, they will refer to '9-day' or '9-9-day' market (for 8-day markets). For this reason, one writer has objected to the use of the terms '4-day' and '8-day' markets as they are used in the present study.[6] Educated Yoruba, however, increasingly use the terms '4-day' and '8-day' to refer to these time periods; and the terms '5-day' and '9-day' can in fact only be justified by counting the same day twice within two consecutive periods. Furthermore, comments in official publications have been found to use the terms '4-day' and '5-day' indiscriminately to refer to the same interval.[7] To avoid this confusion, and to facilitate a real comparison within Yorubaland and with areas outside, only the terms '4-day' and '8-day' will be used here.

Periodicity is an essential element of the local indigenous market-structure of most under-developed countries, as it was of medieval Europe. Certainly the basic 4-day period is a common phenomenon in the southern parts of West Africa today, and is related to time factors operating prior to the adoption of the 7-day week towards the latter part of the nineteenth century as European control extended inland from the coast. The traditional Yoruba week, like that of so many other West African peoples, is a 4-day week. According to Kroeber, the fairly compact distribution of this African 4-day week points to a common origin. The early Romans, he notes, observed a regular 8-day market and semi-holiday; but though this might be connected with the African institution, it cannot be historically linked with it.[8]

Four is the sacred Yoruba figure and their standard unit for calculations. This is rooted mainly in the Yoruba religion, one day being set aside for each of the four major deities and their local variants. As Oduduwa represents the creation, it is quite natural that the Yoruba should consider his day as first in their week:

1. Oduduwa (Ogun)
2. Sayo (Jakuta)
3. Obatala (Orishala)
4. Orunmila (Awo, Ifa, Eshu)

In some localities, the most popular local god was used in the past to mark the beginning of the week; but later on the economic importance of the market tended to make market-day the first day of the week and so the standard reference for all other days. To the Yoruba, as to the Konkomba and many other West African peoples, markets are a method of assessing space and time. Thus the market-day in Ado-Ekiti is known as *ọjọ ọja* ('market day'), the second day of the week as *ọjọ keji ọja* ('market's second day'), the third day of the week as *ọjọ kẹta ọja* ('market's third day'), and the last day of the week as *oja d'ọla* ('market-day is tomorrow'). Moreover, in large settlements where each of the three days separating market-days is given up to small-scale marketing in some quarters of the town besides the central market place, the days are named after the quarter markets.[9] In some areas, certain days are important for marketing; but generally speaking the first day of a 4-day period is regarded as the most propitious for marketing, and this means that the largest markets and the largest number of markets commonly occur on the first day of each market 'week'.

This cycle of four days constitutes the Yoruba week, four of which (16 days) constitutes one month. In this context, then, 2-day markets are 'twice-weekly', 4-day markets are 'weekly', 8-day markets are 'fortnightly', and 16-day markets are 'monthly' markets.

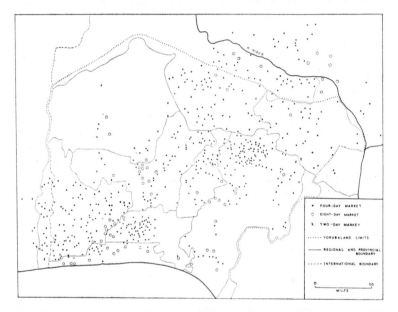

Fig. 10   Distribution of periodic markets in Yorubaland.

The distribution of periodic markets in Yorubaland today (Fig. 10) reflects in general the broad pattern of population distribution in that it is most continuous in the crescent-shaped area of relatively densely populated country stretching along an axis running from Lagos, through Ibadan and Ilesha to the east of the Yoruba country (Fig. 5). More precisely, however, there seems to be a critical density of population of about fifty persons to the square mile, above which there is a regular pattern of periodic markets and below which there are very few indeed. Within the 'populated crescent', however, periodic markets are distributed fairly evenly at distances from each other averaging some 7.2 miles. Higher densities of periodic markets are to be found in two major areas—Ekiti and Ijebu—where the average distance between periodic markets is only 5.7 miles. This is particularly interesting, fitting in as these two areas do with those two areas of Yorubaland where subordinate towns and village settlements respectively are much more important features of the settlement pattern than elsewhere in the Yoruba country[10]. In the Ekiti area the high average density of periodic markets may be correlated with the large number of subordinate towns which reflects the remarkably fragmented social and political structure of the Ekiti Yoruba; and in the Ijebu area the high density of periodic markets may be seen to reflect the high proportion of village as distinct from the normal Yoruba type of rural hamlet settlement.

Thus, whereas the general distributional pattern of periodic markets within Yorubaland reflects the general pattern of population distribution, variations in the density of these periodic markets within the heavily populated 'crescent' seem to be associated most closely with areal differentiation in the *patterns* of settlement rather than with variations in the *density* of population.

In detail, the distribution of periodic markets shows little correspondence either with the distribution of population or with the distribution, size or hierarchy of rural or urban settlements,[11] this in spite of the fact that the population lives almost entirely in compact settlements of one form or another. Several of the largest periodic markets are not in settlements at all, or are only in very small villages; and many of the more important settlements have no periodic markets. The bulk of the population, in fact, lives away from the actual market sites; and this phenomenon has frequently been noted: 'I will here give my impressions of my first visit to Atigeri . . . There is no town at Atigeri. And when the market is not on, there are not many persons around. On market day, however, there are thousands from all over'.[12] This supports the contention that the village *per se* is not at all an important unit of economic organisation in Yorubaland, however important a role it may play in the social organisation.[13]

The network of periodic markets in Yorubaland, then, cannot be compared to patterns of market centres described in Europe and America by Christaller, Dickinson and Brush,[14] and the size and distribution of periodic markets cannot be used as a valid criterion in the definition and hierarchy of settlements—either urban or rural —in Yorubaland. In spite of the seven-mile average distance simi-larity with the markets of medieval Europe—a fact which is presumably associated with the average convenient walking-distance — the evenly spaced pattern of traditional periodic markets in parts of Europe and America is quite different in that it is clearly and casually related to the pattern and hierarchy of settlements. Most important, no relationship between periodic markets and urban settlements — the growth and function of towns — can be distinguished in the Yoruba country.

Why this last fact should be so is an interesting question, and opens up an as yet untouched field of research for the social geographer in underdeveloped lands. No more than tentative suggestions can be made at this stage. To some extent the explanation may lie in the Yoruba concept of urban life.[15] This lack of correspondence between the location of periodic market sites and the location and hierarchy of town, village or hamlet settlements is at first sight surprising, for it would appear that both market sites and settlements would be to some extent subjected to the same principles of location. The explanation of this paradox, it is suggested, may lie in the difference in area over which the factors of location operate, as between markets on the one hand and town or village settlements on the other. The location of the large villages and town settlements depends on much wider considerations than does the location of a market, which is determined by convenience of access from *all* settlements, however large or small, within a radius of some five to ten miles. A market, then, is a focusing point of a very different order from that of a settlement. As Brasseur has noted of the Dahomey section of Yorubaland, markets may be independent of the *existence* of a village even when they are located in villages. This is true, for instance, of Avoinko market in Katagon.[16] Formerly, when the density of population was much lower, markets were generally in the open countryside, and the origin of many markets as neutral points of exchange in a warring countryside set the tradition of a market's location being away from a settlement. Today, with permanent buildings being built around even the most isolated markets, market-places give the impression to the casual observer of being nuclei of population—that is, settlements. But much more, however, markets are nuclei of communications, especially of bush paths and roads.

Another fact to be noted from Fig. 11 is the distribution of the various types of periodic markets — 2-day, 4-day and 8-day. The least common type is the 2-day market, noted particularly in the south-west across the Dahomey border. These 2-day markets commonly represent the merging of two 4-day markets. In Porto Novo, for instance, there were formerly two 4-day markets — Ono and Eru — providing markets every other day between them. In 1918, however, the Chief merged the two into one, the surviving market, now a 2-day market, taking over the functions of both markets. At Dangbo, the original market was every eight days, and the 2-day markets are simply the markets that used to take place in nearby sites but have now been taken over by the more powerful Dangbo market. It should be noted here, however, that a number of places, commonly believed to have 2-day markets, do in fact still have two quite separate 4-day markets occurring alternately every two days. An example of this can be seen in Ketu — Akabidina and Ojapanu markets.

As for the 8-day markets, these occur in very definite groupings. The most important concentration lies to the north of Ibadan but south of Oyo township, though there are other groupings in Ondo and in the Ijebu-Remo area. Finally, there are a number of 8-day markets along the northern side of the coastal lagoon waters, stretching from Badagry in the west to Epe in the east.

It has been suggested in conversations with the Yoruba that the 8-day market is usually larger and more important than the 4-day market. In north-eastern Yorubaland, Agboola has noted that the 8-day markets are regarded as the more important markets, the lesser ones being held every four days, though he finds this truer of the Nupe than of the Yoruba people.[17] Admittedly one of the theoretical advantages of the 8-day market is that it can give traders time to organise trade over a much wider area than they could cover with a 4-day interval; and there is some evidence for the view that the shorter the interval between market days, the more limited the area over which a market can operate. But on the other hand, an analysis of Yoruba markets shows that on the average the 8-day market is by no means larger than the average 4-day market. Indeed, there are a number of examples of markets, such as Agunloye (Ado) and Erekesin (Ado Ekiti), which have changed from 8-day to 4-day markets as a result of an increase in the size and trading importance of the surrounding settlements. Certainly today, 4-day markets dominate the pattern of periodic markets in Yoruba country.

One possible explanation for the groupings of 8-day markets may lie in the fact that with the exception of the lagoon-side markets they all lie at the junction of different groups or sub-groups of the Yoruba-speaking people. If the view expressed in an earlier chapter — that markets can arise only out of the demands of external contacts or long-distance trade between peoples — is correct,[18] it is probable that these 8-day market groupings represent the original foci of the market network in their location at junction zones between the

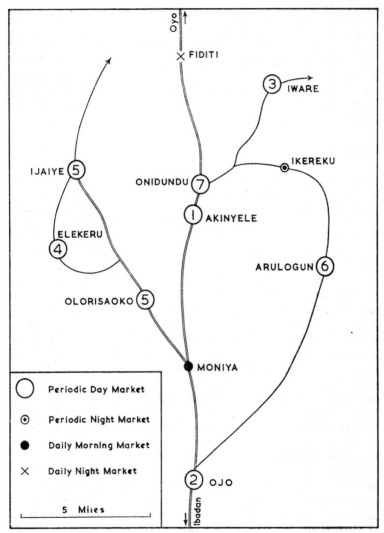

Fig. 11   *The Akinyele market ring or circuit.*
         The figures refer to the order in which the markets operate.

Egba and Ijebu; between the Ibadan and Oyo (proper) Yoruba; and between the Ife-Ilesha, Ekiti and Ondo Yoruba (Fig. 10). Once in existence, it is difficult for groupings of 8-day markets to change to groupings of 4-day markets, if only because of the limitations to change imposed by the system of patterns of integrated markets indicated by the existence of market rings in Yorubaland. As for the lagoon-side 8-day markets, these, too, have clearly been perpetuated since slave-trading days when many of them, such as Badagry, acted in effect as ports and the points of contact between external sea and long-distance land routes.

Market Rings

Most periodic markets in Yorubaland operate on a ring system, each ring being composed of a complete and integrated sequence of markets taking place over 4-day or 8-day periods. In the first ring in which this phenomenon was examined closely,[19] eight periodic markets were noted, seven taking place at 8-day intervals, and one at a 4-day interval (Fig. 11). These markets operate on successive days in such a way that each of the seven 8-day markets take place on a day on which it is the only one of the seven operating within the ring. After all markets have had their turn, there is one market-less day, after which the process is repeated in the same order. The eighth market occurs every four days and operates simultaneously with one market on the first day and with another on the fifth day of each 8-day period. This ring also operates in such a way that successive markets are not normally adjacent markets. The first market is at the centre, the second at the extreme southern edge, and the third at the extreme northern edge; then there are subsequent further movements back and forth until the seventh day, when the market near the centre takes place before the eighth, or rest day. In this way the timing of marketing activities is evened out over the whole ring, so that no hamlet or other settlement is far from a market for more than three days. This integrated timing and pattern of markets is most logical and convenient. It is a wholly indigenous phenomenon, expressing an intelligent mutual self-interest among neighbouring village chiefs, or *baḷes*. A ring or cycle of integrated markets is an expression of the need to contact a wider and more varied section of people and goods than is possible when only one market is involved.

Similar market rings are characteristic of most parts of Yorubaland, though the most common type—the 4-day market ring, normally involving a maximum of four markets—is not nearly so striking a phenomenon as is the 8-day market ring. Nevertheless, the same basic features can usually be observed. North of Ijebu-Ode, for example, the Ajegunle ring—consisting of Ajegunle, Ago, Mamu and Omu markets—is elliptical rather than circular in shape but still shows the same feature of spreading the timing over the whole area: first the central market, then the market in the south-west, followed by markets in the north and south. A similar feature is characteristic of the Lagos ring of periodic markets examined by Mabogunje.[20] Another example is the Oke-Oyi market ring in Ilorin division where the central market is held on the first day of the 4-day period, Pamada on the second day, and Agbeyangi on the third day. The fourth day is a rest day.

Very few market rings, admittedly, are in any sense wholly self-contained; and adjacent market rings often impinge on one another, resulting in a loose chain-mail pattern of rings stretching over most of Yorubaland. But there is by no means a complete system of interlocking cycles, and there are more physically isolated rings than might be expected.

The one considerable area of Yoruba country where the system of periodic markets and associated rings does not occur is in north-western Oyo. As already suggested, this lack of markets is to some extent a reflection of the low density of population; only where the density of population is high enough, presumably, is personal face-to-face contact of large numbers of people within ready walking distance of one another possible. Moreover, a low density of population, as in north-western Yorubaland, seriously restricts the possibilities of economic diversification and any large degree of regional specialisation of production. In this corner of Yorubaland the people are more or less self-sufficient in most items; and here, too, road transportation is very poorly developed.

Daily Markets

The essence of daily marketing is that it is continuous as distinct from periodic, though the daily market may in fact last throughout the entire day or only through the early morning or evening. No general map of the distribution of daily markets in Yorubaland is possible, however, because these markets are so numerous and are commonly concentrated within very small areas, notably in towns or nucleated settlements of one kind or another.

Morning markets are perhaps the most widely spread and varied kind of daily market. They occur both in rural areas and in towns and vary widely—from the small morning market in a village, town's quarter or wayside junction, to the small 'morning feeder' markets around the edge of a town. Morning markets usually begin soon after dawn and may continue up to 11 a.m.

Night markets, beginning about 6.30 p.m. and lasting till about 10.30 p.m., are in some areas the dominant type of market. It is commonly supposed that the night market is a peculiarly Oyo Yoruba (proper Yoruba) phenomenon, and it is true that the most famous night markets—Ilorin, Iseyin and Oyo—are all in the former Oyo Province or in the adjacent part of the Northern Region. Night markets are peculiarly important among the savanna towns of northern Yorubaland, and appear always to have been so. Clapperton in 1825, for instance, found seven night markets in Old Oyo (Katunga).[21] Other parts of Yorubaland, admittedly, also have night markets, but these are normally only very small affairs, much more social in function, and are subordinated to day, morning or periodic markets.

The day markets of Yorubaland include the largest markets: for example Dugbe market in Ibadan where perhaps 20,000—30,000 people pass through in any one day. These large day markets normally take place from about 8 a.m. to 6 p.m., though in the smaller towns or villages they may peter out around mid-day.

For the geographer one of the most striking features about daily markets is that, unlike periodic markets, they show a clear correlation in their location with the distribution and hierarchy of settlements. In brief, the larger the town the more numerous and larger daily markets it is likely to contain. Yet there is no such thing in Yoruba country as a 'market' town as distinct from a 'non-market' town, and the history of almost every Yoruba town is intimately associated with the founding of a market outside the house or palace of the first or most powerful ruler of the settlement. All towns have some kind of daily market; and here lies another virtually untouched field of study for the social geographer. The whole body of central-place theory, in particular, needs most careful re-examination in the context of an area like Yorubaland.

* * *

The above classification of markets suggests, perhaps, a sharper geographical distinction between periodic and daily markets than does in fact exist. Not only will a settlement—especially a town of some size—possibly have both kinds of markets, but the two kinds may even occur on the same piece of ground. This phenomenon can be illustrated from Ikare (Ekiti) which contains several markets—

two 8-day markets, four 4-day markets, and a number of morning, day and evening markets, some of which occur on the same site as the periodic markets.[22] Nevertheless, the classification of Yoruba markets put forward here appears to be both convenient and useful, since it allows the market network to be broken down for analysis into two main types, each of which has its own distributional characteristics and economic functions. The next chapter attempts to examine these economic functions.

NOTES

1. This chapter has appeared in an almost identical form in the *Scottish Geographical Magazine*, Vol. 81, 1965, pp. 48-58.
2. P. Bohannan, *The Tiv market place*, 1961 (unpublished manuscript), p. 7.
3. L. W. Shannon, *Underdeveloped areas*. New York, 1957, p. 132.
4. R. E. Dickinson, *The West European city*. London, 1951, p. 325.
5. B. W. Hodder, 'Rural periodic day markets in parts of Yorubaland', *Trans. Inst. Brit. Geogr.*, No. 29, 1961, pp. 149-159.
6. G. Marshall, 'Some patterns of trade among women in Western Nigeria', *N.I.S.E.R. Conference Proceedings*, 1962, p. 157.
7. See, for instance, Federal Ministry of Commerce and Industry, *Handbook of commerce and industry in Nigeria*. Lagos, 1962, pp. 216-218.
8. A. L. Kroeber, *Anthropology*. New York, 1948, p. 489.
9. G. A. Ojo, op. cit., p. 109.
10. This point is made in P. C. Lloyd, *Yoruba land law*. London, 1962, p. 10
11. Hodder, op. cit., p. 5.
12. E. Ward, *The Yoruba husband-wife code*. London, 1938, p. 130.
13. R. Galletti, K. D. S. Baldwin, and I. O. Dina, *Nigerian cocoa farmers*. London, 1956, p. 58.
14. W. Christaller, *Die zentralen orte in suddeutschlands*. Jena, 1933; R. E. Dickinson, *City region and regionalism*. London, 1947; J. E. Brush, 'The hierarchy of central places in south-western Wisconsin', *G.R.*, Vol. 43, 1953, pp. 380-402.
15. See, for instance, S. Goddard, 'Town-farm relationships in Yorubaland: A case study from Oyo', *Africa*, Vol. 35, 1965, pp. 21-29.
16. P. Brasseur-Marian, and G. Brasseur, 'Porto Novo et sa palmeraie', *Mem. de l'IFAN*, Vol. 32, 1953, p. 46.
17. S. A. Agboola, 'Some geographical influences upon the population and economy of the middle belt west of the Niger'. M.A. Thesis, University of London, 1962 (unpublished).
18. B. W. Hodder, 'Some comments on the origins of traditional markets in Subsaharan Africa', *T.I.B.G.*, No. 37, 1965, pp. 147-159.
19. Hodder, op. cit. (1961), pp. 149-159.
20. A. L. Mabogunje, 'Lagos: a study in urban geography'. Ph.D. Thesis, University of London, 1962 (unpublished).
21. H. Clapperton, and R. Lander, *Journal of a second expedition into the interior of Africa from the Bight of Benin to Soccattoo*. London, 1829, p. 59. A great many reasons may be advanced to explain this phenomenon—the greater difficulty of finding shade against the hot sun in these northern savanna areas and the greater tradition of 'family' farming outside the town during the day among the Oyo Yoruba, for instance—but none as yet can be accepted as really convincing.
22. Information collected in the field with the help of Mr O. Obadofin during his work on the markets of the town.

CHAPTER SIX

Economic Functions of Periodic and Daily Markets

I. PERIODIC MARKETS

THE dominant economic function of periodic markets is the collection, bulking and distribution of local food products, the products of local food processing, and local craft industrial products. Local foodstuffs, such as maize, cassava, yams, bananas, kola and vegetables like tomatoes and okra; locally made palm oil and palm wine; and pots, calabashes, firewood and bundles of wrapping leaves: all are carried into periodic markets by women, chiefly from within the market ring or rings in which the market lies. It will be noted that the two crops of perhaps the greatest cash value in Yorubaland—cocoa and palm kernels—do not enter the local rural market economy to any significant extent. Whereas kola, like most other crops, first enters the exchange economy chiefly through these local markets, cocoa and palm kernel buying stations are not commonly associated with market places. These buying stations are located in villages or at strategic points in the network of paths through the bush, and are not subjected to a 4-day or 8-day cycle of activities in any way. There may be buying stations, concrete drying platforms and produce scales in a village where a market is held, but the location of these buying stations, platforms and scales is not dependent in any way upon the location there of a market.

The secondary, though still important, economic function of periodic markets is as distributing points of goods imported from other parts of Nigeria and from abroad. Thus, beans from the Kano area or cloth from England may have been bought in the larger towns by market women who then carry their goods into the periodic markets for resale.

Movement of Goods and the Ring System

The movement of local farm or craft produce into the periodic markets is not a simple movement of women from their husbands' farms to market, though in a few cases this does happen. More commonly a woman has acted as a first-level intermediary, buying

71

goods from a number of farmers to sell at the markets, and even in some cases buying from women who already have bought from the farmers. In a polygamous family, agricultural products destined for sale are carried home from the farms by the several wives, and the marketing of these products may be supervised by the senior wife. Yet most of the women who buy produce from the farmer before beginning their marketing activities are not in fact related to the farmer. Most farmers believe that they will get better prices by selling to unrelated women traders than by allowing their own wives to do the actual marketing of their produce. Although the various types of products thus brought into the market from the immediate environs within a ring appear to move to market quite haphazardly, in fact there is usually some kind of specialisation in the various feeder areas. Thus at Ijaiye (Ibadan) the following specialisations have been noted:

Commodity	Feeder village or hamlet	Distance in miles from Ijaiye
Cassava flour and yams	Imini	11
	Ajaja	9
	Fayunwa	3
Pepper and fowls	Laleye	4
	Oretu	5
Baskets	Adetola	11
	Olowode	13
Palm Oil	Elekuru	5
Tomatoes	Ajibode	8
Maize	Idigba	2

The other main movement of goods into a periodic market concerns the movement from the main towns of imported goods not obtainable in the immediate locality of a market. Individually the scale of trading may again be very small, a woman's entire wares of imported goods often being contained in a suitcase; yet these traders clearly serve an important function in bringing within reach of the rural population cloth, imported stockfish, matches, salt, sugar, and all those goods otherwise obtainable only in the main towns. These women, of whom there are many, normally visit several markets within a ring before returning to town to replenish their stocks.

In analysing the movement of goods away from the market, three categories of movement may be distinguished (Table I). First, there is the movement to the surrounding settlements in the market ring area. When a woman leaves a market, she will rarely leave without having bought something, even though her main purpose in attending the market was to sell and not to buy; for the market is also her local shop where she can buy her requirements of food, imported materials and the products of local craft industries. In the second place, there is the movement of women to other markets in the same or neighbouring rings. These women, buying at one market and selling at another, perhaps after some form of bulking, are clearly aiding the movement of goods through Yorubaland on the ring system. Finally, goods will be taken out of a market by bulk buyers from the towns, and even in some cases by individual buyers from the towns who come to buy goods which are either unobtainable or too expensive in towns; or they may be women who have come to buy goods for sale in the urban markets.

The key to the understanding of the economic as well as the non-economic functions of periodic markets lies in the existence of the ring system which clearly involves what in sum constitutes large daily movements of people and goods. Within a ring area the majority of women attend more than one market and may in fact attend most of them. A woman living near Abeshe in the Akinyele (Ibadan) ring, for instance, normally attends Akinyele, Iware, Olorisaoko, Arulogun and Onidundu markets. She thus walks up to nine miles a day to market, usually with a basket or calabash of goods on her head and with a baby on her back, and is occupied in travelling and trading in the markets five out of every eight days. This is not unusual, few women attending less than one market within each 4-day period anywhere in Yorubaland. In the Akinyele ring, about 10,000 women, or 35% of the total population in the ring area, are estimated to move to and from market every day. Over the whole of Yorubaland, at a most conservative estimate, over half a million people move daily along paths and roads to and from markets. In any one market-place the population is likely to increase from a handful of people on the evening preceding the market to some 3,000 to 4,000 by midday on market day itself.

Table I
THE DISTRIBUTION OF FARM PRODUCE

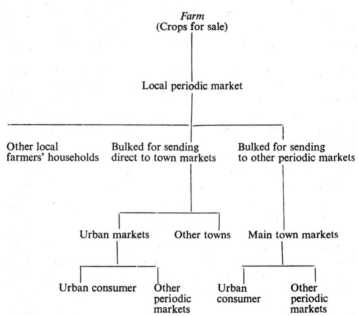

Farm
(Crops for sale)

Local periodic market

| Other local farmers' households | Bulked for sending direct to town markets | Bulked for sending to other periodic markets |

Urban markets   Other towns   Main town markets

Urban consumer   Other periodic markets   Urban consumer   Other periodic markets

The frequent repetition of activities in a periodic market is the result of a number of factors, of which perhaps the two most important are the lack of storage facilities—both on the part of the producer and the consumer—and the elementary methods of transport. In this humid tropical climate there are few commodities which can be stored for long without the danger of serious deterioration. Women go to the market to buy only a few days supply, in the case of most commodities, knowing that in a day or two they can buy a further supply in the same or related market. The daily repetition of movement to and from market is also necessary where methods of transport are still dominated by headloading, as occurs in Yorubaland. Most of the goods brought to and from periodic markets are transported by headloading, and the loads that can be carried by women on their heads along bush paths for several miles are limited. A woman is commonly believed to be capable of headloading 80 lbs compared with 120 lbs for a man, though heavier loads are not uncommon. Nevertheless, headloading does severely restrict the scale of individual marketing operations, and consequently the frequent repetition of these operations is essential for the effective distribution of local produce.

The bicycle plays little or no part in the transport of goods to and from market in Yoruba country; but the use of motor lorry transport is increasing rapidly. Though some periodic markets are not accessible by motor road at all, and many are only accessible during the dry season, an increasing number of periodic markets are being reached by motor transport, and some women—especially those bringing imported goods from the town and travelling from market to market—make some use of lorry transport on market-days. Yet lorry transport has not as yet had any significant effect on the operations of most markets because most women, while only too ready to use the motor lorry to transport themselves and their normal headloads, do not seem able, either for reasons of capital or tradition, to take advantage of the opportunity to carry larger loads. An analogous situation is that of water transport. At Badagry, for example, an analysis of boats and canoes arriving at the quayside on market day showed that 112 small canoes and 20 large canoes tied up during the day, but that over 90% of the women coming off the canoes—large and small—carried loads no larger than a normal headload. The women were using the canoes as they would lorries—merely as a form of transport for themselves and their normal headloads. The same can be said of the railway; and it appears certain that while the more modern means of transport allow some women to benefit in terms of time and energy, these means of transport will for long continue to have little effect on the total amount of goods carried per woman.

The movement of people and goods to and from periodic markets in Yorubaland today is affected by the international boundary to an increasing extent, and it is significant that the real economic and social disadvantages of the European partition of the Yoruba country should not really have become serious until after political independence. It is becoming increasingly difficult to evade customs, more especially with the general increase in motor traffic which tends to be restricted to certain roads, though most of them are only dry-season roads. At Irocogny (Dahomey), for instance, an average of between 100 and 150 women visit from Nigeria on market-day—that is, every four days. Farther south, however, at Aba, there are some 250-300 women from Nigeria every market day, Aba being accessible from Nigeria by an all-season motor road. Between the Northern and Western Regions of Nigeria, between the various provinces and divisions, and between the various groups and subgroups of the Yoruba, however, people and goods move quite freely. Many market rings lie athwart the boundaries between different groups of the Yoruba: for example some of the Ikire markets by the Oshun River are shared by Iwo people; and Sekonna market, on the road to Ede, is shared with Ede people.

Finally it must be noted that Yoruba women do not only trade within Yorubaland; they also travel long distances to trade in neighbouring areas. Ndagi has noted their presence in Bida markets, where they deal chiefly in non-foodstuffs, especially in imported textiles, Yoruba dyed cloth, cigarettes, bowls and plates, beads, matches and other European goods. In many cases, moreover, they own shops around the market place.[1] Yoruba women also trade eastwards and westwards into neighbouring territories, being found for instance among the Konkomba of northern Togo, where they have similar functions, travelling with non-perishable, imported and high-cost goods.[2]

Market Characteristics

(i) *Forestalling*   Around most periodic markets are to be found a number of forestalling points, placed at a distance of anything up to two miles from the market place itself. The forestallers are women who place themselves at strategic points on the paths leading into the markets and try to induce women going to market to sell certain items to them. As the forestalling point is in fact a bulking point, the forestaller concentrates on one or two commodities only and allows women carrying other goods to pass without comment. When sufficient bulk has been formed, the forestaller will go into the market to sell to another intermediary or even to one of the town traders. The forestaller may also take her goods to the periodic market occurring on the following day if she estimates that she will get a better price there, and if the distance and trouble are not too great. She may also have been commissioned to cream off certain commodities by someone in another market. At the forestalling point, a woman will receive only slightly lower prices than those obtaining in the market; but she may feel it is worth her while to shed her load, or part of her load, and so have some ready cash with which she can buy things in the market. Another operation that sometimes occurs at a forestalling point is that a woman going to market with little or no load may be asked to sell something in the market and bring back the money—less some commission—to the owner.

(ii) *Age and areal specialisation of commodities*   There is some specialisation of activities by age among market women, the older women dealing with most of the imported goods, or with goods of high value in relation to bulk. Certain commodities, notably cloth of various kinds, are taboo to the younger women in a number of markets. But much clearer is the areal specialisation of commodities within a market site. The degree of areal specialisation varies from market to market, but does not seem to reflect either the age of the market or the degree of social development around the market. Areal specialisation by social groups within the market was always, and to some extent still is, a traditional feature of Yoruba markets; and this in itself does tend to bring about some degree of commodity areal specialisation in the sense that women from one area are likely to have one dominant commodity to dispose of. Regional specialisation of production in the countryside around a market, then, tends to encourage areal specialisation by commodities within a market-place and so is not necessarily inconsistent with social group areal specialisation. Moreover, there are obvious advantages accruing from some form of commodity areal specialisation which must have been recognised at an early date. A similar feature, of course, occurred in the medieval markets of Europe where stalls of traders were arranged in a definite order according to two practices: (i) all traders of the same commodity were placed together in the same stall or row, and (ii) traders were arranged in streets representing the towns or countries from which they came. Certainly commodity areal specialisation was commented upon in Yoruba markets by the early travellers, and in some markets the various parts of the market are referred to as, for example, *Isọ Alaṣọ* (the stalls of the cloth dealers).

From the economic point of view, areal specialisation on a commodity basis has four main advantages. First, it engenders a spirit of healthy competition and rivalry among buyers and sellers, and in particular protects the buyer from victimisation. Secondly, areal specialisation by commodities facilitates price regulation as well as the enforcement of rules among members of a particular trade association: serious undercutting, for instance, is made very difficult. Thirdly, it facilitates the bulk buying and selling of commodities—such as kola nuts and gari; and finally, it makes for quick assembly, packing and loading into lorries.

(*iii*) *Bulking and servicing*   A great variety of bulking operations occur. Thus a woman may come to market with a handful of tomatoes and sell them to a woman who is intending to buy a few more small lots before selling to other women who may then sell to a town trader on the spot. This kind of bulking may sometimes occur on a larger scale and as a result of the ring system. At Ijaiye, for instance, a large number of women were seen sitting behind small lots of tomatoes, but nobody showed any interest at all in selling these lots. The women were in fact mostly buying small lots and bulking them up into baskets which they intended to take to the next day's market where they knew the price would be substantially higher. In other words, Ijaiye was acting primarily as a collecting centre on that day as far as tomatoes were concerned.

In association with this bulking process, facilities are increasingly being provided for the machine milling of maize or cassava. The mill is usually in a permanent building on the edge of the market site, and the milling of maize and cassava is carried out both for the individual farmer and for bulk buyers. Other services include the bulk packing and selling of an increasing range of commodities, though so far it is most common with two commodities—kola nuts and cassava flour. The operations are carried out almost exclusively by men: kola packing by Hausa, and cassava-flour bagging by Yoruba town traders.

Finally, there is the provision of a host of miscellaneous services. At Akinyele (Ibadan), for instance, there are normally some five tailors working in the village, all of whom complain of poor custom, which hardly improves on market-day because of an influx of some twenty-five itinerant tailors. Similarly, there is an influx of about eight carpenters on market-days to compete with the one permanent local carpenter. Such itinerant craftsmen are a feature of the periodic markets, and they visit the different markets together with the itinerant traders already referred to. In servicing of this kind, as in the actual marketing itself, under-employment is clearly an endemic feature. Oje is not unusual in having a permanent population of only 400, in which there are 3 carpenters, 3 blacksmiths, 1 goldsmith, 5 tailors and 3 barbers—and this on non-market-days.

Commodity Structure of Markets

Using the criterion of dominant commodity in a market place by sellers, it is possible to build up a picture of some geographical interest; and this picture must necessarily reflect to some extent, and in a rather unusual way, the regional pattern of economic activities in Yorubaland. Certain markets, naturally, are 'noted' for one commodity or another; and these variations must commonly reflect micro-variations in economic life over quite small areas and indicate the degree of specialisation which is so characteristic of the Yoruba. In the Akinyele (Ibadan) ring, for instance, Arulogun is 'noted' for kola and palm oil, Olorisaoko for cassava flour and yams, and Oje for yams, cassava and kola. Much work remains to be done on this idea of the market as a window through which to view the economic geography of an area, and it is certain that the difficulties of carrying out such work are formidable. For instance, the commodity structure of periodic markets is affected by diet preferences, which vary from area to area and are reflected in the pattern of demand in markets; thus while flour from plantain and cassava is very popular with the Ekiti, yam flour is more popular with the Oyo and Ibadan Yoruba.

Table II summarises the commodity structure of a number of periodic markets. Using the criterion of percentage of sellers of foodstuffs in a market, it is clear that most periodic markets are in fact dominantly foodstuffs markets, the percentage averaging about 60%. This is logical if the observation already made—that periodic markets are dominantly collecting and bulking centres for local foodstuffs—is valid.

Table II

ANALYSIS OF SELECTED PERIODIC MARKETS
(BY SELLERS)

Name	Number of sellers	% of foodstuffs	% of non-foodstuffs	% of European goods
Adja Were	333	80.5	19.5	10.9
Ado	206	62.6	37.4	29.2
Aiyede-Ekiti	397	62.0	38.0	12.3
Ajegunle	414	71.5	28.5	22.4
Alade	690	62.1	37.9	17.8
Badagry	1462	57.5	42.5	12.1
Ejidongari	284	84.5	15.5	9.3
Erekesin	1786	59.0	41.0	29.3
Eruwa	313	54.3	45.7	20.7
Ibefun	204	59.3	40.7	21.5
Ijurin	397	72.3	27.7	5.9
Iloro-Ekiti	1139	59.4	40.6	9.7
Ire	272	71.3	28.7	27.3
Maya	540	57.8	42.2	19.0
Ojido	237	81.8	18.2	8.0
Oko	927	56.6	43.4	18.3
Olla	594	57.4	42.6	21.5
Osasa	123	68.3	31.7	15.5
Sakete	662	69.3	30.7	18.3
Shagamu	912	60.7	39.3	30.6

II.   DAILY MARKETS

While many Yoruba towns contain periodic markets, the most important and common type of market to be found in the towns of Yorubaland is the daily market. As indicated earlier, the daily market is almost exclusively urban in its location, and may be one of three main types—morning, day or night.

Morning Markets

Morning markets are generally located on the outskirts of a town and take place very early in the morning, beginning about 6.30. a.m. and finishing about 11 a.m. These 'feeder markets', as they may be called, are normally only very small, containing perhaps 150 women or so, but they serve the function of providing a place on the edge of a town where a woman from the surrounding farmlands can dispose of her goods easily and early in the day. In many cases, these morning markets have grown out of 'forestalling points' on the roads leading into the towns. Very few of the goods in morning markets are bought retail, for they are normally bulked up into larger lots for transport to the day or night market inside the town. These morning markets, however, do provide a few imported goods and 'town' products which can be bought here most conveniently by the women who have come from the farms with their produce.

Day Markets

This class of markets includes most of the great urban markets of Ibadan and the other large towns of Yorubaland. It also includes the small day markets of many smaller towns and villages; and these latter markets may peter out about midday and in general appearance may be indistinguishable from morning markets. The day markets include the most highly organised and planned markets of Yorubaland; but many of the poorer, unplanned day markets are in appearance more like the most isolated periodic markets and may, in fact, as at Faji in Lagos, continue to be held under the aegis of a local chief, to whom the sellers pay rent.

The main economic function of this kind of market is to assemble in a central place within a town the various commodities required by the inhabitants. As already shown, these commodities may come from a very wide source area: like the periodic market, there is nothing 'local' about the source of the bulk of goods in a day market. But unlike periodic markets, even those within a town, day markets serve chiefly the needs of people from within a small area: the town and its immediate environs. Day markets are attended chiefly only by people from the town or part of the town in which the market lies; but the high density and essentially urban nature of the population means that continuous as distinct from periodic trading is possible. The selling, moreover, is dominantly retail as distinct from the

dominantly wholesale buying and selling in periodic markets
(Table III).

Whereas the bulk of the day markets contain a wide and balanced
selection of goods—foodstuffs and non-foodstuffs, both indigenous
and imported—there are certain specialised markets which require
some separate consideration. There are numerous small examples of
such markets: for instance *Ọja Kako* ('market of the pots') in Owo,
where pots from certain compounds in the town are sold and
exported to all parts of Yorubaland; and daily meat markets, such as
Oyingbo market at Ijebu Ode. But the chief examples of specialised
day markets are probably the kola nut markets. At Shagamu,
especially, there is a very large day market (*Shagamu Sabon*) where
virtually nothing else is sold. The interesting thing here is that such
markets act almost entirely as collecting centres for distribution
elsewhere—in the case of kola nuts, to the Northern Region. Many
farmers around Shagamu derive more than 60% of their annual
cash income from kola nuts, which pass through a number of
intermediaries before being sold on a wholesale basis in Sabon
market. These specialised markets, in fact, are mostly wholesale
rather than retail markets; and the same can be said of those large
day markets in the largest towns, like Ibadan, which specialise
in the wholesale trading of foodstuffs.

Table III
ANALYSIS OF SELECTED DAY AND NIGHT MARKETS (BY SELLERS)

Day Markets

Name of market	Number of sellers	% of foodstuffs	% of non-foodstuffs	% of European goods
Ondo (Moferere)	1979	64.8	35.2	19.7
Ogbomosho (Arowomole)	209	65.0	35.0	5.7
Oke Igbo (Ọja Ọba)	280	70.0	30.0	13.0
Offa (Owode)	401	52.0	48.0	11.5

Night Markets

Name of market	Number of sellers	% of foodstuffs	% of non-foodstuffs	% of European goods
Ogbomosho (Jagun)	716	55.4	44.6	9.5
Oyo (Ashipa)	477	89.7	10.3	5.5
Idanre (Idale)	159	88.0	12.0	6.5
Osasa (Ita-Ale)	124	83.9	16.1	31.5

Night Markets

The relative importance of the night market in northern Yorubaland
has already been commented upon; and the general decline of the

night market elsewhere has been associated with the increase in sophistication. The social significance of the night market has also been emphasised. Many young men come regularly to these night markets with the primary motive of meeting and making friends, both men and women, and chatting.

Economically, however, the night market's functions vary with the kind of night market it is. Where the night market is in a settlement of some size and importance, then it functions as an assembly point for foodstuffs and other goods in rather the same way as does the day market. This is true of northern Yorubaland, especially in Oyo Province and Ilorin Division where the night market is normally the dominant, if not the only form of market institution. There are other kinds of night markets, however, which chiefly provide prepared and cooked foodstuffs for use over the following 24 hours. These markets are important for the average Yoruba housewife and provide further opportunities for petty trading on the part of a large number of women.

Market Operations

Although daily markets, by definition, do not operate on a ring system, they are clearly similarly dependent on one another in many ways and show an event sequence of some interest and importance. There are many similarities in characteristics and functions between the various types of daily markets, and between daily markets on the one hand and periodic markets on the other. But significant functional differences do exist; and these are to some extent based upon the differing forms of movement of women and goods into the markets.

As far as the products of indigenous farming and craft industries are concerned, six main ways of marketing or of moving the goods into the daily markets of the main towns may be recognised. In the first place, buyers in the town may go directly to the farms to buy produce and then transport it into town. For example, yams may be offered for sale at the farms, and bought on the spot by urban middlemen. This method of cash sale is popular with farmers because it provides large amounts of cash at a time. It is also popular with those farmers whose farms are so far away from markets that they cannot get enough women to help with the transportation. But it does imply both that the farmer has a large plot and that the trader has enough capital to indulge in the large-scale buying and movement of crops from the farms to the town markets.

A second method is for middlemen buyers (*alarobọ*) to intercept those women carrying goods from the farm to the main daily market of a town. This method has advantages for both buyer and seller. The buyer, unlike the seller, is conversant with the current price in the town market and can adjust his or her buying price accordingly. For the seller this method is convenient in that she does not have to waste time and energy in going into the market to sell, perhaps piecemeal rather than in bulk. This aspect of marketing is in essence similar to the forestalling practised around many periodic markets. Wayside markets have in many cases developed out of these fore-stalling points along the main roads leading into the towns.

The third method involves the movement of women who sell in the main daily markets, the sellers comprising women from the town (both those who have already bought from the wayside markets and those wives of town farmers who go to the farms to fetch the produce) and those from the villages around who have preferred to come right into the main markets themselves.

The fourth type, involving those who go to one or more periodic markets in an adjacent market ring, has already been noted, and is the most important kind of movement in terms of volume of produce carried. Local produce will already have been bulked up to a certain point in the periodic markets and it can thus easily be brought into the town daily markets by lorry.

Fifthly, there is the long-distance movement of goods — farm or craft industrial products — from one part of Yorubaland to another, in which such goods as Yoruba pots, Yoruba cloth, yams or *gari* may be transported by lorry from the main source areas to the main markets of the larger towns. Thus most of the pots found in the Ibadan daily markets come by lorry from northern and north-eastern Yorubaland — the Ilorin, Oyo, Ogbomosho and Ekiti areas — all of which produce different types of pots.

Finally, there is the long-distance movement of goods by lorry or train from other parts of Nigeria into the daily markets of the larger towns of Yorubaland; and one good example of this — the movement of beans by train from the Kano area into Ibadan — will be discussed in the next chapter. Another example is the movement by lorry of palm oil from Nsukka and Onitsha in the Eastern Region of Nigeria into the larger towns of Yorubaland.

As for goods imported from outside Nigeria, these are imported initially by large European firms for the most part. In most cases the goods are landed at Lagos and passed through landing agents into the warehouses of the main importing firms, notably U.A.C.,[3] C.F.A.O.,[4] S.C.O.A.,[5] U.T.C.,[6] P.Z.,[7] Leventis, G.B.O.,[8] and Gott-schalk. From here the goods are sent to depots in the main towns from where they eventually enter the main distributive channels.

There is a similar outwards movement of imported goods from the main towns to the smaller towns and markets, the range of this kind of movement depending chiefly on the marketing organisation of each expatriate firm.

Yet the movement out from daily markets in the towns to the markets of other towns and rural areas is not simply one of imported goods. The areal specialisation of crop and craft industrial production in various parts of Yorubaland means that no area is self-sufficient in more than a very narrow range of commodities, and all areas have to get perhaps the bulk of the food they require from other parts of the country. These foodstuffs will normally be collected and redistributed through the larger wholesale daily markets such as that of *Oritamerin* in Ibadan.

Though there is some movement by headloading into the daily markets of the larger towns, and headloading still entirely dominates the movement between daily markets within a town, the bulk of the produce brought into the markets of the larger towns is more commonly transported by lorry or rail. Many of these daily markets, in fact, are located close to lorry parks and railway stations.

The Growth of Retail Shops

One of the most interesting considerations arising out of a study of Yoruba markets is the close association of day markets with the growth of retail shopping districts. At its simplest, this can be seen to be the logical development of trading from periodic markets, which are dominantly wholesale in economic function and are attended by people from over a wide area; through the daily markets in towns, which are non-periodic and cater dominantly for the retail trade and for those living over much smaller areas (though of course the *number* of people involved is likely to be greater); and finally to retail neighbourhood and permanent retail shopping areas. Though there are large European or Asian retail stores in most of the larger towns, these serve directly only a very small fraction of the African population. Most African customers of such stores are intermediaries who deal chiefly with the wholesale sections of the expatriate firms and begin the distribution process by reselling to others until the final link in the chain of distribution is reached in the markets. Markets then, and especially the large daily markets, are an important feature of the retail structure of the largest towns.

Though these large daily markets are predominantly retail, they already include some element of wholesale trade in them; and this feature is likely to increase rapidly. With the accelerated growth of the retail trade in certain commodities — notably imported and non-perishable goods — towards shops rather than markets, the daily markets are likely to become more specialised and more wholesale. In Lagos, for instance, markets now tend to handle most of the trade in foodstuffs, vegetables and animal products.[9]

This point is all the more interesting in that it relates to a process which occurred similarly in Western Europe, notably in the eighteenth and nineteenth centuries.[10] Covent Garden, for example, almost entirely changed its functions with the expansion of London: 'from being a favoured retail centre of Old London . . . its retail functions have narrowed more and more with the enormous increase of fruit and vegetable consumption, and the consequent growth of the more convenient peripheral markets, until it has become mainly concerned with wholesale distribution'.[11] Similarly, the Paris *Halles*, now chiefly the headquarters of the wholesale trade, was originally a food market of the primitive type in which townsmen bought from peasants. At the same time, this development of specialised wholesale markets was taking place parallel to the growth of retail shops. These shops began to take over many of the functions of the earlier markets. Many sellers began to take shops which at first perhaps only opened on market days, but which served as stores for the wares they hawked in the surrounding villages on the non-market days. Signs of these kinds of changes are already very clear in and around many of the larger daily markets of Yorubaland; and this point will be given further attention in Chapter Seven.

III. Market Areas, Prices and the Economic Sense

Market Areas — Periodic and Daily Markets

Some major differences in characteristics and functions between periodic markets on the one hand and daily markets on the other are summarised in Table IV under the headings of commodity structure, the dominance of retail or wholesale trading, the size of the source area, and the size of the service area.

The commodity structure is perhaps the most variable feature and the least reliable single indicator of market type. Periodic markets commonly contain about 60% foodstuffs sellers and about 10%-15% imported European goods sellers, whereas the main day and night markets average about 40% foodstuffs and some

25% imported European goods. This difference is clearly explained by the suggestion already made, that whereas periodic markets are chiefly collecting and bulking centres for food or craft products produced locally, the day and night markets are chiefly distributing centres, particularly of non-foodstuffs, including those imported from outside Yorubaland. As for the many morning 'feeder' markets, their very low percentage of imported materials and high percentage of foodstuffs and cooking materials such as palm oil, firewood and wrapping leaves, is indicative of their bulking or forestalling functions.

The dominantly wholesale characteristics of marketing in periodic and daily morning markets is contrasted with the largely retail functions of the non-specialised day and night markets in the town.

Table IV

COMPARATIVE ANALYSIS OF MARKET TYPES

Market type	Commodity structure (% foodstuffs sellers)	Over 50% wholesale or retail	Av. radius of source area in miles	Av. radius of service area in miles
Periodic	65	Wholesale	0 - 50	0 - 30
Morning	85	Wholesale	0 - 10	0 - 10
Day Retail	45	Retail	over 30	0 - 5
Day Wholesale	85	Wholesale	over 50	over 30
Night	45	Retail	0 - 5	0 - 10

Note These data, gleaned from work on forty markets in Yorubaland, are only very average figures and estimates for an average day over one year (1962). The service and source areas are in both cases immediate areas in the sense that no account is taken of the movement of goods changing hands from one intermediary to another intermediary not in direct contact with the market involved.

The reasons for this difference are complex, but lie fundamentally in the fact that periodic markets are in origin most characteristic of food surplus areas while day markets are most characteristic of food deficit areas; in other words, periodism in marketing may perhaps be equated with the dominant interest in selling rather than in buying, a feature which is associated to some extent with the processes of 'bulking up' rather than 'breaking down' of commodities. It is indeed a common observation made by visitors to Yoruba markets that 'nobody ever seems to be buying'. Although this is of course a gross exaggeration, it is certainly true that most women in a periodic market are selling to a relatively small number of women who are bulking the smaller lots into larger lots. If this notion is correct, it suggests that the day market in a town is more of a service unit in that it is there for people to visit any time they wish to buy their immediate needs, whereas the function of the periodic market is primarily the injection of locally produced goods into the distributive network. To put this difference another way, it can be suggested that in periodic markets most women do not 'go to market' in the western sense of the term: that is, they are not primarily housewives doing the family shopping. In daily markets, however, most women *are* doing just that.

Of the four characteristics analysed in Table IV, it will be noted that only in the case of the source area is the periodic market at all similar to the day market; in both cases the source area is large compared with that of the morning feeder market or local night market. The day market, however, has normally an even larger source area for most of its products than does the periodic market; for whereas the periodic market may get its main commodities— foodstuffs and craft industrial products—from up to thirty miles away, the day market gathers its chief products—imported goods and long-distance foodstuffs—from perhaps many hundreds of miles away.

In the size of the service area, however, the periodic market covers a very much larger area than does the daily market. While the majority of goods in a periodic market are destined to reach the ultimate consumer in the larger towns or in other parts of Yorubaland and even further afield, the day market caters chiefly for the local population.

These contrasts between periodic and daily markets are most clearly evident in a town where the two exist side by side. In Abeokuta, for instance, apart from the great day markets, notably Ẹrekekin, there are two 4-day markets—Iberekodo and Isabo— whose chief economic function is undoubtedly to provide a dominantly wholesale meeting place for urban and rural products. This distinction is even clearer when comparing night and periodic markets, which are perhaps the complete antitheses in this respect: Shaki, for instance, has two markets—the night market catering for very local and immediate needs, and the periodic 4-day market (Ogidigbo), which is attended by traders from Abeokuta, Ibadan, Oyo and Ilọrin. This contrast in the size of service area can also be seen within one market site—Ado Ekiti's Ọja Ọba market, which takes place daily but which has a 4-day periodic section to which people come from far away. At Lagos, too, Oyingbo market is both an 8-day periodic market and a daily market, which takes place on the other seven days on the same spot, though it is then much smaller, almost wholly retail, and has only a very local service area.

Prices

Two major difficulties in the collection of price data must be noted here. In the first place a European finds it impossible to discover real prices for himself in field investigations; for as there are no ruling prices for most commodities, both buyer and seller must be ready to haggle by a time-consuming process. The difference between the price originally quoted for an article by a seller on being approached by a prospective buyer, and the figure at which it finally changes hands may be as much as 200%. Buyer and dealer must be equally skilful; and the seller attaches as much importance to the haggling process as she does to the actual sale.[12] For a number of reasons, apart from language, the European cannot expect to find out many of the facts about prices for himself.

In the second place, Yoruba measures are by number — for instance an *ile* (three) of yams — or by container, such as a cigarette tin (Table V). Weighing, in fact, is completely unknown as far as market operations are concerned, and this leads to variations and anomalies which make any comparative study of prices most difficult. Apart from the lack of uniform measures, moreover, the measuring container may perhaps be dented by the seller to give less quantity, while the buyer may use her hand to support more flour in a can than it could otherwise hold. Tricks of this kind are legion, though deliberate lowering of quality is almost unknown.

Though no ruling prices operate for the majority of local food-stuffs and craft industrial products, there is usually some fixing of prices at a minimum level within each market on any particular day. Above this level, prices are determined largely by haggling, in which certain rules apply. Thus a hesitating customer may be

Table V

PRICES AND MEASURES OF GOODS AT AKINYELE MARKET (IBADAN), DECEMBER 1962

Commodity	Price	Measure
Stock fish	8d.	2 pieces
Dried meat	2/6d.	6 pieces
Bush meat (dried)	1/6d.	4 pieces
Snails	3d.	each
Green vegetables	1½d.	2 bunches
Rice	6d.	cup
Cooking pots	7d. - 1/3d.	each
Dried caterpillars	3d.	60
Cloth	2/6d. - 3/6d.	yard
Coconut oil	3/-	beer bottle
Kola nuts	5/-	basket
Yams	12/6d.	20
Oranges	1d.	6

Cassava	12/-	sack
Eggs	3d.	each
Okra	1d.	9
Corn	6d.	basin
Yam flour	2/-	calabash
Chewing stick	½d.	length (*c.* 10″)

accosted by two or more sellers at the same time; but according to Fadipe once she stops before one of them, however prolonged the haggling may be, rival traders must make no attempt to invite her over to their stalls. While it is open to any individual to extract any price, however high, from the customer as long as the latter agrees to it, yet should no business be done, it is open to the next dealer to agree to a price considerably below her rival's upset price. The fixing of a minimum price, however, means that no serious undercutting can take place.[13]

In general, prices within a market — at least for the bulk of commodities produced locally — seem to be determined by reference to head market women, usually head women of the sellers of one group of commodities or guilds. This is best seen in some of the larger periodic markets, such as Badagry, where a great number of head market women can be distinguished. But over and above such women, however, there may be, as there is in Badagry, a group of head market women who are members of a market committee — the other members being the market master and a number of local government officials — which deals with the more serious disputes about price regulation and which controls prices at a higher or lower level when they find it is in the interests of the whole market to do so. Thus at Badagry the committee will control prices through the major market woman, who controls the head market women, who in turn control the sellers under them. But this control from the committee is such that it is only invoked and imposed on rare occasions such as when there is a severe shortage of farm commodities, either because of crop failures or because of very wet weather. The aim of control, then, is simply to protect the consumer from having to pay the very high prices which a seller could demand, which could bring the market into disrepute.

This kind of regulation is very similar to that practised in medieval markets in Western Europe where, because of physical conditions, such as rain, it was sometimes impossible for many buyers or sellers to meet, and 'at such times the price of the commodity is really settled by a bargain in which one party can take the full advantage of some accidental circumstance which gives him an advantage in haggling. This was the very thing which medieval regulation had been intended to prevent'.[14]

All price variations, of course, express the operation of a vast number of factors such as rainfall, yield, crop variety, supply, demand, transport, storage capacity, susceptibility of a commodity to storage, changing diet habits, and the occurrence of festivals. To this extent, therefore, price changes are controlled or at least influenced by extraneous factors over which the market women or the market committee have little or no control.

The working of supply and demand in price changes can be most clearly seen, perhaps, in the annual fluctuations of prices of subsistence goods with the agricultural calendar. Although prices are fairly uniform at any one time over a limited area, there is no mechanism save the working of the market which fixes the price. The seasonal fluctuation of prosperity is important in this context. In much of Yorubaland, this is controlled by cocoa: October to March is the period of greatest average prosperity; but April to August are normally lean months for marketing because there is a general scarcity and low circulation of money, this being the season when cocoa earnings are lowest and when the rains demand that farmers invest in their farms in planting. The only relief of importance so far is the peak palm-kernel season in the March-July period, though diversification of primary production and industrialisation generally are tending to even out the flow of economic activity throughout the year.

Throughout the day, prices also vary in response to a number of factors such as demand, whether the seller expects to get a better or lower price the following day, and on the condition of the commodity, especially if it is perishable. The first sale of the day, too, is traditionally made at a rather lower price in order to ensure a good day's trading; and the last sales of the day may also be made at a low price for perishable goods. In periodic markets, however, especially in the more rural areas, the loss of prestige to a woman who sells at too low a price may be sufficient to deter her from selling her goods cheaply even if they will clearly be useless the following day. Here is an instance of the non-economic functions and processes outweighing the purely economic functions in marketing decision-taking.

In the geographical distribution of prices of local foodstuffs the operation of areal variations in rainfall, supply, demand, diet habits and, above all, transport costs and crop types, can clearly be distinguished. A few apparent anomalies appear, however. It might be thought that foodstuffs would be cheaper in rural periodic markets than in the main town markets. But this is not generally so. In general, foodstuffs are dearer in places away from urban centres than in the towns. At Sagbe (Ibadan), for instance, it was found that all the foodstuffs in the market, with the exception of vegetables, were brought from Ibadan and Iwo by the townspeople. In other words, it is often the towns that directly supply many of the food-stuffs to rural areas; and this is clearly a function of the areal specialisation of crop production already referred to. Contrary to what might be expected, and contrary, moreover, to what some writers have claimed, even in rural areas most people do *not* grow most of their own food. Only in north-western and north-eastern Yorubaland is there any approach to self-sufficiency in food supplies —either in volume or variety—within any one market area. In most of Yorubaland, then, the retail trade in foodstuffs is carried a step further in periodic markets. At Sagbe, all the foodstuffs sellers interviewed disclosed that they never sold beans, *elubo* (yam flour), *gari* (cassava meal), or maize in *denge* measures, in which they buy in Ibadan. At Sagbe they use smaller units of measure-ment—the *kango*, for instance, which is about one third of a *denge*.

Imported goods, on the other hand, usually show relatively little variation in price over Yorubaland, except in so far as strict comparability between the Nigerian and Dahomeyan sections of Yorubaland is impossible in this connection. An importing firm like U.A.C., for instance, commonly lays down a 'regional' price which is an average of the economic price at Lagos and all other parts of the country. The 'regional' price thus takes into account such differences as areal variations in demand and transport costs and represents a figure which can operate over the whole area but yet will allow a certain profit margin to be made. Even so, this average 'regional' price, which is fixed by the importing firm, operates only at the point where intermediaries buy from these firms. Lower down the distribution channels many of the same factors of distance, transport costs, and demand once again enter the picture, so that in a market place the same imported product may be sold at a different price from that operating in a neigh-bouring market.

Economic Sense among the Yoruba

While the social importance of the market, as discussed earlier, must not be forgotten in any analysis of the economic functions of markets in Yorubaland, this is not to say that the economic 'sense' of the Yoruba is underdeveloped. While it is important to remember that many African societies are still only beginning to separate out 'economic' from other activities, it would be utterly false to assume that they lack economic sense. Where the Yoruba have a real chance of understanding the issues involved, they have shown a shrewd sense of economic advantage; and there is certainly no evidence among the Yoruba of that 'absence of any desire to make profits from production and exchange' which Thurnwald sees as the characteristic feature of primitive economies.[15] The economy of the Yoruba is neither a developed nor a primitive economy, but what may be called an 'intermediate' form of economy in which the economic sense has long been in operation.

It might be argued that the large-scale movement of women to and from market with local foodstuffs and cottage industrial products is wasteful in time and energy. In many cases, articles have been seen to change hands as many as five times during the course of a day, and the profit made at each transaction has been thought to be negligible. The 'large numbers selling in the markets, and the small margin of profit with which most of them seem to be content, suggests that there is much underemployment of labour, a liking for trade as an activity among Yoruba women, and few other activities offering returns for the capital and labour commanded'.[16] Admittedly, the *per capita* turnover each market day is small and slow for the majority of market women. Because of head-loading, the volume of goods taken into market by each woman each day is small; and as the goods are commonly simply subsistence foods, they are low-priced goods, yielding very limited returns. A typical headload of low-priced foodstuffs, like *elubo* or *gari* will sell for perhaps anything between 15/- and 20/-.

On the other hand, the observation that this system of distribution is apparently wasteful of time and energy does not necessarily imply that the system is inefficient. Admittedly there is a frequent repetition of processes and an inordinately large number of intermediaries. In developed countries a great deal of capital is spent in the various stages of the distribution process; but in Yorubaland capital is scarce and unskilled labour abundant. Before a commodity reaches the periodic market from a farmer's farm, it may have gone through two or three intermediaries, each of whom must make her profit. Yet the 'profits' made by all these intermediaries are small, often infinitesimal, and it is by no means certain that the final retail price would be lower if only one, rather than say, three intermediaries were used. Traders have few overheads and can operate on very low profit margins (rarely over $2\frac{1}{2}$-5%). Moreover, for a host of reasons, market women traders provide a service which could not at the moment be given by shops or stores. Most consumers prefer to buy from market women rather than from the retail stores of European firms, which cater largely for the European or wealthier class of Africans. Many of the popular kinds of goods are only to be found in the markets. Illiterates are more at ease in markets where there are no price tags and where bargaining is expected. Bauer, indeed, goes so far as to argue that in the prevailing social and economic context in West Africa, the present system is the most efficient.[17] In conveying goods from producer to consumer, Yoruba market women substitute labour for capital; and in the process they are provided with a source of cash income in a situation where alternative forms of employment are few or entirely lacking.

NOTES

1. A. Ndagi, *Bida markets*, unpublished manuscript. Ibadan, 1963.
2. D. Tait. 'The territorial pattern and lineage system of Konkomba', in *Tribes without rulers* (eds. J. Middleton, and D. Tait, London, 1958, p. 183.
3. United Africa Company.
4. Compagnie Française de l'Afrique Occidentale.
5. Société Centrale de l'Ouest Africain.
6. Union Trading Company.
7. Patterson Zochonis.
8. G. B. Ollivant.
9. Mabogunje, op. cit. (1962).
10. Ashton, op. cit.. p. 68. In the early 18th century in England food retailers were normally content with a market stall; but as the population grew many began to take shops.
11. G. E. Wallis, 'History of Covent Garden Market', *Economic History*, Vol. 2, No. 7, 1932, p. 375.
12. Fadipe, op. cit., p. 556.
13. Ibid., p. 557.
14. W. Cunningham, *The growth of English industry and commerce*. London, 1947, p. 460.
15. R. C. Thurnwald, *Economics in primitive communities*. London, 1932, p. xiii.
16. Galletti, Baldwin and Dina, op. cit., p. 65.
17. Bauer, op. cit.

CHAPTER SEVEN

The Markets of Ibadan[1]

THOUGH Ibadan, as the largest city in tropical Africa and the capital of the Western Region of Nigeria, already contains important western-type shopping and trading areas, the bulk of the trading within the city still takes place through market-places, the large number and variety of which constantly surprises and interests the visitor. Ibadan markets, indeed, include examples of most market types, both periodic and daily, to be found within Yorubaland.

Periodic Markets

Surrounding Ibadan are a number of periodic markets and market rings,[2] each of which lies athwart one of the main roads leading into the town. The one main road which does not have its own market ring is the Ife road, where there is only one periodic market at Egbeda; but in practice Egbeda is related to the Akanran and Iwo road rings lying immediately to the south and north respectively. Most of these rings, it will be noted, impinge on one another in such a way that a few markets can be considered to be in more than one ring; but there is no regular or complete system of intersecting rings. The size of rings and the density of markets also varies widely, from the large ring containing only five periodic markets to the west of the town, to the small northern ring with some eleven periodic markets. These variations are to be explained largely in terms of population density and the history of settlement in the areas concerned.

It must be noted here, however, that the pattern of markets and market rings is always subject to change; and a number of these have occurred and are still occurring in the Ibadan area. Alabata market, for instance, began in April 1962 as an 8-day market fitting into the Akinyele ring system; and the establishment of Alagba market, also in the Akinyele ring, is still under consideration. The application of the local community to start a market there indicates something of the meaning and importance of such markets to the life of the town of Ibadan:

'I have the honour most humbly and respectfully, to speak to your honour on behalf of my people *Alagba Community*, a district in Ibadan Division. There is a new construction branched at Akinyele Market westward by the left which was constructed by themselves to their own village. After finishing the road, walkable [*sic*] by any vehicles, they want to establish a local produce buying station, and new market of every nine days in their village, in order to be increasing produce tonnages in every year, and foodstuffs for the general public in our great city IBADAN.

Being that I am their son, they ask me to bring a weighing machine to the place, to be buying Cocoa and Palm Kernels, and they are now busy cutting the bush for the market proposed.

Will your honour kindly put the matter into the project of this year? Awaiting favourable reply and approval. May God crown your efforts Amen.'[3]

All these periodic markets and rings, indeed, must increasingly be thought of as suppliers of farm produce and other locally produced commodities to the large urban population of Ibadan City. And just as within each ring there is some specialisation on a commodity basis between markets, so there is a tendency for some commodity specialisation between rings around the city: Omi-Adio ring, and its adjacent Ibarapa ring further to the north-west, for instance, specialise in the production of pepper, cassava flour and yam flour for the city markets.

Within the city of Ibadan there are today only two periodic markets, both of which are held at 8-day intervals: Ibuko (Bode) market at the southern edge of the town on the main Lagos road; and Oje, lying just off the main road leading in from the north-east. These two periodic markets take place on successive days in such a way that Ibuko market immediately follows Oje market day; but in composition and function they now differ radically. Ibuko still retains the characteristics of periodic markets in any rural part of Yorubaland, being primarily a wholesale collecting point for foodstuffs for a source area extending for about thirty miles to the south of Ibadan.

Oje market, however, is nowadays very much a specialised indigenous cloth market.[4] Up to the middle 1930's, Oje was rather like Ibuko in being dominantly a collecting and distributing centre for food crops and the products of craft industries from the surrounding farm districts. In the late 1930's, however, people from Iseyin, Oshogbo and Oyo came to settle nearby and introduced into Oje market the products of their traditional weaving industry; and from this beginning the trade in Yoruba cloth became the dominant aspect of marketing. In the 1940's, a wide tarred road leading in from the north-east of the town was constructed and passed within a few yards of Oje market; and this road greatly facilitated the contact by motor lorry between Oje and the weaving centres of northern and north-eastern Yorubaland. Though part of Oje market still operates in rather the same way as Ibuko, this is very much subordinated to the main function of Oje market as a market for Yoruba cloth.

Oje is a specialised market in a unique way in that the indigenous cloth 'fair', as it is commonly called, takes place every *sixteen* days, that is every other market day, while on the intervening market day Oje operates as a specialised market or 'fair' for black soap. Thus while Oje is strictly an 8-day market, it is a dual-purpose specialised market, each of two products of local craft industries—cloth and black soap — dominating on alternate market days.

Oje is noted as perhaps the greatest market for indigenous cloth in Yorubaland, some three million yards of cloth being sold there during the course of an average year. The cloth comes from Ilorin, Oyo, Iseyin, Ede and Oshogbo, and the market is attended by up to 1,500 traders from as far away as Ghana to the west, Ilorin to the north, and Enugu to the east. The two main types of cloth are *ofi* (locally woven cloths) from Iseyin, Oyo, Ogbomosho and Ilorin districts; and *adire* (traditional patterned fabrics) from Oshogbo and Ede. From Oje the cloth goes into other Ibadan markets and through a chain of intermediaries to other parts of Yorubaland and beyond. Most of the selling is wholesale, often on a credit basis, and the larger wholesale traders — some 300 of them — are all men.

The local weavers in Iseyin, Oyo or Ilorin have their work very much tied to the Oje market cycle. Most of them are full-time weavers who work only to the orders of Oje market traders; so that their fortunes from the weaving industry and the extent to which they have time for occasional farming depends on the demands of Oje market. Fluctuations in the volume of trade throughout the year are in fact very considerable. The supply of cloth is lowest during the July-September period when rain and lack of sunshine make *adire* pattern dyeing very difficult and often interfere with hand-loom weaving. Trading is most vigorous during the November-May period, when weather conditions favour weaving and pattern dyeing and when, moreover, the occurrence of the various traditional, muslim and christian festivals raises the demand.

The cloth fair has had a number of effects on the environs of Oje market. A number of local people have taken to weaving; and most compounds in the area now have a cloth merchant (*Baba alaṣọ oke*).

Adirẹ cloth patterning and dyeing units, too, are now commonly seen. Within one mile of Oje market over sixty women work on about forty looms and have been estimated to produce between 3,000-4,000 yards of cloth a month.[5] As people attend the market from so far away, moreover, the cooked foods trade and the provision of overnight lodgings have become important occupations among the local people of Oje. Finally, the piece cloths to be sold in the market are in some cases made up into Yoruba clothes; and this gives some employment to tailors.

The black soap fair is not only much smaller than the cloth fair, but is supplied from a much smaller source area, the main sources of black soap being the oil-palm producing areas around Ibadan — Akanran, Araromi, Lalupon, Lagun, Egbeda and Jago — where surplus palm oil is to be had. Here, too, however, the fair has had an effect on the activities of those living in or near the market site, for there are today over thirty women engaged in the making of black soap in eight soap-making units within half a mile of Oje market.

These two local craft industries — Yoruba cloth and black soap manufacture — are on alternate market days the life blood of Oje market. The cloth fair, however, is not only much larger: it is also increasing over the years and is clearly assisting in keeping alive the weaving industry in northern Yorubaland. The black soap fair, on the other hand, is declining in importance, for the industry is finding it impossible to compete with factory manufactured soap.

Daily Markets

Most of the markets of Ibadan are daily markets and, like those of other parts of Yorubaland, are of three types: morning, day and night markets.

(*i*) The *morning* markets include Ago Taylor, Eleiyele, Mokola, Idiape, Agugu, Elekuro (Labo), and Ibuko, the last being sited immediately adjacent to the periodic market. These morning markets operate between 7 a.m. and 11 a.m. and are best looked upon as feeder markets. They act primarily as regular daily meeting places for town and country traders. Farm products such as yams and cassava are brought in together with cooking materials such as palm oil, firewood and wrapping leaves. These goods are in most cases bought wholesale by women traders from Ibadan who intend to resell in small lots, in many cases after having prepared them into a variety of cooked foods. The women who have brought in the farm produce, or have simply collected wood and wrapping leaves, sell their goods for cash which they then normally use in buying

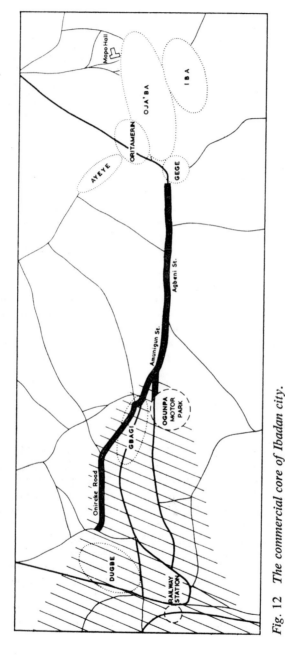

Fig. 12   *The commercial core of Ibadan city.*
The dotted areas refer to the markets; the black strips refer to the indigenous shop areas; and the shaded area refers to the main commercial core, with large European-type shops, banks and commercial houses.

cooked foods or small daily necessities for their home use.

The historial associations of many of these morning feeder markets are indicated by their location on or very near the old town wall. Agugu, for instance, lies only a few yards inside the old wall and according to tradition was begun some one hundred years ago during the inter-tribal wars as a collecting point for goods from outside the town walls. These markets still function as important meeting places between town and country; for although individually these markets are quite small, having perhaps only about one hundred sellers and probably no more than 250-300 women in the market place at any one moment, their daily repetition gives them a much greater significance than these figures would suggest. As far as firewood and the perishable wrapping leaves and green vegetables are concerned, moreover, these daily morning feeder markets are essential to the life of the town.

The dominance of certain other commodities in these morning feeder markets reflects the districts from which the farm women come. Elekuru market, for instance, is noted for palm oil and lies at the junction of the Akanran-Olojuoro roads leading from the main palm oil producing areas to the south-west of the town. These morning feeder markets, however, are rarely supplied from more than eight miles away and are almost invariably attended only by women headloading their goods into market. The contrast between the Ibuko periodic market, where large numbers of lorries bring goods and traders from as far away as Epe and Oyo, and Ibuko morning feeder market, which is attended only by women who have walked into market with their goods on their heads the same morning, is particularly striking in this respect.

(*ii*) The *day* markets of Ibadan are by far the most impressive marketing institutions in the town and with one exception are located in a belt stretching from Dugbe, by the railway station in the west of the town, to Oja'ba in the centre of the old town. Within this commercial core lie the main day markets of the city, the central motor lorry park (Ogunpa), the main shopping districts, both Nigerian and European, and the main commercial offices and banks (Fig. 12).

The one exception is Mokola market which lies to the north of the town and has a quite separate origin in being associated with the old Hausa Sabo settlement in this area. The Hausa Sabo market was originally the main market, and served the Hausa who were interested chiefly in the kola trade and in the importing of cattle from the north through their cattle fair. By 1945, however, this cattle fair had been moved farther away up the Oyo road. This move was designed to prevent congestion at the busy Mokola junction; but the old cattle fair site was quickly taken over by a quite spontaneous and unplanned but vigorous daily market. This new market soon dominated trading in the area and led to the decline of Sabo market into a small night market. By 1960, however, the siting of Mokola market at what had become a very important and busy roundabout was condemned and a new, planned market was built outside the old wall a few hundred yards to the north of the road junction. Today, Mokola is a thriving, well organised market which is typical of day markets in being interested primarily in retail trading, but has an unusually high percentage of foodstuffs sellers, reaching to cover 80% of the total.

Dugbe (Jubilee) market, like all the day markets, opens daily including Sundays and all holidays, from about 9 a.m. to 6. 30 p.m. or so. Dugbe market began in 1919 on the site of a small market and slaughter slab, but in origin Dugbe is believed to have been one of the traditional gate markets around the town wall. The building of the railway station nearby in 1901, however, gave it a much greater importance as the nearest market to what was then the main means of long-distance commercial transportation. In 1919, finally, it was proposed 'to mark out a certain area at Ibadan between the present Government land and the Ogunpa stream, into trading plots with suitable dividing roads to conform with existing Sanitary roads and in such a way that Firms can acquire more than a plot if desired'.[6] Revenue from the market rose from £16. 6. 0. in 1920 to £198. 5. 0. in 1926.

Today Dugbe is one of the largest daily markets in Ibadan, containing between 5,000-6,000 sellers and visited by some 30,000 people on an average day. Dugbe market performs the function of supplying foodstuffs and other items to consumers buying chiefly for family units; and around the market there is already some development of Nigerian stores and shops. Dugbe, however, is not the most popular market for the bulk of the poorer classes in Ibadan. Not only is this market too far away from the oldest, most congested sections of the city, but Dugbe is reputed to cater especially for European and Nigerian middle class people. In fact, however, even the poorest classes use Dugbe for certain special items, notably imported china, pottery or enamelware.

At the other end of the commercial core lie the daily markets of Qja'ba and Gege-Oritamerin. The main function of this marketing complex, however, is quite different from that of Dugbe in that the bulk of it is devoted to the collection and wholesale buying and selling of foodstuffs from over a very wide area of Yorubaland and beyond. There is a section of Gege market called 'the housewives market' which is popular in having the highest quality, greatest variety and lowest cost foodstuffs in the town; and part of Qja'ba is also dominantly retail in its functions. But the bulk of the marketing complex here is devoted to the wholesale trading of foodstuffs.

This whole marketing complex has developed between the older Gege and Iba markets at the western and eastern ends respectively. Up to the early 1940's the trade in foodstuffs was not at all an important aspect of marketing at Qja'ba market. But by 1950 the foodstuffs trading at Oje and other peripheral markets declined with the great increase in motor lorry traffic and the construction of tarred roads into the centre of the town. The foodstuffs trade now shifted to Qja'ba market, centrally placed at the junction of major roads near the traditional heart of the town. The motor lorry parks at Bẹrẹ, Oritamerin and Ayẹyẹ were convenient termini. Goods brought into Ibadan by lorry could in fact now most easily be conveyed to the growing foodstuffs stores in and around Qja'ba market. Gradually the foodstuffs section of the market extended away from Qja'ba downhill towards Gege to create the present maze of paths and stalls in the Qja'ba-Gege-Oritamerin foodstuffs marketing complex.

Probably the bulk of the local foodstuffs consumed in Ibadan now come into the town initially through the Gege-Oritamerin foodstuffs market. This is particularly true of yams, yam flour, cassava flour, beans, corn, peppers, and onions. Travelling merchants, each attached to a group of traders specializing in one or two particular commodities, collect and bulk the foodstuffs from periodic markets or other marketing centres and transport them by lorry or train into Ibadan's Gege-Oritamerin market where the goods are deposited at the stores of individual wholesale traders. The goods are then sold to bulk purchasers in bags and standard measures of one kind or another. Whereas most of the travelling merchants are men, most of those selling in the market itself are women.

Of the three main foodstuffs markets in Ibadan—Dugbe, Mokola, and Gege-Oritamerin — the last is easily the largest and most important. In fact, many foodstuffs sellers in Dugbe and Mokola get their supplies wholesale from Gege-Oritamerin in the first place. Gege-Oritamerin is not only a major foodstuffs collecting centre for the city of Ibadan, but also a major centre of redistribution of foodstuffs for Yorubaland and beyond; yams from Ilesha and Ekiti, for instance, will be sent to Ibadan, Ijebu and Abeokuta districts through intermediaries in Gege-Oritamerin.

The composition and amount of trading done at Gege-Oritamerin market fluctuates noticeably throughout the year in response to seasonal fluctuations in food crop production in the various parts of Yorubaland. Though the farming calender varies slightly from area to area within the country, more goods are certainly brought into the market between November and March when most food products are harvested. Only yams, harvested chiefly in the August-December period, and cassava, which is harvested throughout the year, are important exceptions to this rule, though the recent widening popularity of crop storage in most parts of the country is tending increasingly to even out the flow of most crops into the market.

Oja'ba market is perhaps best known as a night market, but one part of it is an all-purpose day market, including a large section for goats, sheep and hens. One of the most interesting sections of Oja'ba market, however, is the kola nut centre at *Iba* which is primarily a collecting and distributing centre for a cash crop which is produced locally but is destined for the markets of Northern Nigeria. The kola nuts are brought by lorry into the market here to be sold wholesale to Hausa traders who pack the nuts and send them off by rail or lorry to the north, often, however, sending them first to the Sabo kola centre at Mokola. Ancillary industries — rope making, the collection of wrapping leaves, the making of baskets — are to be found thriving in and around the kola market site at Oja'ba; but this section of the market only has importance for the Hausa elements in the population of Ibadan and the surrounding Hausa settlements in Akanran, Araromi, Akinyele, Ikereku, Lalupon, Igbo Elerin, Maun and Iware.

In this respect, the Oja'ba market is similar to the Sango cattle market, which is also a specialised daily market monopolised by Hausa elements in the population. Located to the north of Ibadan, near to the Veterinary Department's control point along the main Oyo road, Sango receives cattle from the Northern Region; and these cattle have either come down on the hoof or have been conveyed to the railway station at Ibadan before being brought up to Sango. From Sango cattle are sent not only to the slaughter slabs of Ibadan but also to many other parts of the Western Region. Whereas the Oja'ba kola market, then, is a point at which the Hausa elements collect local kola nuts for sending to the north, Sango cattle market is the point at which cattle are received from the north for distribution in and around Ibadan.

(*iii*) As for Ibadan *night* markets, these are of two types: the central night market of Oja'ba, and the small local night markets.

Qja'ba night market is simply one part of the main Qja'ba market site, and is still a striking institution characterised by the same economic and social functions as those of the larger towns of northern Yorubaland — notably Ilorin, Iseyin and Oyo. Yet during the last six years or so, the size and significance of the Qja'ba night market has been steadily but rapidly declining, and there seems little doubt that the growing sophistication of urban life in Ibadan will eventually, as in Lagos, lead to the disappearance of what was once the main centre of social life for the bulk of the population of the town.

The local night markets hold from about 400 to 800 people each evening. There are about twenty well-known markets of this type in the city, but numerous other smaller marketing centres of the same kind can also be found. These local night markets are fairly evenly distributed throughout the town at intervals of about half a mile. Their function is primarily to distribute ready-made dishes, cooked meals and petty articles of food to people living in the neighbourhood of the market site. The sources of goods are in the morning feeder markets and large day markets from which women purchase foodstuffs like maize, yams, rice, cassava flour or beans; cooking materials such as palm oil and fire wood; and leaves for wrapping the food. Many of these women then spend the rest of the day processing the foodstuffs into ready-made dishes (bean bread, *ękǫ, amala, ęba,* or *dundu*) for sale in their local night market; or they may simply break down their purchases into small units for resale at perhaps 1d, 3d, or 6d a unit.

This kind of night market, in which women connect their local communities with the town's main sources of foodstuffs, can only be understood in the context of the local Yoruba habits of feeding. The bulk of the working-class population eats food that has not been prepared in their own homes. The normal practice is for all members of a family to eat breakfast at a cooked food stall in the morning, to have the midday meal at least partly prepared at home, and to have the evening meal either in the local night market or to bring food from the market into the home to eat. Yoruba food, moreover, takes a long time and much energy to prepare; and it is most economically prepared in larger amounts than any one person or family can usually eat at a time. The explanation of this pheno-menon of outside cooking and eating, however, is also bound up with the fact that women put trading first in their interests.

Place of Markets in the Chain of Distribution

It is now possible to illustrate rather more precisely the movement of goods into and out of markets. It is useful to distinguish three main channels of distribution along which goods move into and through the markets of Ibadan to the ultimate consumer. First, there is the movement of goods from farms into the surrounding periodic markets from where the goods are collected and brought into Ibadan, either by headloading to the morning feeder markets, or by lorry to the day markets. In some cases the farmer may by-pass the periodic market altogether, especially if he lives near to Ibadan. An example of a crop moving in this way is *gari*. Prepared in the farms by the grating, pressing, drying, and sieving of cassava, *gari* is probably the most commonly used foodstuff in the township, and is widely used over most parts of Yorubaland. *Gari* from the farms near Ibadan is brought into the surrounding periodic markets and then into the morning feeder or day markets of Ibadan. If the distance is not great, headloading of small quantities is practised, but if the quantities are large and the distances involved great, lorry transport is always used and the *gari* deposited at Oritamerin market. There some of it is bought retail by housewives, but the bulk of it is sold wholesale to traders — perhaps a whole series of some four or five intermediaries — for eventual retailing in any of the markets of the town. Some of it, moreover, may be bought wholesale by traders for distribution in other parts of Yorubaland, or perhaps to a periodic market in one of the rings surrounding the town. The variations, in fact, are infinite; and a whole series of trading operations may intervene between the moment when *gari* is delivered by lorry at Oritamerin and the moment when it is finally sold in very small lots to individual retail buyers. Even then, the *gari* may be used to prepare cooked foods for selling at a local night market. Any comments on the prices of *gari* are therefore difficult to make with any precision, except for a particular place at a particular time of the year; and this difficulty will be found to apply to most foodstuffs sold in the towns. To give some idea of the way in which prices are made up, however, it can be stated that in July 1962 the wholesale price of a bag of *gari* at Oritamerin was £6 (for *oloyọ*) and £4 (for *itoko*). To these prices transport costs of about 4/- a bag, store rents of 2/- a bag and profit margins of 6/- a bag were added to the wholesale price to fix the retail price of the *gari*.[7] This meant that a bag of *oloyọ* resold at Dugbe for £6. 12. 0. and a bag of *itoko* sold for £4. 12. 0., giving differences of 10% and 15% respectively between the wholesale and retail prices of the two main types of *gari*.

Secondly, there is the long-distance movement of goods into Ibadan from producing areas far distant from the town. Some of the *gari* consumed in Ibadan, for instance, comes from as far away as Ekiti or Oyo whence it is brought by lorry into Oritamerin market. But an even clearer example of this kind of movement is provided by beans. Beans, unlike *gari*, are not produced in the immediate neighbourhood of Ibadan in significant quantities commercially; but the importance of beans in the diet of Ibadan people is indicated by the fact that over 60% of the population of the town take beans at least twice a day. Most of the beans consumed in Ibadan are imported from the far north of Nigeria—notably from Kano, Bornu, Jos, Nguru, and Yola. Only a few black-eyed beans from Ilorin, Ogbomosho, Oyo and Iseyin are imported into Ibadan from within Yorubaland. Most of the supply from farther north comes down to Ibadan by train. Telecommunications are widely used to keep traders in Ibadan in touch with their personal representatives in the major centres of bean production in the north. These personal representatives go to the farms and villages, buying in small amounts and gradually accumulating enough bulk in the main centres for bagging and sending down to Ibadan by train. Once in Ibadan, beans are normally taken from the railway station to Oritamerin market stores. From Oritamerin Market, beans enter into the same varied channels of distribution as operate in the case of *gari;* but in the case of beans, which are not important in the indigenous cash crop economy of Yorubaland, there is also a more definite movement out of the town into the surrounding market rings as well as into the towns of many other parts of the country.

The third type of movement involves those goods imported from overseas. Such goods are normally imported by large expatriate firms through Lagos and sent to their Ibadan depots for distribution. Stockfish, for instance, has over the past ten years become very much a part of the average man's diet in Ibadan and, although imported, is cheaper, generally preferred and more plentiful than fresh meat, fresh fish or locally dried fish. Most of the different types of stockfish consumed in Ibadan are Norwegian in origin. Initially imported through Lagos, stockfish enters the distributive channels in Ibadan through the large wholesale dealers which are mostly expatriate firms, like U.A.C. Inlacks and P.Z., having their headquarters in Lagos. Most of the stockfish is then purchased by small wholesale traders who are invariably Nigerian traders with sufficient capital or credit standing to purchase several bales of stockfish at a time. These small wholesale traders in many cases operate from shops in Agbeni Street; and in front of these shops and elsewhere in the markets of Ibadan sit the vast bulk of the stockfish traders — the petty retail traders, who get their supplies from the small wholesale traders, mostly in Agbeni. Some of the more prosperous retail traders are women who have by-passed the small wholesale dealers and bought direct from the large wholesale dealers, so that their margins of profit are higher than for the majority of women retailers in the markets of Ibadan.

The source area of Ibadan as far as local foodstuffs are concerned stretches northwards into the far north of the Northern Region and southwards to the coast; but except for palm oil, it does not reach into the Eastern Region of Nigeria, and excludes for most purposes, too, the Mid-west Region. Westwards, there is today only very limited and local movement of foodstuffs across the international boundary. To the geographer, this north-south elongation of the source area for foodstuffs is interesting in that the variety of environments — both natural and social — is much greater in this direction. In particular the latitudinal climatic differences allow a wider range of commodities to be grown. It is also true, of course, that the road and rail network encourages economic relations between Yorubaland and the north rather than between Yorubaland and her eastern neighbours. But this is not true for the Dahomey section of the country with which there is at least one good road connection. In this case, the international boundary has been made, especially since independence, to function more efficiently as a political boundary, but at the same time this has made economic exchange much more difficult than it ever was in the past.

The Growth of Retail Shops

Mention has already been made of the tendency for small permanent shops to develop around many of the market places of Ibadan. But in between Dugbe market at one end of the commercial core and the Gege-Oritamerin-Oja'ba market complex at the other end, quite independent areas of indigenous street and shop trading have developed over the last twenty years or so. The street trading and shop areas, however, deal almost exclusively in non-perishable articles, especially imported manufactured articles of one kind or another. Gbagi, in particular, specialises very much in imported textiles, the women selling their goods on the sides of the streets in front of textile shops which, admittedly, are still dominantly European or Indian owned. The small Nigerian shops in Agbeni Street, on the other hand, sell a much wider variety of goods, though again imported non-perishable goods dominate. Agbeni Street is in fact the chief street for African shopkeepers in Ibadan as Lebanon and New Court Road are for European and Indian shopkeepers.

More recently, small Nigerian shops have spread farther westwards and north-westwards along Amunigun and Onireke Streets.

The interest of this element in the commercial core of Ibadan lies in the fact that it illustrates the various stages of trading from permanent or 'continuous' marketing, through street trading and small-scale indigenous shops to the large-scale European and sophisticated African shops. Current trends in the changing structure of the commercial core appear to be (i) a relative increase in whole-sale trading in the day markets; and (ii) an increase in the number and size of permanent retail shops owned and run by Nigerians.

The commercial core, including as it does the largest markets of Ibadan street trading areas, indigenous and large expatriate shops, and the chief motor park and railway station of Ibadan, is a highly congested area and constitutes a serious problem for planning in the city. Of the markets, only Dugbe is in any sense a planned market site. Like the older markets of many Yoruba towns—for instance Itoku market in Abeokuta—the Gege-Oritamerin and Oja'ba markets of Ibadan are for the most part confused lines of stalls stretching along the streets and paths of the market sites in between heavily congested dwellings. Agbeni shops are similarly lined alongside the main road leading from Gege to the Ogunpa Motor Park, and Gbagi 'market' is no more than an area where street traders squat down in front of European and Indian shops.

This last problem—that of the Gbagi traders—has been frequently discussed by the town authorities. In 1962 the Council considered moving Ogunpa Motor Park to some less congested part of the town and building at Ogunpa a new retail market for textiles to which the Gbagi traders would have to move. This plan was formed in response to a petition of 1962 from Lebanese and Indian shopkeepers, who contended that they were 'not opposed to these women buying and selling . . . ; nor are we afraid that, taken together, they might constitute serious competition in our field [*sic*] . . . ; but what we do object to is that they constitute themselves into a nuisance . . . by making such awful noise when they advertise their wares by crying "Gbanjo, Gbanjo!" . . . and by using the walls of our shops, and the drains alongside, as their urinals.'[8] So far, however, nothing has been done.

In Oja'ba market, on the other hand, plans to construct a properly planned market site with permanent stalls, adequate access roads, and proper sanitation, have now been drawn up. Certainly at the moment, physical conditions in the market are as bad as any to be found in the most isolated market in rural Yorubaland. But improvement at Oja'ba, though generally desired, is made peculiarly difficult by its long existence as the oldest market in the town. Still controlled, as shown earlier, by local chiefs, who collect rent directly from the customers, Ọja'ba lies outside the immediate jurisdiction of the City Council; and until the Council is empowered to collect fees of some kind or another from the traders, plans for the development of the market site are unlikely to be implemented.

It has been observed in the previous chapter that the trends observable in the retail trade of Yoruba towns, and especially perhaps of Ibadan, are in many ways comparable to those that occurred in Western European towns during the eighteenth and early nineteenth centuries.

Yet whatever changes do take place, and in particular however rapidly Nigerian shops develop in the commercial core, and however completely markets like Oritamerin take over the wholesale trade in foodstuffs, there is no doubt that open markets will for long continue to dominate the retail structure of Ibadan. It is perhaps too easily assumed that such markets are out of place in a modern city; and it is often forgotten that the change from markets to shops in most European towns took place only slowly over a century or so. Moreover, it is by no means certain that open markets are not ideally suited to the prevailing physical, social and economic conditions of Yorubaland. Town Planning in Ibadan can perhaps only realistically be developed on the assumption that open markets will continue to dominate the retail structure. Ibadan markets are not unfortunate anachronisms. The periodic markets make possible the distribution within Ibadan of local food products and the products of craft industries from over a wide area. The morning feeder markets allow easy trading contact between the town and the surrounding rural areas and their market rings. Local night markets provide the Yoruba household with much of its daily cooked food requirements. The large wholesale sections of the day markets make possible the distribution within the town of local food-stuffs from a very wide area stretching northwards to beyond Kano. Finally, the retail sections of the great day markets still serve, and will probably continue to serve, as the main sources of all kinds of commodities for the bulk of the population of Ibadan City.

NOTES

1. This chapter appears in a rather different form in *The City of Ibadan*, edited by P. C. Lloyd and A. L. Mabogunje. Cambridge, 1967.
2. A market ring in this context is composed of a complete and integrated sequence of markets taking place over 4-day or 8-day periods.
3. *File T.*49/3, 20 January, 1954. Ministry of Trade and Industry, Ibadan. I am indebted to the Minister of Trade and Industry for allowing me to look through all the relevant files in Ibadan. The phrase 'nine days' in the letter quoted here refers to the '8-day' period used elsewhere in this study.
4. I am grateful to Mr O. Aremu for his help generally in my work on the markets of Ibadan. In particular, see his *Ibadan Markets* (unpublished essay submitted for the B.A. Honours Degree of the University of London, 1963), on which I have drawn freely.
5. These and other data for Oje market from Aremu, op. cit.
6. N.R.O., *Oyo Papers*, 1919.
7. This information supplied by Mr A. Adediran, of the Ministry of Trade and Industry, in the relevant files, but especially in *T.*49/3.
8. *File T.*49/3, 20 January, 1954. Ministry of Trade and Industry, Ibadan.

Part II

Markets In Iboland

CHAPTER EIGHT

The Iboland Setting

Land and Climate

This study refers to the Ibo-speaking part of the Eastern Region of Nigeria, an area bounded to the west by the Niger river, to the north by Igala and Tiv country, to the south by Ijaw country, to the south-east by the Annang and to the north-east by a number of smaller groups. Only in the west, then, is Iboland taken to have any definite physical limits; yet even the Niger river itself is in fact a most arbitrary boundary, for Ibo-speaking peoples extend westwards across the river into the Mid-Western Region of Nigeria (Fig. 13).

As defined for the purposes of this study, Iboland is an area of gently rolling country and plains, hemmed in by fringing waterways in the west and south, and by more rugged country to the north and east. Very generally, the area rises from the south-west inland in an easterly and north-easterly direction, but is interrupted by a recurring succession of scarps and ridges, uplands and basins. The major topographical landmark is the easternmost and highest of these scarps—the Nsukka-Awgu escarpment, with its southerly and south-easterly extension through Okigwi and Ohafia to Arochuku. Geologically, Iboland is underlain by sedimentary rocks, successively older rocks outcropping in the general direction of uplift so that on the surface there is an alternation of sandstones and shales, ranging from Holocene alluvium on the coast to Albian and older shales in the extreme north-east. These features have some significance for many of the elements of the human landscape, such as the spread and distribution of population, the local differences in agricultural production, and the development of transportation routes.

Iboland is cut off from the Bight of Biafra by the creeks and swamps of the Niger delta, which fans out from its apex about seventy miles from the mouth of the River Niger south-south-eastwards to the mouth of the Imo river at Opobo. On the western side the study area reaches to the River Niger's floodplain, which varies in width from 10 to 15 miles and is broken only at Onitsha. To the north the Anambra tributary flows into the Niger near

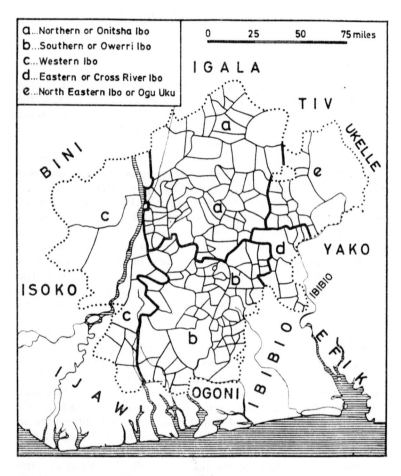

Fig. 13   *Ibo-speaking peoples and adjacents groups.*

Onitsha and provides access to the river for lands adjacent to the floodplains. To the south the River Orashi, together with numerous minor distributaries, connects the mainland with the Niger valley, delta and coastal creeks. A radial pattern of distributaries and creeks and a maze of linking waterways provide routeways from the otherwise land-locked Iboland to the sea. Two of the largest creeks, the Sombreiro and the Kalabari (New Calabar river), break through the swamps to firm land, and are joined by two rivers of the same names originating in the southern half of Iboland. More important still is the Imo river, farther east, which provides nearly a hundred miles of canoe waterways leading to the sea at Opobo. East of the mouth of the Imo the coast is relatively straight but is backed by a system of parallel creeks.

In Vine's classification of Nigerian soils,[1] the soils of Iboland come under three main types. First come the freshwater swamp soils; then the areas of yellowish-brown friable porous sands to sandy clays, lying mostly on the wet coastal plain sands; and, finally, soils of the rest of Iboland which are characterised by predominantly reddish, friable and porous sands to sandy clays. A sub-regional type is found on the drier shales of the Aboine basin and the Adaba valley where soils are indurated with concretionary ironstones. Acid soils are dominant but a wide range of parent materials and contrasting topography have combined to produce a complex variety of soil conditions which have become associated with differences in cropping patterns.

Climatically, Iboland is by no means uniform. Rainfall is very heavy in the delta and forest lands of southern Iboland but decreases rapidly westwards, falling from 150″ in Brass to 100″ in Ahoada and Port Harcourt just inside Iboland. The decrease inland is more gradual. The driest part is the Nsukka plateau and the Adada basin where the amount of rainfall is under 70.″ As with temperatures, the amount of rainfall can be said to be everywhere adequate for the growing of the principal staple food crops—yams, cassava and cocoyams. Yams do well with less than the amount generally available—60″ to 70″ is believed to be ideal—but cassava and cocoyams are tolerant of heavy rainfall and do not find amounts of over 90″ excessive. Citrus and other fruits, however, do rather better in the drier areas. Different vegetables have different moisture requirements and there is a marked regional pattern in their distribution. The water-leaf, the fluted pumpkin and the gourd are to be found mainly in the wetter south, while the bitter leaf and the angara occur in the north.

More critical to the regional pattern of agricultural production than the total amount of rainfall over the year is the seasonality of rainfall in Iboland. Typically there is a tendency to double rainfall maxima with a break in August, though this is most marked in the south where the rainy season is much longer. The number of dry months (with rainfall less than 2.4″) ranges from under three in the south to five in the north-east. The critical value would appear to be four months. The isoline more or less coincides with the 80″ isohyet and is criss-crossed by the southern limit of the derived savanna. North of it a wide variety of grain and seed crops — maize, beans, pepper, cotton and even millet — can be grown, the long dry season enabling seeds to ripen. Where yams are grown only one crop is normally possible. In the south, however, the rains last longer, yams become dominant, and they are mature enough by the August break in rainfall for harvesting and the sowing of a second yam crop.

Population and Settlement

Iboland in Eastern Nigeria is one of the largest population nuclei and has the highest local rural densities in Nigeria. In 1952 the average population density in Iboland was 346 persons to the square mile as against 249 for the whole of the Eastern Region, 151 for the Western Region (1965 boundaries), 100 for the Mid-West Region, and 60 for the Northern Region. At the local level, average divisional densities in Iboland are often very much higher still. In 1952/3 the lowest divisional density—143 persons to the square mile in Ahoada Division—compares with the median of 150 in the Western Region and is surpassed in only four of the Northern Region's 38 divisions. The only area of comparable densities is in Ibibioland, contiguous with Iboland in the south-east; but except in this direction, Iboland borders on areas of low population density. With so many persons on the land the balance between agricultural production and food demand is precarious. Excessive pressure on the land underlies many features of Ibo social and economic life: a readiness to change from agriculture to other occupations when possible; a willingness to try out new ideas; and a tendency to migrate to towns or to less crowded rural areas.

Within Iboland the distribution of population is very varied Local differences in population density derive particular significance from the fact that ownership of land is vested in the traditionally autonomous village group. Hence local density gradients tend to be self-perpetuating, in spite of the fact that a great many people migrate seasonally to the better endowed areas.

Outright sale of agricultural land is rare. However long his sojourn, the migrant farmer with his annual leases granted by the land-holding kindred units has the status of a squatter. With the recurrent juxtaposition of food surplus and food deficit village groups, the scope for trade at even the local level is very great.

The main axis of population concentration is a solid block of country extending south-eastwards from the Onitsha-Awka axis into Umuahia Province. The northern edge of this block correlates remarkably closely with the scarped, ridged and gullied edges of the central Ibo uplands. Beyond it, densities fall away very rapidly in the Mamu and Imo valleys, local differences between upland and valley reaching to over 400 persons to the square mile. Although there is a gradual transition from the uplands to the coastal plains in the south, the change in population densities here is just as abrupt as in the north. The line of the steepest density gradient is followed very closely by the 400 ft. contour and by the Onitsha-Owerri road. Within the block of highest densities the most densely populated area is in the Isuama country in the southern parts of Orlu and Okigwi divisions, where there are over 1,200 persons to the square mile. Population densities are low in the coastal plain sands and riverain areas except near the modern town of Port Harcourt, at the head of the more important Oil Rivers creeks, where many of the old trading towns are clustered. North of the Mamu and Imo valleys, population densities rise again in the Awka, Udi and Nsukka plateau, culminating in over 800 persons to the square mile in Igbo Eze county. Population densities are generally low east of the escarpment, in the Cross River basin, but there are outliers of heavily populated country in the Ezza country and in the southern part of Nkanu county.

Grove has noted a close correlation between the incidence of high population densities and the occurrence of acid sands on the upland areas,[2] and various attempts have been made to deduce from this a causal relation between the two factors of population density and soils. Morgan postulates the relative ease of clearing the light forest with the sands as well as of working the sandy soils. He also suggests the need for shelter from attack, which is amply provided by the forest.[3] These factors are certainly important, but that other factors may also have been at work is suggested by the existence of very high densities in Ibibioland on the coastal plains sands, as well as by the sharp contrasts between the densely populated Ezza country and the sparsely settled Izzi country on the heavy clays of the Cross River basin. Anthropological research suggests an historical explanation in terms of waves of migration from outside into the area—from across the Niger and from the savanna north—as well as its dispersal from a heartland in the Nri-Awka area moving south-east and north along lines of least resistance.[4] Other historical factors, such as the effects of the Arab and the European slave trades in the selective depopulation of the country, have also been advanced.

At the present state of knowledge, all explanatory discussion on the population distribution must necessarily be largely speculative. Very little is known of past patterns of population distribution. Local oral histories are understandably if sometimes systematically biased, the aim being not merely to record events but also to regulate social relationships. Archaeological research into Ibo history has now started at Awka Nri under the auspices of Ibadan University, and it is to be hoped that this will put the study of the development of settlements and population distribution on a much firmer footing.

The population of Iboland is contained in 2,780 settlement units, only 72 of which contain substantial urbanised sectors, and only 20 having urban sectors constituting more than one quarter of the total population. In order of decreasing size, these 'towns' are Onitsha, Port Harcourt, Enugu, Aba, Oguta, Umuahia-Ibeku, Omoku, Abakaliki, Aguleri, Owerri, Agbani, Ogwe, Nomeh, Omoba, Ogrugru, Ahoada, Obigbo, Nbawsi, Afikpo Road and Umukoroshe. They fall into three main rank/size groups. The first four are outstanding as cities, each with a population of over 50,000 in 1953. The second group of towns—Oguta, Umuahia-Ibeku, Abakaliki, Aguleri and Owerri—come into the 10,000 range; and the rest are aligned in a log-linear continuum in the 1,000-5,000 range. The pattern of distribution of these towns is to be explained largely by their history. The development of urban centres is as yet immature, and outside the big cities there is little correlation between size and function. Furthermore, the trends of development of various towns are disparate, a town like Umuahia-Ibeku growing rapidly while Oguta declines. Excepting the four cities, settlement units in Iboland were all under 35,000 persons in 1953. The median size was 640. Half the settlements were between 230 and 1,800 and 82% under 3,000. The large rural settlements (under 3,000) were locally concentrated in the northern plateau and in the densely populated central Ibo uplands, while most of the smaller settlements (under 230 persons) were in the Aboine basin and the coastal plains.

Production

The economy of Iboland is predominantly agricultural, 78% of the working population (male) in 1952/3 being involved in direct primary production and another 6% in trading activities involving local produce. The distinction into occupation groups, however, is not clear cut. Many farmers engage in trade, as do most women, who tend to specialise in agricultural produce. Many of those who are recorded as engaged in other occupations also own farms. From the point of view of trade and marketing, agricultural production and exchange give rise to the most complex and vigorous pattern of commodity flow and areal interdependence.

But of increasing importance nowadays are the non-agricultural sectors of the economy, notably the new industries associated with the introduction of western technological skills, and the various tertiary activities — administrative, professional and commercial — which have developed with political and economic expansion. Some of the traditional crafts have died out in competition with imported rival commodities but others have flourished with the increase of the market (due to population increase, greater occupational specialisation and rising purchasing power). The regional distribution of all these activities is much more uneven than that of agricultural production.

(*i*) *Agricultural production*   Iboland lies well within the root-crops and oil palm producing region of southern Nigeria, while on its northern borders it touches on the grain economy of the drier north. In relation to the whole country Iboland is a food deficit area. Production per square mile of territory in Iboland is much higher than the average for the country; but this is more than offset by the abnormally high population densities already referred to. Yet while there is a net import of food into Iboland, there are also some movements of staple foods outwards from Iboland to other parts of Nigeria; rice from Abakaliki to Lagos and *gari*, palm oil and fruits to the Ibo concentrations in the Northern Region being the most significant.

Inter-regional trade in foodstuffs is specialised, highly organised and dependent on bulk movement by road, rail and river. Local exchange on the other hand is mostly unspecialised, depending on the movements of thousands of peasant producers and marketers. Such local exchange is more significant for an understanding of rural market development, and its pattern very much depends on local differences in ecology and production. For this reason Iboland has been divided into a number of ecological regions in which the man-land balance and the pattern of agricultural production and needs may be seen to be broadly similar. An examination of these regions and their inter-relationships provides a useful framework for the analysis of patterns of commodity flow and market development in Iboland today.

The ecological region is of course a qualitative concept, a subjective evaluation of a number of associations, some of which are not readily quantifiable. But in view of the intimate relationship between the agricultural character and potential of a region and some key physical and human factors, it is feasible to attempt a delimitation of the region in terms of these factors, always bearing in mind the necessarily arbitrary nature of the thresholds. The main factors which would appear to be significant are topography, climate (especially rainfall), soils and population density. Topography provides the basic organising framework. The ethnic distribution of the population has been somewhat determined by this, and the various tracts—plateau, ridge, valley and plain—correlate broadly with areas of similar soil associations and agricultural practice. Climate and soils are relevant to the periodicity of agriculture, to the choice of crop and crop associations, and to their yields. Population density reflects on the intensity of farming, and is critical in the determination of food-surplus and food-deficit regions.

On the basis of these criteria, Iboland may be divided into nine main ecological regions.

(I) the riverain and delta alluvial swamps,

(II) the southern Ibo plains,

(III) the overpopulated central Ibo uplands,

(IV) the north-western basin,

(V) the northern plateau,

(VI) the northern foothills,

(VII) the Awgu-Okigwi complex and the upper Mamu and Imo valleys,

(VIII) the south-east dissected region,

(IX) the Aboine basin.

Some of the differences in crop production patterns are illustrated in Table VI.

Table VI

REGIONAL VARIATION IN CROP COMBINATIONS 1959/60

Ecological Region	Sample Village	Average No. of Farms	Crop Combinations (% of Farms)								
			1	2	3	4	5	6	7	8	Total
I	Egwe Oguta	3.5	6	27	19	—	42	—	2	3	100
II	Akwu-kabi	1.8	—	—	73	—	25	—	2	—	100
	Amapu	1.6	15	3	64	5	10	—	3	—	100
III	Ichi	2.6	34	2	9	—	—	—	55	—	100
	Ntueke	3.4	4	3	39	—	18	—	36	—	100
	Umueze	3.9	2	2	22	—	33	35	6	—	100
	Unodu Oraifite	1.9	19	4	—	—	13	—	64	—	100
IV	Aku	4.5	6	80	2	—	—	—	12	—	100
	Amokwe	5.9	18	1	22	—	3	—	57	—	100
VII	Awlaw	4.1	6	22	27	—	25	—	20	1	100
VIII	Ahuwa	3.9	1	2	41	1	53	2	—	—	100
	Aman-gwu	3.2	71	29	—	—	—	—	—	—	100
	Okon	2.5	61	14	—	—	5	—	—	—	100
IX	Agu Udene	2.5	48	8	—	—	29	2	6	8	100
	Okposi	3.6	34	8	6	3	12	4	23	9	100

1. Yams, sole crops
2. Yams, and minor crops
3. Yams & cassava
4. Yams and cocoyams
5. Cassava, sole or with minor crops
6. Cassava and cocoyam
7. Cocoyam
8. Other crops

(Based on records of the Rural Economic Survey, Fed. Dept. of Statistics. No data available for regions V and VI.)

(*ii*) *Non-agricultural production* In comparison with other parts of Nigeria, traditional arts and crafts are poorly developed in Iboland, only two centres being noted as important for handicraft industries: Awka for wood carving and Akwette for textiles. These are two industries which have survived better than others the influx of cheaper or more strictly utilitarian imported substitutes. However, there is a variety of rural crafts of local importance, including pottery, wood carving, palm leaf and bamboo work, calabash decoration, metal work, weaving (cloth and raffia), decorative cloth work, rope making, net making, basket making, fishing implements, leather work, and the making of various kinds of musical instruments.

Awka wood carvings are very popular throughout Nigeria and

are much sought after in the world art market. The craft is not confined to Awka village. It is practised over much of the Njikoka and Aguata counties as well as the Nnewi District of Onitsha Division. Products include elaborately carved doors, furniture and domestic utensils, as well as the more picturesque masks, idols and other sculptures. The craft of fashioning ordinary wooden instruments is more widespread throughout Iboland; it is practised wherever there is a sufficiency of timber.

Akwette's importance in the textiles trade derives from its specialisation in a luxury industry — the production of a special kind of hand-loom cloth by a process which is still a closely guarded secret. Ordinary cloth weaving, based on local cotton, was formerly much more widespread but is now confined to parts of Onitsha and Nsukka Divisions.

The making of sleeping mats is concentrated in the Ishielu and Ohozara areas of Okigwi and Afikpo Divisions. It is based on local resources of *tharmatococus*, screw pine and reeds. The oil palm tree is the basis of a large number of crafts — trays, basketry, ropes, boxes and bags among others. The production of these contributes notably to the livelihood of the peasants in the land-starved but palm-tree rich central Ibo upland area.

Leather work and ivory carving are practised in Abakaliki and Nsukka Divisions where more game is available and more domestic animals kept, and where the cultural influence of Northern Nigerian communities is greater.

Pottery is a widespread skill but most of the production for trade comes from communities with easy access to clay, particularly from around the Awgu-Okigwi complex and along the line of the Bende-Ameliki clays. The principal producers specialise in particular kinds of pottery: pitchers and coolers from Ishiago and cheap cooking pots from Ibeku. The expensive black stewing pots come from coastal communities or are imported from the north through Onitsha.

Metal working is locally important. The traditional centres were Awka, Nkwerre, Abiriba and Item; but only the first two are of any importance today, Abiriba and Item people having turned to trading in the big cities. The blacksmiths now depend on scrap iron rather than on iron ore deposits.

As for modern industrial activities, from a recent survey of fourteen towns in the Eastern Region, Kilby estimates that about £3 million is invested in small-scale industries providing employment for about 30,000 workers.[5] Tailoring and carpentry are easily the most important activities, each involving over one quarter of both the number of firms and the total employment. Metal smithing — tin, gold and iron — account for over 10% of the firms and 8% of the employment. Light engineering — repairs, welding, battery charging, radio repairs — together contribute 8.7% of the firms and 9.7% of the labour force. Other important activities include shoemaking and repairs, bakeries and service industries. Most of these activities are concentrated in the four cities and the rapidly growing town of Umuahia-Ibeku. Some of the technically less complex industries are located in smaller towns not included in the survey or dispersed in rural settlements.

There is more complete and precise information on those industrial activities that employ more than ten persons — which in the context of Iboland must be regarded as medium-scale and large-scale industries. Again the position of the four cities and Umuahia-Ibeku is outstanding. Five settlements — Owerri, Nkalagu (cement factory), Okigwi, Abakaliki and Ikeduru each has just one establishment. One of the problems to be considered in this study is the extent to which the concentration of industrial and other centralising functions in a few towns affects the patterns of marketing. The growth of rural industrial centres is a critical factor in the transformation of the marketing landscape of the area.

Consumption

Something of the pattern of consumer's expenditure in Nigeria is indicated in Okigbo's analysis of the National Accounts.[6] These data reflect a low level of economic development, a level at which a high proportion of income is spent on necessities, particularly on food.[7] Indeed the total of 73.8% for food, drinks and tobacco is very close to the figure of 75% which has been claimed to represent 'practically the lowest level of subsistence',[8] although statistics generally available are not really reliable or comparable enough to justify such precise evaluations.

The 1957 figures given by Okigbo represent a continuing change in the pattern of expenditure which is consistent with the conventional views formally demonstrated in Engels' curves:[9] that there is a higher income elasticity of demand for 'luxury' items — usually non-agricultural goods and services — than for food. Both the rising import figures, as well as various studies in Western Nigeria,[10] show a shift in expenditure from food items to imported goods. Although conclusions drawn from statistics of consumption taken over a few years must be treated with caution, Okigbo's figures show an interesting trend in Nigeria's expenditure on various items between 1950 and 1957. The rate of increase of total expenditure was 5% per annum, but expenditure on Nigerian food rose by only 2%, in contrast to imported foods, which had the highest rate of growth — 20% per annum. Expenditure on clothing rising at 6% was close to the total growth rate, but the other items rose much more sharply — 10% for durable goods and 15% for other non-durable goods. To the extent that this trend is maintained or accelerated the patterns of trade are liable to change, with places and institutions associated with the rising lines of business becoming more important.

Another feature which emerges from a study of consumption is its very low mean value. The 1957 figures indicate an average *per capita* consumption of £24. 6s. 0d per annum. Considering that this figure includes the value of usufructure, the vigour of marketing activity in Nigeria is noteworthy. A more meaningful unit of expenditure is, of course, the family. Figures from family budget studies in Eastern Nigeria,[11] show that the expenditure of a rural household is of the order of 9/- to 25/- weekly for food and (a much wider range) 10/- to 60/- for other purchases. Other studies throughout Nigeria show a similar pattern.[12] Taking together the low level of consumption and the known vigour of marketing activity, it is not surprising to note the very low average value of marketing transactions.

NOTES

1. H. Vine, *Notes on main types of Nigerian soils*. Lagos, 1952.
2. A. T. Grove, 'Soil erosion and population problems in south-eastern Nigeria', *G.J.*, 1951.
3. W. B. Morgan, 'Farming practice, settlement patterns and population density in south-eastern Nigeria', *G.J.*, 1955.
4. G. I. Jones, 'Ibo land tenure', *Africa*, 1949.
5. P. Kilby, 'Development of small industries in Eastern Nigeria', *United States A.I.D. Report*. Enugu, 1963.
6. P. N. C. Okigbo, *Nigerian national accounts*. Lagos, 1962.
7. See for example C. Gide, *Cours d'Economie Politique*. London, 1911; also H. Wold, *Demand analysis: a study in econometrics*. New York, 1953; and H. Leibenstein, *Economic backwardness and economic growth*. New York, 1957.
8. C. Clark, *The conditions of economic progress*. London, 1951, p. 421.
9. Wold, op. cit.
10. R. Galletti, K. D. S. Baldwin, and I. O. Dina, *Nigerian cocoa farmers*. London, 1956; J. Heads, 'Urbanisation and economic progress in Nigeria', *South African Journal of Economics*, 1959.
11. Rural Economic Surveys 1959/60. Records of the Federal Department of Statistics, Lagos.
12. See, for instance, A. Martin, *The oil-palm economy of the Ibibio farmer*. Ibadan, 1956.

CHAPTER NINE

The Development of Trade and Marketing

The Social Unit

THE largest effective unit of social control in Iboland is traditionally the village group, which has a population ranging from a few hundred to a few thousand persons and may extend in area from a few square miles to thirty or more. In topographical terms the village group consists of a cluster of villages sharing a market place, which is at once a ritual, political and marketing centre.[1] But the village group is more a sociological than a topographical unit. It is 'the largest local unit, named, and based on a patrilineage or segment of one, whose members claim to be regarded as independent of other groups, even of those sharing a common ancestry; this claim being recognised by other comparable groups, but not being necessarily connected with any true independence of function.'[2] The last qualification underlines the difficulties of definition involved. Operationally defined, the village group is a working arrangement of its constituent villages, an arrangement which is by no means static. Fission of groups and adhesion of constituent villages to new groups is a common feature of the Ibo social dynamics. These structural changes are usually accompanied by changes in the traditional history of the group, a common expedient in non-literate societies where tradition has a duty not only to record history but also to provide mnemonics for social relationships.[3] Hence it is not always possible to reconstruct from oral tradition the previous relationships of various units.

The village group may be regarded as a corporate entity. Preeminently, it is the land-administering unit. Although land normally belongs to the constituent villages, some of it, usually in the centre or on the borders, may be held in common. Also the group has a suzerain interest in the land and may requisition it without compensation, for purposes of common interest. Social life is organised within the framework of the village group. Rituals and reciprocative gift-exchanges, redistributive sharing, periodic meetings and common festivals keep alive the solidarity of the group. The economy is organised within the same context. The farming calendar, from the date of bush-burning to the date of the yam harvest festival, is set for the group. So are the location of group markets and their periodicity. The members of the group have contacts with persons in neighbouring village groups and beyond, but the greater part of their activities are carried out within the village group community and their strongest ties are with other members of it. Territorial sovereignty is given physical form in the institution of *Ogbugbandu* — formal boundaries guaranteed by covenant — which exist only between contiguous village groups and not between their constituent villages.

The village is a more basic unit than the village group and is topographically much more obvious. It is made up of a number of localised patrilineages, which constitute the primary local group. Whether these patrilineages live in compact settlements or in individual homesteads, the congregation of settlement units about a point distinguishes physically the complex from other villages. Structurally there is a greater cohesion between the patrilineages constituting the village, which are usually very closely related, than between the villages in the village group. The village is the principal land-owning unit and usually delegates to the patrilineages the rights to allocate its use. Reciprocal gift-exchanges are an important element of economic relationships within the village. They become more prominent as the web of kinship becomes more closely knit, but commercial exchanges are also significant and remain so down to the family level. The parental family — a man, his wives and unmarried children — may be considered the basic economic unit. Much of the economy lies in the redistributive sector, depending on internal division of labour, mainly according to sex, and on socially prescribed contributions by its members. But commercial exchanges are by no means ruled out. Thus it is normal for wives to buy from their husbands the palm wine and yam they need for their social and ritual obligations.

Trade and Market in Traditional Iboland

The market-place is the principal venue for commercial exchange. Typically, a traditional market is held once in every four or eight days. The ordering of the periodicity is embedded in Ibo culture and derives from Ibo concepts of time. These concepts would appear to be analysable within the categories established by Evans-Pritchard in his studies of the Nuer: structural time, ecological time, and chronological time.[4] The first two are very important in a non-literate society where quantitative reckoning of long periods of time is tedious to make and impossible to store accurately, while in the absence of mechanical aids, precise reckoning of units of time shorter than a day is out of the question. Historical events were stored in social memory in the context of contemporaneous events. In traditional history time was elastic, expanding or contracting to reflect current social relationships.

For day-to-day life in Iboland the units of time were the year (*Afo, Aro*); the moon (*Onwa*); the week (*Izu*) and the day (*Ubochi, Mbosi*). The year is ecological rather than chronological. It is the period from one yam harvest to the next, from mid-dry season to mid-dry season, and lasts between twelve and thirteen moons. The moon (*Onwa*) is related directly to the lunar cycle, being the period between the beginning of the first quarter and the end of the last. Operationally the duration is rather imprecise since it depends on the ability to spot the new moon; sometimes, as between debtor and creditor, luminescence can be subjective. The basic unit of time, the week (*Izu*), is chronological and is not strictly related to either the year or the moon. The *Izu* is a four-day period; the days are known as *Eke, Orie* or *Olie, Afo* or *Aho*, and *Nkwo*, succeeding in that order.

The origin of the four-day unit is obscure. But it is interesting to observe that the quadriform motif is recurrent in Ibo thought and symbolism. The blades of the *Onu*, a cross-shaped knot of palm leaf, the symbol of authority and harbinger of war, are four. A formal address to a community meeting is begun with up to a maximum of four calls or greetings and a corresponding number of responses. Only a person addressing his peers may make the four calls: for example young men addressing meetings at which elders are present may not do so. Kola nuts for ceremonial and ritual purposes must consist of four segments precisely. The number four occurs repeatedly in the liturgy of the priests and incantations of the doctors.

The idea of duality or opposition is also a very powerful one in Iboland. Sociologically it is reflected in Ibo social organisation, notably in the double-descent system, and in the dual organisation of social units.[5] In the realm of concepts dichotomies are prominent, the major oppositions being sky (*Enu*), versus earth (*Ani*); sun (*Anwu, Anyanwu*) versus moon (*Onwa*); rains (*Udumiri, Udumili*) versus droughts (*Okochi*); right (*Aka nri, Aka utala*) versus left (*Akaekpe, Akaibite*); heights or ups (*Enu, Enugwu*) and downs (*Ndida, Agbo*). Horton records from the Nike area an ingenious explanation of the four-day week in the context of a double opposition.[6] According to this account it derives from the opposition of the two most significant polar axes: the path of the sun and moon, and the path of the sky and earth. *Eke* is in the sun-earth sector, *orie* in the earth-moon, *afo* in the moon-sky, and *nkwo* in the sky-sun sector. Although this fascinating concept is probably a latter day invention, it suggests the deep-rootedness of the four-day week in Ibo thought. The four-day week preceded the market institution. Given the need for periodicity it was logical that this feature should develop within the existing temporal framework. Only in two small areas in Iboland — in the Ngbo enclave in Abakaliki Division, and in part of Ikwerre land, both as a result of non-Ibo influences — do we have five-day market cycles. (On the other hand the Igala communities bordering on Nsukka Division are changing from their traditional five-day cycle to a four-day cycle.)

Periodic markets in Iboland are widely believed to have developed out of the custom of the rest day. By this custom, different segments or villages in the village groups have different days within the four-day week or a period of two weeks (known as *izu ukwu*—big week) on which they abstain from farm work. The people stay at home and do household chores, practise crafts or hobbies, relax and entertain one another as well as visitors. Most of the local festivals and ceremonies also fall on rest days. A market system thus found a ready-made institutional framework, each village controlling the market developed on its land—usually in the village square—and held on its rest day. Most village groups have a central market, usually claimed to date from the origin of the settlement, having been 'carried over' from the abandoned settlement, and located in and controlled by the senior village. Not all markets are, of course, associated with the traditional rest days. But the habit of allocating visiting days on the basis of fairness has been transferred to that of fixing the periodicity of the market, which must take into consideration the periodicity of existing markets in the area of authority of the group. The location and periodicity of traditional group markets in each village group thus depend on factors internal to that village group. Hence the group markets constitute independent sets of markets, and we may consider traditional Iboland as covered by a basic order of independent marketing rings more or less as numerous as there are village groups.

Although the group marketing rings were independent of each other in organisation and control, they were not independent in function. As we have seen there was considerable trade between village groups. Typically, no new markets were created to cater for the inter-group trade, but through general competition or special advantages certain markets in each village group emerged as inter-group markets serving not only their village group but also large numbers of persons from outside it. Normally the senior market in the village group, the market at the centre of the group and control-led by the senior village, would emerge as the inter-group market, but it need not always be so. The senior markets of two contiguous village groups might be held on the same day and a minor market in one of them might well take up the inter-group role. Also where a village group is sprawled over a wide area, no one market might be central enough to act as inter-group market for trade with all the neighbouring districts: several markets in one group might then emerge as inter-group markets, each specialising in trade with different communities. Thus the status of inter-group markets was not institutionalised; nor was their emergence consciously planned for. Markets waxed and waned with the state of external trade.

Some qualifications may be made to the pattern outlined above. First, under conditions of unstable relations between village groups, markets owned and controlled by rival groups were deemed too dangerous to visit, and new markets had to be created between them, or at their outskirts, in order to increase the chances of escape from attack. This would appear to be the case among a number of communities in parts of Onitsha, Awka and Nsukka Divisions. Secondly, in the pioneer fringes of Ibo settlement — mainly in Abakaliki and Aba Divisions—few settlements were large enough to support a market. Markets were typically located between rather than within settlements, so as to be as central as possible to the communities using them, and so that they might be seen by all to be common property.

A particular type of inter-group trade, that between the mainland agricultural communities and the people of the creeks and riverain areas, deserves special mention. The location of markets was necessarily linear, on the banks of the waterways, and was particularly unsuited to the operation of the ring system. Secondly, the perishable nature of fish, the principal waterside commodity, necessitated their daily disposal by fishermen. Thus in the contact zone (the *Ogwunabiri*), an early morning daily market took the place of the periodic inter-group market.

Both intra-group and inter-group trade depended mainly on mass movements of peasants who bought one another's goods and did a little trading as well. Long-distance trade depended on the movements of specialist groups. As long as trade was mainly internal, long-distance goods traffic in a largely similar environment, though well established, was not voluminous; an exception was the already mentioned trade between the riverain and inland communities. It was concerned largely with non-bulky or luxury items: salt, beads, ivory and other ornaments, dyes, cloths, carvings (religious and secular), charms and ironmongery. This kind of trade was mostly irregular and can hardly be said to have created new markets within an area. Two systems, however, reached a very high level of organisation: the Awka system and the Arochuku system. The Awka system conformed to a more general pattern. The Arochuku system was better integrated and reached its apogee in a later period when the greater demands of European trade enabled it to make full use of its organisation (Fig. 14).

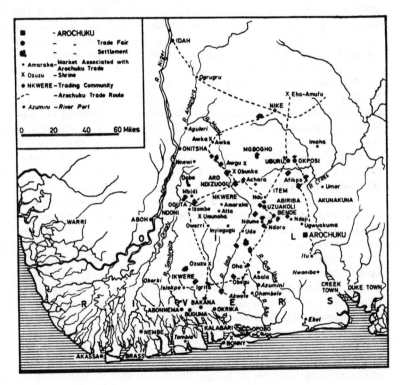

Fig. 14 *The old Ibo trading system.*

We have already seen in the *Ogbugbandu* institution the role of covenants in formalising inter-group relationships. The *Igbandu* was a covenant at the personal level and was the principal means of guaranteeing freedom of movement across the country and safety among strangers. The traveller entered into an *Igbandu* relationship with an influential member of the village group he was visiting or passing through. Details varied regionally, but the ceremony was much after a common pattern. It involved ritual incision on the forearms of the covenanting parties and the intermingling of their blood. Kola dipped in the common blood might be eaten, and there would be a common sacrifice and feast. The parties thus entered into a ritual kinship and were bound not only to do no harm to each other but also to protect each other when necessary. The host protected his guest and generally acted as his agent *vis-à-vis* other members of the community. It was also his duty to have the departing guest escorted to the *Ogbugbandu* with the next village group and formally handed over to the contact there. Thus the traveller was shuttled across the country by a relay of hosts.

The prestige of the Awka people in Iboland derived from the repute of their 'Agbala' deity and from their skill as physicians. They travelled first and foremost as priests, diviners and doctors. The contacts made in these capacities were useful in establishing markets for their wares and services as skilled craftsmen—blacksmiths and carvers, and as inland pedlars of luxury items, notably ivory and coral beads from the Anambra and Igala country. The Awka people did not abandon agriculture, but integrated it with their specialist activities. The village group was divided into two parts between which the monopoly of going on the road alternated annually. In the eighth or ninth agricultural month, shortly after the new yam festival, the travellers whose turn it was would leave. There was no formal division of territory. They travelled in troupes of ten to twenty adults, each of whom had with him two to four apprentices aged between five and twelve years. The area of operation of a troupe would depend on earlier contacts and on the ability of the leaders to open new territory and negotiate new covenants. The tour normally lasted about nine months but travellers were not obliged to return until the seventh month of the next year, about five *Izus* (twenty days) from the new yam festival. From the nature of their organisation the Awka people did not create any permanent settlements or markets, although the Awka man's presence in an area enhanced, for the duration, the importance of the local markets. Nonetheless several markets were very strongly associated with Awka activity.

The Aro Trade System

The long-distance trade associated with the Arochuku people, the most famous trading community in Iboland, contrasts with that of the Awka people. Its primary stimulus was the overseas trade with Europe, which began with the arrival of the Portuguese traders in the Bight of Biafra in the fifteenth century. The response to this stimulus was wholly indigenous, and until the latter half of the nineteenth century the inland side of the trade remained in the hands of indigenous traders, mainly Arochuku people. The establishment of the Arochuku system marked a new phase in the development of trade and markets in Iboland. The distinctive feature was the setting up of a consciously coordinated trading network based on trading settlements, trade routes and fairs. Its operation led to the further differentiation of existing markets, the creation of new ones and the development of new patterns of regional orientation.

Arochuku is an Ibo-speaking village group made up of nineteen villages of Ibo, Ibiobio and Ekoi origin. Traditions of its origin vary, but its location at the tip of a narrow projection of Iboland into Ibibio country lends support to the tradition that its foundation was part of the general movement of Ibo people from the Ibo heartland towards the coast. Talbot dates the foundation between the years 1300 and 1400,[7] when Ibo invaders with some Ekoi allies and mercenaries conquered the Ibiobio aborigines, some of whom were eventually assimilated. A famous Ibiobio oracle, the *Ebinokpabi*, was adopted by the invaders and soon became famous throughout Iboland through the proselytising zeal and acumen of its new agents. In addition to the protection offered by the prestige of their oracle the Arochuku people maintained and extended their influence through a system of military alliances and the extensive use of mercenary soldiers, notably from the village groups of Abam, Ohafia and Ngbo. Their wars of suppression and intimidation became very frequent in the period of the European slave trade and in fact continued right up to the end of the nineteenth century.

Arochuku lies at the end of a ridge running east and south-south-east from the Central Ibo upland region, a continuation of the Awka-Orlu-Okigwi escarpment. The main Arochuku trade route lay along the ridge as far as Awka and thence north and north-eastwards to Nike. Another route from Arochuku went northwards to the north-eastern Ibo areas through Afikpo and Uburu to the Ezza and Izzi country. From Bende and Uzuakoli on the main route other routes linked up the southern parts of Iboland, and from Uzuakoli a northerly route joined up with the Arochuku-Uburu route. The Arochuku colonies were clustered along these routes. Iboland was carved up by the Arochuku villages into spheres of influence so that the various colonies were usually associated with particular Arochuku villages. Arochuku colonies continued to be founded until well into the twentieth century. In the absence of written records it is difficult to be precise about the dates of their establishment. Kalu Umo lists 98 settlements and suggests that most of them were founded in the seventeenth century.[8] The most important colony was Aro Ndizuogu, situated in the heart of the Ibo country with easy access from this broken country to the uplands in the west and north, through gaps in the escarpment to the Cross River basin in the east, as well as to the southern coastal plains. Other large colonies included Ajalli, Isuochi and Okporoenyi and their satellite colonies, all in the stretch of country between Bende and Awka. In this area the Arochuku people formed self-contained communities. In other areas, while retaining their identity they usually sought to be adopted by and eventually to dominate the local groups. Even now many of the new rulers in Iboland, county councillors and second-class chiefs, are or claim to be of Aro origin.

The functional links between the colonies and Arochuku were very strong. The colonists acted locally as agents of the oracle and took instructions from the authorities at home. They relayed intelligence from their territories back to Arochuku. They conducted clients, litigants and ritual offenders to Arochuku and brought back pronouncements, charms and medicines to local peoples. A certain amount of commerce was always associated with the Arochuku system, but at first this did not necessarily give rise to markets. Much of it was administered trade in luxury items — slaves, horses and cattle for ritual purposes, and beads — and did not command a mass market. Hence the colonies themselves rather than the local markets were the main venues for long distance trade. The group and inter-group markets, where they existed, operated largely outside the Arochuku network. Naturally the presence of an Arochuku colony and the attendant commerce enhanced the importance of nearby markets. The rise of the great markets had to do with the development of the overseas trade, the range and volume of which far surpassed what could be dealt with by private contact in the colonies.

The first European traders established themselves on the coast in 1486. But for nearly four centuries, in some places until 1912, Europeans did not penetrate into the interior of Iboland. Rather they depended on exchange with the coastal communities who in turn organised trade with the inland peoples. The coastal communities did not concern themselves with collecting produce or selling merchandise directly in the interior. They relied on water transport and on the strings of posts and buying depots which they established along the numerous creeks and rivers. At these posts they corresponded with the inland trading communities, notably the Arochuku, the Awka and the Nkwerre people, who organised the trade in the interior. The Arochuku people, with their wide and well established network, became their principal customers.

The demands of the new trade imposed some modifications on the Arochuku system. The house-to-house system could not cope with the expanded volume of business and was supplemented by increasing recourse to market-place exchange, particularly for the retail of imported goods—tobacco, spirits, gun powder and textiles. The traffic in slaves tended to keep within the old system so that the Nkwo Ndaro market in Oboro (Bende Division), although becoming an important Arochuku trade centre, was never noted for the slave traffic.[9]

Nevertheless, considerable market development was associated with the activities of Aro traders. The location of the principal markets did not exactly correspond with the Aro colonies. Rather, Aro traders adopted the principal markets in various areas. These markets remained under local administration and control although the Aro people wielded a lot of influence. In areas where there were no markets or where market development was inadequate, particularly among the Ikwerre and Ogu Ukwu peoples, the Aro established new markets.

Most important of the Aro markets were two fairs set up, not at Aro Ndizuogu, the premier Aro colony, but at nodal points in the main area of Aro influence. The first fair rotated between Uzuakoli and Bende, and served mainly the southern part of the country. The second rotated between Okposi and Uburu, two village groups four miles apart in the southern part of the Ogu Ukwu country. Routes from this area led through the gap between the Nsukka-Udi and the Awgu-Okigwi escarpments into Achi and Udi and linked up with the Western Aro trade route. Okposi-Uburu thus served mainly the northern parts of Iboland. The alternation between pairs of sites was for purely strategic reasons. The Aro traders wanted to retain effective control of the fairs; and competition between rival sites for their very profitable patronage ensured that they obtained the most favourable conditions.

The operation of the two fairs was functionally integrated. Each was opened at 24-day intervals and during the period of the system's highest development, in the nineteenth century, lasted for four major days. Their periodicity was dovetailed so that traders could move from one fair (*Agbagwu*) to the other. Fig. 15 illustrates the cycle of trade in the latter part of the nineteenth century when the Uburu and Uzuakoli markets were in operation. The *Agbagwu* season began with the Uburu fairs and was heralded by a large attendance at the Nkwo Uburu market, normally an eight-day periodic inter-group market, on an *nkwo* day, four days before the *Agbagwu* day itself. This market day was known as *Nkworoto*. Long-distance traders, particularly those dealing in imported goods, started to arrive and to display their goods while the Uburu people stocked up provisions in preparation for their guests. In the next three days, trading activity was lax and confined to the evenings while more traders came in. *Agbagwu* proper began on the fifth day and lasted four days. On the last day the journey to Uzuakoli, 40 miles away, began. At Uzuakoli this was the Afor Ngwu market day, similar to the Nkworoto when traders began to come in and their hosts to stock up provisions. The Uzuakoli *Agbagwu* began two days later at Eke Ogbiti market and lasted for six days, the first four of which were the *Agbagwu* proper. The last two days were known as *Bianko*, from the Aro traders from Bianko who traditionally arrived at this time. The nine days between the *Agbagwu* seasons were known as *Oge nta* (small season) and were used for holding subsidiary fairs, one at Uburu following the Uzuakoli season and one at Uzuakoli just before the Uburu season.

The fairs served primarily to coordinate the activities of two groups of Aro traders, the *Aro ulo* (home-based Aro) and the *Aro uzo* (Aro abroad). The *Aro ulo* acted as middlemen between the coastal traders and the *Aro uzo* who organised the local trade. But the fame of the fairs carried throughout Iboland and attracted thousands of traders from afar and peasants from all over the surrounding countryside. Because of the interconnection between the two fairs there was considerable overlap in their hinterlands. Thus a local history of Uzuakoli records that traders came to its market from 'Akaka Elugu, Elugwu Ngwo, Agbaja, Mgbogho, Nnewi, Okaiuga, Obowo, Ibeku, Lekwe, Ndi Okpara, Bende, Ozuitem, and even as far as Ibiobio and Onitsha'.[10] In addition to the trade in slaves and imported goods, the most important items of trade in the fairs were salt, pigs, horses and cattle at Uburu and Akwette cloth and tobacco at Uzuakoli.

The Coastal Trade and the European Contact Phase

Like most Ibo groups the Arochuku people were essentially land-lubbers. Although the Aro trade system was perfected during the period of the European slave trade and was based on the large-scale exchange of slaves and tropical produce with sea-borne European goods, the Arochuku people were never in control of either the ports or the creeks and rivers leading to them. Rather, they communicated

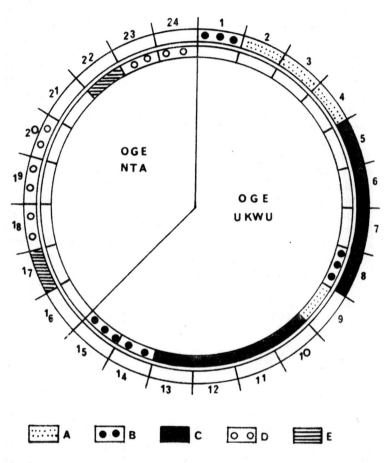

Fig. 15   *Cycle of trade in late nineteenth century at Uburu* (outside)
and Uzuakoli (inside) *fairs.*
A, Lax trading period, usually in evening; B, Market;
C, Agbagwu; D, Subsidiary Market; E, Subsidiary Fair.

with riverain and coastal communities such as the Efik, the Opobo and Bonny people who in turn traded with the European ships. The *Aro ulo* took most of their merchandise to Itu, at the mouth of the Enyong tributary of the Cross River some eighteen miles from Arochuku, and sold to Efik traders who had come up from Calabar. Some of the bigger Aro traders, however, went direct to the coast to sell to Calabar, Bonny and Opobo middlemen. Similarly, some of the bigger *Aro uzo* (colonial) traders by-passed the fairs and took their goods direct to the coast. This was particularly true of traders operating in the Ikwerre, Etche and Ngwa country near the coast.

The traditional trade between the coastal and inland communities has already been mentioned. There was also an interflow of craftsmen and specialists. Awka and Nkwerre blacksmiths were employed for the ironwork of the huge trade canoes. There were ritual links between such coastal deities as that of Bonny and the priesthood of the interior. Jones points out that by the time the first European traders appeared on the coast a regular pattern of trade was well established and flourishing.[11] Certain communities like the Kalabari specialised in the carrying trade, operating from markets along the banks of the waterways. The *Esmeraldo de Situ Orbis*, one of the earliest European records of the Guinea trade, gives some idea of the extent of the commerce. The canoes are described as 'the largest in the Ethipias of Guinea', some of them being large enough to hold eighty men:

> They come from a hundred leagues or more up the river buying yams in large quantities; they also buy many slaves, cows, goats and sheep. They sell all this to the natives of the village for salt and our ships buy these things for copper bracelets.[12]

As long as the European traders were confined to the coast the general pattern of traffic persisted through successive waves of Portuguese, Dutch and English merchants. But by the time of British ascendancy, in the later seventeenth century, structural changes were taking place within the trading communities. At first the effect of the European trade was to set the pattern of trade more firmly. Its much greater volume and regularity required permanent posts on the old routes. Here stocks in trade were maintained and produce purchased; from here inland buyers were financed and produce sent down to the coast. Among the more important colonies were those at Azumini, Ohambele, Akwete, Ndoni, Eleme, Asa, Urantta, Usemodu, Elele, Omoku, Oguta, Obigbo and Owerrinta. Unlike the Arochuku system there was no centralised coordination of operations and competition was as fierce between segments of one trading community as it was between rival communities.[13] The introduction of gunpowder in the mid-seventeenth century was a key event in the evolution of the delta communities. It enabled the rich and the efficient to fight their way to the top of the trade. The communities themselves evolved into oligarchic city states with the heads of the pre-eminent trading firms as the heads of the ruling houses.[14] From the point of view of efficiency there was of course a great advantage in the system. In between periods of inter-House warfare the organisation of each House made for speedy and coordinated large-scale trade. The colonies and their associated markets waxed and waned with the strength of their Houses.

By the beginning of the nineteenth century the British, who were now virtually the only European trading group in the area, were beginning to turn from the slave trade to trade in vegetable oils: a change related to the beginnings of the industrial revolution in Britain and the need for industrial lubricants as well as new markets for industrial products.[15] One of the immediate effects of the shift in emphasis was to enhance the position of the coastal communities nearer the mainland. The supply market for palm produce, the chief attraction in Iboland, is ubiquitous while that for slaves depended on a high degree of organisation and coordination between the coastal communities and the inland agents, such as existed between the Bonny or Calabar and the Arochuku people. Many producers and small traders outside the Aro system could and did take their palm produce direct to the waterside posts. Trading states such as Abonnema and Aboh took on increased importance and new settlements proliferated, particularly on the Imo River (Imo River Station, Owerrinta, Ife, Udoh). The old Aro trade route continued to flourish but the new trade did not use it. Developments in the nineteenth and twentieth centuries further modified the patterns. The nineteenth century saw the penetration of Europeans into the inland waterways and the establishment of direct contact between them and the inland peoples. The twentieth century saw the shift of traffic from the waterways to the railway and later on to the road systems. Each change had implications for the patterns of commodity flow, regional orientations and the development of markets.

The Effects of European Penetration

In 1830 John and Richard Lander discovered the well-guarded African secret that the river Niger's outlet to the sea was through the creeks of the Oil Rivers. This marked the beginning of a new phase in the history of the development of Ibo-European trade and was the precursor of numerous expeditions which were to culminate in British control of the interior as well as of the waterways.[16] At first British official interest in the interior was sporadic, being confined to giving occasional gun-boat support to British traders who took the initiative for penetration. The major British trading interests were amalgamated into the United Africa Company in 1879, by which time many European trading stations had already been established up-river, the most important being those at Aboh Oguta and Onitsha. In 1886, following the Berlin Conference of 1884, the British declared a protectorate over the area of operation of the United Africa Company and granted the Company a Royal Charter to administer it. The Oil Rivers Protectorate—as it was called—comprised the area bordering the lower Niger for some 258 miles from the sea up to Lokoja. The new authority strengthened the hands of the British traders. From securing a foothold on the inland stations the company, now renamed the Royal Niger Company, proceeded by several devices to exclude the coastal peoples from the river trade, choosing to regard them as 'foreigners' in the company's area of authority and thus liable to buy licences for trade and to pay tax as well as import and export duties on their merchandise.[17] The effect of all this was to increase the rate at which the centre of gravity of trade shifted from the coastal ports to the creek and river stations now controlled by the Company.

From the official point of view the system of indirect control proved unsatisfactory and after a period of indecision Britain declared the area a protectorate in 1891 and began to pursue a deliberate policy for the eventual direct administration of the interior.

First, European activity on the known waterways was urged and encouraged. The Government offered to trading companies leases of land at nominal rents (60 years at annual rentals varying between £40 and £60 according to the volume of established trade). The great problem was the Cross River district. Here European activity had been much slower than on the Niger.[18] Until the first decade of the twentieth century 'the trade of the district [was] conducted by down-river people: Efiks, Akunakunas, Inokus and natives of Umon' who came up to Calabar in their big canoes. Contrary to the usual pattern, trade followed the flag. The energetic British High Commissioner, Sir Ralph Moore, set up a station at Itu, the great river port for Aro trade, made surveys and canvassed firms for location at suitable points—Itu, Afikpo, Atani, Obrikom. The fear of possible German acquisition of the hinterland lent urgency to these efforts.[19]

Secondly, a series of expeditions were sent inland from the Oil

Rivers bases. The aim was to make as many journeys inland as possible each dry season, making treaties and surveying; to establish stations whence these places could be revisited; and then to make further advance the following year.[20] Only the two main rivers were navigable far inland, but the heads of navigation of the other rivers and creeks provided starting points for the inland treks. Official bases were established at Akwette, 30 miles up the Imo river from Opobo; at Degema, the same distance up the Sombreiro river from the coast; as well as at Warri and Sapele in the Western Delta. The spirit and aims of the exercise are illustrated by the memorandum to the officers of the 'Aquettah Opobo' expedition, which instructs:

> in moving about the country you should keep your eyes open to see if there are any rubber trees or you can discern any economic indigenous plants or products. The direction from which trade comes should be noted and inquiry made if the trade routes are free . . . . . It must be distinctly laid down (to the natives) that all the roads and waterways of the country are free for trade and no tolls must be levied on those using them because they don't happen to belong to the country through which they pass.[21]

The incursions were strenuously resisted by coastal interests but by the turn of the century the British had succeeded in concluding 'treaties' with numerous Ibo communities guaranteeing freedom of trade, guarantees which, however, were not always respected.

The reports of the expeditions recount the importance of the inland markets. Thus the Obegu market, a 4-day periodic market in southern Ngwaland, is described as containing thousands of people coming from immense distances. The Aro presence is noted and the commodities observed include palm oil and kernels, yams, goats, dogs, fowls and metal work. Other important markets through which goods from Obegu reached Opobo are also noted—Akwette, Ohambele and Asa.

The twentieth century saw a shift in British official interest from exploration to 'pacification'. The great military expeditions were started in 1902. The most dramatic event was the destruction of the Ibini Ukpabi shrine at Arochuku, an act which it was hoped would bring down Arochuku influence.[22] By the end of 1906 the whole of Iboland had come under effective British occupation.

Meanwhile efforts were being made to extend the range of the waterways by clearing hitherto unnavigable stretches. The work was to be carried out jointly by the chiefs of the locality and a Government demolition party, the local people doing the initial clearing and the demolition party completing the job. The aim was to make all the waterways navigable for canoes and as far as possible for launch traffic. By 1911 the Otamiri river had been cleared up to Owerri, the Imo river up to Udo and the Sombreiro river up to Ikoi.[23]

By the end of the first decade of the twentieth century, then, a new pattern of trade had been established. The new and expanded markets on the waterways were drawing in palm produce from their immediate hinterland and distributing a wide range of imported merchandise. The farther inland, the greater was the influence of the old Arochuku network which, contrary to British expectation, the destruction of the Ibini Ukpabi had left largely unimpaired. For the inland peoples the European factories represented a new experience. They were permanent centres and offered daily opportunities for exchange, in contrast to the traditional periodic markets. Business fluctuated with the days, since the people had to fit in marketing at the 'beach' with the local periodic system. But with their great advantages of opportunity and frequency, these centres and their associated markets grew rapidly at the expense of the traditional markets. This was the heyday of such trading centres as Ogruru, Aguleri, Oguta, Osomari. The old network was used exclusively for luxury items and the clandestine trade in slaves. On the coast the effect of the new developments was to enhance the position of the ports where the British firms had their warehouses, at the expense of other ports.

In the course of the subjugation of the interior, several operating bases were set up, some of which eventually became headquarters of administrative districts — Owerri, Bende, Awka, Okigwi, Aba, Afikpo, Abakaliki, Udi and Orlu. Some, like Okpoga and Umuduru, were later abandoned in favour of other sites. The chief criteria for siting a Government station seems to have been as follows: (1) reasonable proximity to the next post. The usual day's march for Government troops was about 40 miles and this is the average distance between stations; (2) nodality and ease of access to the surrounding country; (3) proximity to a large market; (4) where possible, high ground well above the surrounding country to provide a strategic, well-drained, airy and pleasant site for the official residences and barracks.[24]

The establishment of administrative centres was an important development for trade and marketing. It did not greatly affect the external trade, nor the old markets and routes associated with the coastal trade. But it increased the scope for trade in local produce in the interior, particularly food crops. The garrisons and the administrative personnel constituted a nucleus of a non-rural based population dependent on the countryside for food. Traders and persons engaged in other service occupations as well as men who came in originally as conscripted labour all settled near the Government station.[25]

Like other permanent stations, the administrative nuclei and their associated settlements offered to the rural communities a new kind of opportunity different from that offered by the traditional periodic markets. There was daily demand for goods. Reaction took several forms. Where there were large periodic markets, as at Bende or Afikpo, these became even more important. In addition to their normal periodicity they developed daily sectors selling mainly foodstuffs. Where there was none, a new market sprang up. At Nsukka the traditional market was over a mile from the site of the station and was not particularly large. The important markets in the area were the Oyo Orba and the Nkwo Ibagwa markets. The new Nsukka market, the Ogige (gate) market, has a daily sector but its most important days are *Eke* and *Oye*, when the two great rural markets are not on. At Amawbia (Strangerville) and Awka Government settlement, an official attempt was made, with very limited success, to persuade the local people to adopt the market as a district market open on *Eke*, the market day for the great traditional market at Awka village group.[26] On the whole, the impact of the administrative centres was only of local significance. More important was the function which most of these centres assumed as nodes of a communication system and as the focus of other centralising institutions such as schools and hospitals. The subsequent development has depended on this. Two centres, Udi and Bende, which are distant from the main lines of movement in Iboland, have deteriorated rather than grown.

Meanwhile the economy itself was expanding rapidly. The external trade was taking an increasing proportion of Ibo trade. The increase reflected the growth of cash-oriented economic activity under the stimulus of greater opportunities for sale and an expansion of demand due to a widening choice of new goods. The introduction of a common currency over Iboland played an important part in easing the flow of goods. Hitherto several currencies had circulated, their acceptability and exchange ratios varying from place to place. The principal currencies were brass rods, manillas and cowries. Their bulk alone was a hindrance to trade. British silver coins were introduced in 1913.[27] They circulated side by side with the old currencies until they were withdrawn after the war, but the sterling equivalence provided a regional unit of account and standard of value.

Direct taxation was introduced in the twenties. Although taxation is widely believed to have a catalytic effect in the development of an exchange economy, in Iboland where commerce was already well established its effect can only have been marginal. The poll tax was between 3/- and 6/-. It stimulated brief seasonal spurts of extra cash-earning efforts and characteristically produced target selling rather than any fundamental restructuring of economic behaviour. The fact that it involved every adult male, however, made its pressure felt in every village and household.

The establishment of Hausa settlements in Iboland belongs to this phase in the development of trade and marketing. Hausa contact with the northern part of Iboland pre-dates European trade. The Igala affinities of the Nsukka area and the Lower Niger Valley as well as the Niger-Benue riverain trade brought these areas into direct communication with the Hausa people. In the north-east there were also trade links, particularly in horses and cattle for ritual and ceremonial purposes. Outside these connections the Hausa were attracted by big game, particularly elephants, and by the trade in ivory. They brought down beads, leather goods and medicines. But it was in the decade following the declaration of the Protectorate of Southern Nigeria that Hausa settlements proliferated, usually as appendages of the European factories or the army barracks. Most of the soldiers were Hausas or Muslims and Hausa traders catered for them. Hausas also provided labour for the factories, for example the head-load carriers between Oguta and Abonnema. Hausas set up as craftsmen, tailors and leather-workers especially, as well as intermediaries for exchange with local communities. Similarly Hausa contractors provided much of the labour for both the railway and early road-building programmes, and more Hausa settlements followed the establishment of railway towns. By the end of the twenties Hausa settlements were flourishing at Ibagwa, Awka, Aguleri, Abakaliki, Enugu, Onitsha, Elele, Omoku Oguta, Port Harcourt, Aba, Umuahia-Ibeku, Omoba, Mbawsi and Afikpo Road.

Hausa communities are highly specialised. From the twenties onwards they were almost exclusively traders and craftsmen. Their distribution shows the location of important retail centres in Iboland in the pre-war period. The settlements provided a permanent base, a central place where goods and services could always be obtained, but the Hausaman also travelled about in the countryside peddling his wares and still does. The development of the cattle trade in the thirties stimulated more Hausa immigration into already existing centres like Abakaliki and Umuahia but did not greatly alter the overall distribution pattern. Hausa traders are still dominant in the cattle trade but are otherwise not now a very important feature of the Ibo economic landscape. They are concerned mainly with selling leather goods, crafts and medicines or buying kola nuts for the northern markets.

Post-War Development

The post-war period has seen an accentuation of the trends already evident between the two world wars, an accentuation due in part to the exigencies of war and in part to the new economic conditions of the post-war era. Up to the second world war British official interest was focused on encouraging export crop production and trade with the metropolitian country. The disruption of normal trade during the war years and the need for increased local produce for the war effort created high food prices and led to the entry of numerous specialist traders and producers into the local food market. War conditions also highlighted regional differences in food production and food prices—differences arising partly from the as yet fragmented nature of the market. Price control measures introduced for the principal food crops and abandoned after the war had the long-term effect of reducing abnormal price gradients for locally produced foods and thus facilitating the creation of a regional market for foodstuffs.

The war also accelerated urbanisation. Most of the demobilised soldiers returned with capital, new skills and a determination not to return to the rural life. They tended to remain in the towns, going into trade or business. Some of them set up their relations as well, as did some of the beneficiaries of the post-war boom in tropical agricultural produce.

The most significant post-war development was the revolution in transport. The railway, constructed between 1914 and 1917, cut through the heart of the Ibo country to the new-found coal mines at Enugu (later to become the capital of Eastern Nigeria) and gave this area for the first time direct access to the coast at the Port Harcourt railhead. Eventually it linked northwards with the grain and meat-producing savanna country of Northern Nigeria. From the point of view of external trade the most important result of railway con-struction was the establishment along the route of European firms after the manner of the riverain and coastal stations. Indeed, so close was the similarity that the stations were known locally as 'beaches', and still are. These firms rapidly attracted markets and trading communities around them and formed the nuclei of new commercial towns. Where, as at Aba, both administrative and commercial centres coincided, the two functions complemented each other and the urban community flourished. Where there was competition between a commercial and an administrative centre, as between Enugu and Udi or between Umuahia and Bende, the commercial centre prevailed, eventually taking over the political functions of the vanquished town.

Up to the end of the twenties, the waterways and the railway line bore the bulk of the long-distance traffic. In 1926 the Government was still considering the practicability of building feeder railway lines from Oguta to Aba or Port Harcourt.[28] By the beginning of the thirties, however, it had become evident that improvement in road transport was necessary to increased production and trade, the bulk of the population being concentrated away from both the waterways and the railway. Plans for road development were prepared but had to be shelved during the second world war. The post-war era saw a huge road-building programme, the road mileage more than doubling between 1937 and 1960.[29] At the same time the number of motor vehicles registered annually increased more than eleven times. Road development led not only to a greater integration of the region but also to a change in orientation of the interior areas from the waterways and railway to the road system.

From the first, motor road development was geared to the demands of long-distance travel. The provision of facilities for movement within a village group or between nearby village groups was purely incidental. The motor road pattern thus cut across the bush path alignments. The motor road network started from a skeletal grid connecting the administrative centres. The main consideration seems to have been topography; construction along ridges and watersheds cut down the number of bridges and culverts necessary and minimised problems of drainage and maintenance. The skeletal grid was completed in the twenties and has dominated road development and borne the bulk of motor traffic ever since. Government road building since the war has been concerned primarily with road improvement, particularly with road-widening and tarring. The enormous increases in road mileage are the result mainly of local effort.

Today there is a dense network of roads connecting rural settlements to one another as well as to the commercial and administrative centres, and to the main arterial roads. The network is particularly underdeveloped in the coastal or riverain areas and in the north and north-east. In the Nsukka plateau the road density is only 30 to 45 miles per 100 square miles as compared with 60 to 80 in a comparable area in Owerri Division. The Aboine basin is also poorly served, except for a strip of country bordering the trunk road from Okigwi to Afikpo. The highest densities are around Onitsha and Aba, the central Ibo area between Okigwi, Orlu, Owerri, Aba and Umuahia, and the area of cross roads between Udi and Awka.

If the density of roads in an area indicates its accessibility, the patterns of road alignments reflect the patterns of spatial orientations. The motor road network of Iboland does indeed reflect the weakness of centralising links. The most important ones are at the chief urban administrative centres, the nuclei of the system. In addition to these a number of rural cross-roads have become important as transportation centres on the more heavily used roads. Most of these are found in the central Ibo upland area. There is also a relatively high concentration of road junctions on the Udi plateau between Enugu Ngwo, Iwollo, Oji River and Ozalla, where the east-west routes cross the north-south plateau routes; but elsewhere road junctions are fewer and more widely spaced. Where the density of the road network is low and road junctions few, the location of road junctions—usually determined by topographic considerations (the head of a valley, a pass or intersection of ridges)—tends to develop into a rural centre. But the relationship is not always such that junction creates centre. Thus Inyi is the focus of a great many routes from the Agwu plateau as well as from across the Mamu valley, largely because it was already an important rural market. On the other hand Ngwo, Angara and Akeze are examples of centres developing because of the cross-roads.

In places where the road alignment is dominantly linear—particularly in the riverain and coastal plain areas—cross-roads are few and far between and are not necessarily significant as centres. The new road alignment is often transverse to the traditional routes so that there are two main types of movement existing side by side: the traditional trade between nearby regions using the traditional routes, and the long-distance trade focused on the main road. The important locations are thus at the crossing points of the two systems of routes.

Road development affects spatial orientations and the development of exchange institutions in other ways. Traditional markets may flourish on periodic incursions of pedestrians, but shops and fixed central places rely very much on regular day-to-day traffic and are tied to the motor road. It is not surprising that rural centres are most common in the central Ibo upland area. Also the accessibility of rural markets to motor traffic makes a lot of difference to their importance relative to other markets in the area. In Bende Division, for instance, the Uzuakoli market, in addition to its importance as an old trade centre, dominated the long-distance marketing of the Elu and Owuwa counties because of its railway and road connections with Umuahia. The re-building of the Umuahia-Ohafia road—now tarred—has meant that the local people do not have to carry their produce all the way to Uzuakoli but can sell to visiting lorries in their own local markets. The emergence of the Nkwo Ndielu and Afor Oputu markets in Ugwueke, and the Eke Ozuitem and Eke Ndioji Ozuabam markets as important food markets for Umuahia traders, dates from this reconstruction.

The pull of the road has of course meant local changes in orientation. In areas of dispersed settlement, where there is greater freedom to build, the tendency for new buildings to be built along the main road has been much more pronounced than in areas of nucleated settlement where social pressures oblige most people to put up their fine new edifices alongside the humbler huts of their relations. But the overall trend is towards concentration along the road. Irrespective of the settlement pattern, all the new amenities—schools, hospitals, dispensaries, post offices and so on—are built on the main roads. Where the traditional market is located away from the new road, market development has often meant a move to a new site on the road.

* * *

The present economic landscape of Iboland derives from various traditional elements and historical processes. The broad pattern of development in so far as it affects marketing institutions may be summarised briefly. The basic framework was the traditional pattern of small village groups with internal marketing systems based on periodic group markets and, in a largely undifferentiated economy, concerned mainly with exchanges between masses of peasant producers-cum-consumers. Inter-group exchange led to differentiation of certain markets within the group systems. Through these inter-group markets the various marketing chains were interlocked. The resulting chains did not have the social recognition and stability of the group systems, but changed with competition between markets. For long-distance trade, traditional society depended on specialist trading communities, notably the Arochuku people, whose activities took on new importance with the establishment of commercial contacts with European merchants trading on the coast. Rural periodic markets became further differentiated in relation to the long-distance trade and their proximity to the trade routes. In certain areas new markets were founded. The creation of the great *Agbagwu* fairs introduced a third order into the rural marketing hierarchy. With European penetration into and subsequent control of the interior, the system of specialist traders declined, the old trade routes giving way to new trade centres on the waterways which fringe Iboland, and eventually on the railway and motor roads. The creation of administrative centres, urban development and the closer internal integration of the entire area stimulated the growth of specialised local production of food and increases in inter-regional trade. The European trade introduced a new type of institution— the daily shop or warehouse—into the marketing landscape. Most of these are located in the towns, but some are now to be found in rural centres and not always on the site of existing markets. On the other hand, market places became established in the new urban and trade centres.

On the basis of this historical and formal analysis of the develop- ment of trade and marketing, then, it is possible to classify settlements into seven formal types:

    i. ports,
   ii. cities or metropolitan centres,
  iii. major urban centres,
   iv. minor urban centres,
    v. administrative centres not otherwise classified,
   vi. rural service centres with urbanised sectors,
 vii. rural settlements.

Each of these types is associated with a particular combination of certain kinds of central-place institutions and market places. On the whole, ports, metropolitan and urban centres have daily markets, some of the smaller markets operating in the evenings only. Traditionally, rural markets are periodic—rural periodic inter- group markets or rural periodic group markets—but rural daily markets and rural evening markets have also come into existence. The minor urban centres and rural service centres may have daily or periodic markets.

In the next chapter we shall attempt a detailed analysis of the present-day marketing landscape, paying particular attention to some of the implications of the peculiar features of marketing activities in market places.

NOTES

1. D. Forde, and G. I. Jones, *The Ibo and Ibibio-Speaking Peoples of South-Eastern Nigeria*. London, 1950.
2. E. W. Ardener, 'Lineage and locality among the Mbaise Ibo', *Africa*, 1954.
3. J. Goody and J. Watt, 'The consequences of literacy', *Comparative studies in society and History*, 1963.
4. E. E. Evans-Pritchard, *Nuer: a description of the modes of livelihood and political institutions of a nilotic people*. London, 1940.
5. See C. M. Meek, *Report on social and political organisation in the Owerri Division*. Lagos, 1934; and E. W. Ardener, 'The kinship terminology of a group of southern Ibo', *Africa*, 1954.
6. W. R. G. Horton, 'God, man and the land in a northern Ibo village group, *Africa*, 1956.
7. P. A. Talbot, *The peoples of Southern Nigeria*, (4 Vols.). London, 1926.
8. K. Umo, *History of Aro settlements*. Lagos, 1949.
9. The partial separation of the slave-trading network from the market-place sub-system was responsible for many of the difficulties encountered by the British authorities in suppressing the slave trade in the interior. In places like Uzuakoli, where a large slave traffic had developed, Government pressure forced the trade back to the house-to-house system. Thus the trade continued long after it was considered closed.
10. F. W. Dodds, 'Notes on early days in Uzuakoli', in A. J. Fox, *Uzuakoli a short history*. London, 1964.
11. G. I. Jones, *The trading states of the Oil Rivers*. London, 1963.
12. Quoted in G. I. Jones, op. cit.
13. K. O. Dike, *Trade and politics in the Niger Delta*, 1830-1885. Oxford, 1956.
14. G. I. Jones, op. cit.
15. H. Stilliard, 'The rise and development of the legitimate trade in palm oil.' Unpublished M.A. Thesis, Birmingham, 1938.
16. K. O. Dike, op. cit., p. 62.
17. Sir Henry Galway, 'The rising of the Brassmen', *Journal of the African Society*, 1935; and E. J. Alagoa, *The small brave City-State, a history of Nembe-Brass in the Niger Delta*. Ibadan, 1964.
    A revolt by the Brassmen against the imposition met with reprisals strong enough to discourage similar resistance elsewhere.
18. The time lag between the activities of European traders in the Niger and the Cross River waterways contributed to the persistence of the Aro trade system, which was linked more with the latter.
19. Sir Ralph Moor's Correspondence: Letters to Secretaries of the African Association, A. Miller and Bros, 21 Feb., 1901. Calprof 9/2 Vol. 1 (Ibadan Archives).
20. C. J. Gertzel, 'Commercial organisation on the Niger Coast 1852-1891', *Leverhulme Inter-Collegiate Conference 1960: Historians in Tropical Africa*. Salisbury, 1962.
21. *Consular Paper:* Calprof 8/2 dated 26 Feb., 1896 (Ibadan Archives).

22. J. C. Anene, 'The Protectorate Government of Southern Nigeria and the Aros 1901-1902', *Journal of the Historical Society of Nigeria*, 1956. According to Anene (p. 21) the British had gradually built up the idea of Aro enmity into an obsession. A Government report (Annual Report 1899/1900) complained that the Aro were 'scattered all over this part, sometimes in twos and threes, sometimes in settlements from the Cross River to the Niger . . . Their influence is predominant over these pagan tribes and as they have no good to say about the Government, their presence is a continued thorn in the side of the Government'.
23. P. A. Talbot, op. cit.
24. Sir Ralph Moor's Correspondence on the opening up of Afikpo Government Station outlines these requirements clearly. C. Calprof 9/2 (Ibadan Archives).
25. S. O. Ottenberg and P. Ottenberg, 'Afikpo markets 1900-1960', in P. J. Bohannan, and G. Dalton, *Markets in Africa*. Evanston, 1963.
26. Awka Divisional Files AW/533 (Enugu Archives).
27. Sir F. D. Lugard, *The dual mandate in British Tropical Africa*. London, 1929.
28. The voluminous correspondence with European firms is preserved in Enugu Archives Ref. C. 10/27.
29. *Annual Abstract of Statistics*, 1960. Lagos, 1963.

CHAPTER TEN

The Marketing Landscape

Markets and Central Places in Developing Countries

THE distinguishing factor in the institutional framework for commercial exchange in Iboland is the central importance of market places. Although the historical geography of market places has been recorded for many areas, detailed studies of the operation of a system in which they play a part are rare. Traditionally, marketing geographers have been concerned with exchange in modern Western-type societies. Here, typically, production is very specialised both as between persons and as between areas. Integration is achieved through the activities of financial and commercial agencies depending on a highly developed system of transport and communications. These agencies are typically located 'in some kind of combination (with other institutions) in a permanent and compact settlement'.[1] From the village shopping centre to the central business district of the metropolis, these complexes are essentially urban features. Each can be analysed as a system of nodes of varying size, range and complexity, in a system of functional areal organisation. Because they are so integrated with other urban features, their study has usually been approached within the general framework of urban functions. On the theoretical level this is also generally true; indeed Christaller's pioneering central-place studies were intended 'to explain the size, number and distribution of towns'.[2]

In central-place studies the key idea seems to be that of the urban hierarchy, each town being the node of a region, and the centres of a lower order together with their complementary regions becoming in turn oriented to a higher order centre. Although there is some doubt about the general applicability of the numerous empirical and deductive models,[3] and, more fundamentally, some doubt about the reality of breaks in the central-place rank/size gradient — and hence about the validity of the concept of the hierarchy itself[4]—the urban orientation of the analysis is unchallenged. Even studies based on rural communities have as their end product the evaluation of rural centres, which are at the bottom of the central-place hierarchy, and the delimitation of their service areas.[5]

In Iboland the role of fixed central places is not as marked. As we have seen, traditional Ibo society was rural and agrarian. Organised within the context of extreme fragmentation of social and political units, interaction between communities led, not to the development of large centres, but to a proliferation of small ones. As the oft-repeated association of market place, shrine and meeting-place shows, these centres were multifunctional and thus analogous to the central places of the modern Western type. But so simple were the organisation and the technical requirements of the various activities that there was often no fixation of activities and physical structures about these centres, no Christaller-type 'crystallization of mass about a nucleus'.[6]

Their roles remained passive, to provide venues for periodic meetings for the various activities. The organising centres for these activities, the home of the priest, the artisan, or the trader, remained in the settlement unit functionally untied to specific centres but related to a number of them.

Urban development was subsequent to European economic and cultural invasion. Some of the towns of the creeks and the Niger valley were developed under the stimulus of European trade and also by internal evolution. More akin to the Greek city-states than to the modern town, their relationship with the hinterland was restricted to specialised trading functions. The other components of centrality, social and administrative, were lacking. The patterns of areal organisation in the hinterland remained largely unaffected. Similarly restricted in role were the Aro settlements and fairs. Concerned primarily with the long-distance trade, their role in spatial integration at the level of local communities was peripheral. The towns—developed as a result of European penetration into and control of the interior—were established initially as ports or administrative centres. Their establishment had little to do with the internal organisation of economic activity. Given the initial advantages of good communications and external contacts, as well as nuclei of inhabitants in secondary and tertiary occupations, these towns developed in varying degrees central—place functions and institutions of the Western type. So did some of the older towns, which had new sectors grafted on to them. But over wide areas, no towns exist. The centralising institutions are located at rural centres, the association of church, school or health centre with a market site being a recurrent one. However, quite often the character of rural society—the fragmentation of units and the need to balance group pressure—makes it necessary for institutions serving a number of communities to be located on neutral ground, away from settlements or any place too closely associated with any one settlement. Even where public utilities and services are attached to settlement units, the political pressure for equity ensures that there is a diffusion of them rather than any agglomeration at a common centre.

Thus if one thinks of the space economy of Iboland in terms of the conventional framework of a hierarchy of nodes and regions, one finds that the structure is very immature. The hierarchy is truncated below the level of the minor towns. The upper tiers are missing in large areas; at the lower levels there is insufficient coincidence of locations to mark out particular centres as central places in a general sense, although they may be important for specific functions. Furthermore, where a centre is, so to speak, fortuitously grafted on to a rural settlement, there is little correlation between its rank and the size of the settlement. In the language of central-place studies, the non-basic component of the size of the settlement is dominant. This is the general framework in which our system of exchange institutions is set. The central-place type of institutions such as wholesale warehouses, buying stations and permanent department stores and retail shops, are an entirely new phenomenon. Most of them are located in the towns. Some are dispersed in rural centres, on market sites in settlements or away from them. Market places exist both in towns and in the rural areas. For analytical reasons we may regard the exchange system as made up of two sub-systems, the central-place sub-system and the market-place sub-system. For each of these there is a certain hierarchical structure depending on the type and variety of goods and services obtainable at the various centres, and on the size of the service area. The two sub-systems are functionally integrated. Some goods tend to remain in one sub-system or the other, moving up or down the hierarchy in their circulation, while others use both channels simultaneously or at different stages.

In the previous chapter an attempt was made to distinguish different kinds of centres and market places in Iboland on the basis of history, form and periodicity. For a study of the operation of the exchange system, however, a formal classification is inappropriate. There are obvious connections between history, form and function, but in a dynamic context form and function are often out of step. A declining centre—say, an old trade centre or a rural periodic inter-group market—may retain some features from its glorious past, while the growing importance of a centre may outstrip its formal standing. Considering the central places, the cities and the major urban centres are sharply differentiated functionally by the concentration of particular facilities in them. The importance of the other centres varies with the type of trade. Regarding market places, the periodicity of a market is no indication of its size, the range of commodities sold within it, or the size of its service area. A small local market for sauce ingredients may be held daily but the principal market in the area may be held only once in eight days. Also, the integration of Iboland in modern times has gone a long way to reduce the friction of social distance between village groups, thus diminishing the economic significance of in-group and out-group identities and the relevance of considering market visiting patterns in those terms.

An attempt has therefore been made to classify the various institutions on purely functional criteria. Very simply, we may consider the following:

1. the location of the centre, whether it is urban or rural;
2. its functional rank — metropolitan, central (i.e., regional) or local;
3. sub-system to which it belongs.

The empirical evidence suggests five categories in each sub-system as follows:

Central-Place Sub-System A	Market-Place Sub-System B
1. Metropolitan Centre	Metropolitan Market
2. Urban Centre	Urban Central Market
3. Urban neighbourhood shopping district	Urban local or neighbourhood market
4. Rural regional centre	Rural central Market
5. Rural local centre	Rural local market

This is a very generalized summary statement of a complex pattern. The type and number of institutions belonging to each category, the level of differentiation and the patterns of linkage between them vary for different commodities. The details will be considered in the next chapter.

The Significance of Marketing Periodicity

From the point of view of functional areal organisation, one of the most significant features of the operation of the market-place sub-system is the periodicity of rural markets. It has been shown how in Iboland the periodicity of traditional markets reflects the organisation of the village group. In some African societies, such as that of the Tiv in Northern Nigeria,[7] the Konkomba in Ghana[8] and the Konso in Ethiopia,[9] the day takes its name from the market place. Thus a marketing sequence provides time referents for the communities using that set of markets. It follows that recognition of a particular market-day calendar can be used to define a marketing region as an area of conscious interaction; the area over which a market-day name is current being regarded as at least partially oriented to the named market place.

From the point of view of economic function, the periodicity of markets has been described as a superficial trait; a convenient device which conceals a characteristic of more fundamental importance — the itinerancy of the traders and their merchandise.[10] Contrary to this view, the evidence from Iboland suggests that the periodicity of markets is of fundamental importance both to the pattern of movements of traders and their wares and, even more significantly, to the patterns of areal orientation and the nature of trade competition between centres. Periodicity of markets and itinerancy of traders sustain each other. Together they make possible the passive role of the market place in the exchange process and inhibit the crystallization of central-place type institutions about the market place. In this sense, the transformation of a market from a periodic régime to daily activity is, in effect, a change in its nature, making it a fixed centre analogous to the conventional central-place. Furthermore, the transition enables central-place type institutions, properly speaking, to be located on the site of the assured daily source of business. Alternatively, the development of a central-place usually calls into being a daily market to provide those lower order needs not usually catered for by shopping institutions.

From the point of view of functional areal organisation, a consequence of periodicity is the partial substitution of temporal for spatial competition between centres. The periodicity of markets permits a greater number of them to be maintained at a higher level of activity per market day than otherwise. It enables scarce resources of traders and trade goods to be offered more widely. But it poses a different problem of choice for the individual consumer. In the short run, the Christaller economic landscape can be regarded as a fairly stable honeycomb of nodal regions, each focused on a central-place. A consumer, and hence his place of residence, is, other things being equal, oriented to that centre where he can obtain goods and services at minimum cost or maximum advantage. With periodic markets, the opportunities which are open to a given area vary systematically from day to day within the periodic cycle. The marketing landscape becomes, at best, a panorama of honeycombs in regular periodic circuit.

Two implications of this feature are of immediate interest. The first is that the consumer tends to visit a large number of market places for any given commodity and that the total range of market visits is very wide. This is borne out by the two rural case studies in Chapter Twelve, the number of different markets regularly visited during an eight-day cycle being about twenty in each case. The average number of markets visited per marketer was 4.2 for Umunakanu and 3.6 for Ugwueke na Ezeukwu. Similarly in a questionnaire survey of 56 rural settlements, the average for various settlements ranged between two and four markets, the mode being about three markets per marketer. The patterns of market visiting in Iboland are examined in Chapter Twelve.

The second implication of periodicity is that differences in price level between different markets may be partly absorbed by differences in their periodicity and hence their temporal convenience to a given area. This implication may be examined with the aid of a theoretical model.

Consider that there are five markets A_0, A_1, A_2, A_3, A_4, at which a consumer is free to buy goods. In the tradition of classical economic analysis we would expect him to buy at the least-cost market. Graphically we may express his order of preferences by a series of equal-cost curves, relating market price to economic distance, since lower prices at certain markets may be offset by higher costs of getting there. In our example A_1 and A_3 are the cheapest markets, and are equally cheap. There are thus equal chances that the consumer will visit one or the other. But if all five markets are held on the same day there is no rational economic incentive to visit any of the other three markets. If there is a relative increase in cost at either A_1 or A_3 it is automatically displaced from consideration. Thus we may state as a general rule that for any group of markets held simultaneously, only those markets are likely to be visited where the cost is at a minimum, and the probability for each likely market is $\frac{1}{n}$ where n is the number of such markets.

With periodic markets a third consideration (i.e., in addition to market price and economic distance) comes into the consumer's calculations—the cost of waiting. The cheapest market may not be held on the day he takes his decision to buy, and he then has a choice between buying at the cheapest available market that day and postponing his purchase for a day or more so as to buy at a still cheaper market. The longer the waiting period the greater the money saving or other benefit demanded as compensation. We could express graphically, by indifference curves, the relation between price and willingness to wait for various levels of satisfaction. The level of satisfaction rises as the curve values decrease, and the optimum position is the lowest possible curve.

The effect of this may be illustrated very simply. Using the markets A_0, A_1, A_2, A_3, A_4, with the name price levels determined, let us plot these price levels against the indifference curves above. Suppose that A_0 is a daily market, but that A_1, A_2, A_3, A_4, are periodic markets held successively in that order once in a four-day cycle.

On the first day of the cycle the choice for the buyer is to buy at A_1 or A_0 or to postpone purchase for 1, 2, or 3 days in order to buy at A_2, A_3 or A_4. A_1 is evidently the best choice since it offers a better price than A_0 and as good a price as A_3 without the inconvenience of waiting. The others combine less desirable prices with some inconvenience of waiting. Thus the probability that the consumer will decide to buy at the market amounts to a certainty for A_1 and zero for the others.

A buyer taking a decision on the second day, when A_0 and A_2 are held, will prefer A_0 to the higher-priced A_2. But he will be equally prepared—*vide* the indifference curves—to wait for a day and buy at a still better price at A_3. There is no other choice which is as good or better. Hence the probability is 0.5 each for A_2 and A_3 and zero for the others. In the same way we can work out a table

Table VII

THE EFFECT OF CHANGES IN MARKETING SEQUENCE ON THE PROBABILITY OF VISITS TO COMPETING MARKETS

	Market	Day Held	Price Level in Ascending Order	Probability of Choice on successive Days of Cycle				Probability of Choice
				1st day	2nd day	3rd day	4th day	Day Cycle
1st Sequence	A_0	Daily	3	—	—	—	.25	.0625
	A_1	1st	1	1.00	—	—	.25	.3125
	A_2	2nd	2	—	.50	—	.25	.1875
	A_3	3rd	1	—	.50	1.00	.25	.4375
	A_4	4th	4	—	—	—	—	—
2nd Sequence	A_0	Daily	3	—	.33	—	—	.0833
	A_1	1st	1	1.00	—	—	—	.2500
	A_2	3rd	2	—	.33	.50	—	.2083
	A_3	4th	1	—	.33	.50	1.00	.4583
	A_4	2nd	4	—	—	—	—	—

of daily probabilities for all the markets in the four-day cycle assuming that the same number of decisions are taken each day (Table VII). As the table shows, the effect of periodicity is to increase the number of probable markets in our example from two to four, but unlike in simultaneous markets, the probabilities are unequal. The probability of each market deviates from $\frac{1}{n}$ partly by reason of its cost schedule and partly by reason of its periodicity. By altering the order of the markets in the cycle while keeping costs constant we obtain a different pattern of probabilities (Table VII).

Several unrealistic simplifying assumptions have been made in the construction of this model. In the first place, given periodic markets, the daily incidence of decision-making will not be randomly distributed throughout the periodic cycle. People will tend to adjust their buying habits so as to make most of their purchases on the most convenient day, thus economising on both money and time. In any case the price willingness to wait poses serious problems of measurement. It has to be inferred from behaviour rather than noted directly. It also varies from commodity to commodity and from time to time. It is, however, often marginally decisive of whether a market or number of markets are to be visited or not.

Competition between periodic markets is thus partly spatial and partly temporal. A new market established on or near the market-day of an existing market stands a poorer chance of success than one planned for a gap in the local cycle. It is unlikely to survive unless it offers lower prices or decreases economic distance to market sufficiently for a wide enough area. As a general rule the principal markets in an area of, say, 20 miles radius, have their market days staggered, as in Bende Division, so that we may speak of them loosely as forming marketing rings. The staggering is due in part to differential development of local markets in this kind of competition.

The concept of the marketing ring must be applied with caution, since it suggests an institutionalized order and a uniformity which may not exist. A marketing ring has relevance only to the individual marketers in a given area. For the areal unit as a whole, the ring is meaningful only as indicating the markets most frequently visited by the people in that unit. In view of the variation in the range of goods and in the requirements of different types of marketers, it is useful to distinguish between different types of rings. Three types are suggested for Iboland:

1. the primary or village-group ring,
2. the local or neighbourhood ring,

3. the rural trading ring.

The primary or village-group ring is of historical rather than functional significance. It is the set of markets found within a village group. Some of these markets may be traditional. In that case they are intimately connected with the social and cultural life of the people, and may continue to perform their ritual and social functions long after they have ceased to possess economic importance. The bases of rural marketing in Iboland are the local ring and the trading ring. Hardly any marketers nowadays confine themselves to their primary ring. The local ring concerns the great majority of marketers. It consists of the chief markets visited by the inhabitants of a village group in their capacity as producers or consumers. The rural trading ring links the more important rural central markets and is the range of markets visited by dealers in imported goods and high value staples. In Chapter Eleven a study of some rural markets illustrates the operations and scope of these two kinds of marketing rings.

The Distribution of Centres

(*i*) *The central-place sub-system*   The unit of location in the central-place sub-system is the individual establishment; the number and the rank of institutions in a place determine its rank. The details of location are therefore discussed under various kinds of trade.

Central-place institutions are of peripheral significance in the internal trade in agricultural produce. This trade takes place almost entirely in the market place, although there are direct supplies by producers or food contractors to institutional consumers such as schools and hospitals, and some agricultural produce—mainly fruits and vegetables—are sold in local shops in the larger urban centres.

The produce buying agents, in whose hands lies the organisation of the movement of export crop produce, operate in much the same way whether they are located in town or country. Only Port Harcourt, which receives produce coming from other buying stations for export, may be differentiated as a metropolitan centre for this activity. There is little correlation between the size of the settlement and the amount of produce bulked. Onitsha and Enugu, for example, rank very low in the list of produce buying stations. Oil mills may also be considered as central-place institutions. Their location depends on local factors of site—nearness to a large stream—and accessibility, and need not be near a large, or indeed, any settlement. The differentiation of centres is most definite in the case of the trade in imported goods. The four cities stand out as metropolitan centres, with services of a higher order—banking, finance and advertising, as well as certain goods like heavy industrial machinery concentrated in them and serving the whole region. Most region-wide marketing organisations have their regional headquarters in one or other of the cities. Shopping facilities are fairly well developed in the major urban centres and some of the establishments do considerable wholesale or sub-wholesale business with traders from the town itself and from the surrounding country. Otherwise the shops outside the four cities which are involved in the trade in imported goods are usually local shops, retailing every day goods to consumers.

Rural service centres are difficult to identify or locate. The best index would appear to be the official list of shops selling beer. The sale of beer is controlled by a Government Licencing Board. Proposed premises have to be inspected and approved and a licence fee of £5 a year is charged. Thus only the more successful shopkeepers can afford licences. But in most places where there is a concentration of shops, beer-shops are generally to be found. A concentration of beer-shops then suggests an important shopping centre. In addition to the local shop there are a number of establishments typically to be found at a rural service centre—the carpenter, the bicycle repairer, the tinker and the dressmaker being the most prominent. Larger centres may have a photographer or two, some barbers, as well as some eating houses and some palm-wine bars. Fig. 16 indicates the distribution of beer-selling centres in Iboland in 1963. There is a remarkable concentration in Orlu Division with an average of about two centres per settlement unit. The rest of the central Ibo upland area, including Owerri, Awka and Onitsha Divisions as well as parts of Okigwi and Bende Divisions, also has a high density of centres. This is in sharp contrast to the Aboine Basin (Afikpo and Abakaliki Divisions) where there is scarcely a centre per 100 square miles and two (Abakaliki) or five (Afikpo) per 100 settlement units. The other areas are intermediate. These differences reflect the varying rates of development of permanent centres in different parts of Iboland. The larger centres (empirically determined as those with four beer shops or more) are usually located at major road junctions or attached to the more important rural central markets.

The above outline shows the inadequacy of the central-place sub-system as an organising framework for exchange, and points to the vital role of market places. The market places attached to the minor urban centres, old trade settlements, administrative centres and rural centres, are functionally akin to rural central markets, sharing in the characteristic of having periodic régimes. They are

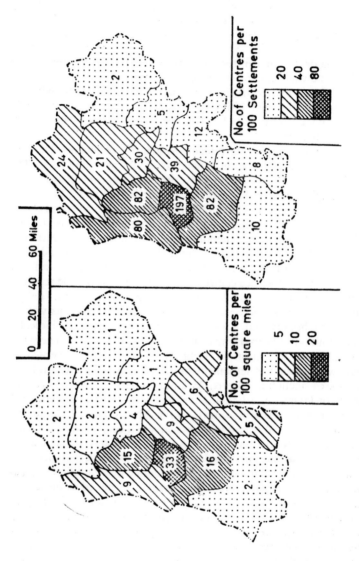

treated by both traders and peasants as part of the rural marketing rounds. These market places, rather than the local shops, are the principal venues for the central functions performed at these places.

(*ii*) *Distribution of principal markets.* On a regional scale a number of markets stand out among the hundreds of rural central markets. In spite of the impracticability of quantitative evaluation, there is little difficulty in identifying them. In every locality the principal markets are known by common repute and are usually ranked by persons interviewed in much the same order. Written replies by county officials to questionnaires made it possible to confirm the information in most counties. Responses to question-naires on market-visiting habits also revealed the fact that certain markets stand well above others in the extent of their service area. Other evidence includes the Eastern Nigerian Ministry of Agric-ulture's list of principal markets, and the official list of licenced beer-shops, a number of which are usually to be found in the larger markets.

Fig. 17 shows the location of the principal markets. The striking feature is that they are not evenly distributed throughout the area but tend rather to be concentrated along the major routes. This points to the importance of long-distance trade in the size and competitive vigour of markets. The most significant factor is location in relation to the long-distance trade in foodstuffs. The bigger traders in imported goods and manufactured articles restrict their activities to the principal markets.

We have already noted the relationship between markets and settlements in Iboland. Looking at the area as a whole one finds that there are regional differences in the density of markets. As may be expected from close links between markets and settlements here, the density of markets appears to be related to the population density and settlement pattern. There is a concentration in areas of high population density, where there are many settlements per unit area. Areas of nucleated settlement tend to have more markets than areas of dispersed settlement, the number of markets in a village-group area depending partly on the number of topographi-cally distinct units constituting the group. The forces of change have caused a general decline in the number of markets and the differential development of existing ones—the markets favourably situated in relation to new channels of trade becoming important. New markets have sprung up in places. But the regional differences in the density of the distribution have persisted through these overall changes.

Physical Aspects of the Marketing Landscape

In their spatial organisation the metropolitan and major urban centres are not markedly different from Western cities. This is generally true of the new cities in Africa, designated by Southall as 'type B' towns,[11] founded by European administrations and developed under modern conditions. The main morphological features of the new towns may be briefly outlined. The business district, an association of the main shopping districts, the market and the transport terminals—lorry parks and, where relevant, the railway station or port—form the central business district. On one side of this is the 'Native Location'. On the other side and kept separate from the business district by a strip of open space is the 'European Reservation', in which the Administrative Offices are also located. Political developments have made obsolete the division between 'Native' and European quarters, and urban growth has complicated the pattern of functional areal association within the towns. But the underlying uniformity of pattern may still be observed. The morphologies of individual towns are examined in case studies in a later chapter.

Rural centres are essentially rural settlements which have developed strong urban sectors. Morphologically they retain the rural framework which is clearly distinguished from the new centre. The new centre is marked by a very high density of buildings along the main road or at cross-roads and by the concentration of shopping centres, etc. Unlike in the rural sector the population may be largely immigrant, and even those from the village groups do not live in kindred units but in parental family units once they have moved into the centre. The most common facilities are provided by carpenters, tailors, bicycle repairers and shops. These depend on the surrounding countryside as well as on motor traffic for business. Hence they are strongly attached to the motor roads.

The old trade settlements show in their compact settlement pattern their unplanned character. Most of the older houses are of mud and thatched roofs and the houses are built without proper street planning or drainage. There is strong concentration on the major roads, where the streets are occupied by shops, the density of buildings falling away from the road. The centre of economic activity is the 'beach', as in the case in the railway towns, and this is the main focus. The people tend to use the residential area mainly as a dormitory, carrying out most of their business in the market or 'beach'.

Administrative centres like Udi, Awka and Bende started with the Government Reservation separate and distinct from the rural settlement. The accretion of new centres was by the encroachment of settlements on the original centres, depending ultimately on the importance of the place as a centre.

Since the majority of rural markets were established in the context of the traditional society, their number and location are clearly related to rural settlement patterns. On the other hand, the disparate trends of modern development—in particular the varying regional rates of the growth of central-place type institutions and the fixation of periodic markets—have introduced another level of differentiation. Following from the regional contrasts, the pattern of interaction between the central-place sub-system and the market-place sub-system, as well as their relative significance, vary from place to place. Iboland may be divided into four major rural settlement types based on an analysis of the various elements of settlement and on the general geographical background. The usual disclaimer may be made: that the classification is ultimately that of convenience, suitable, it is hoped, to the purpose of this study. The four types are:

1. Coastal and Riverain clusters
2. Regions of Nucleated Settlement
3. Regions of Dispersed Settlement
4. Regions of Continuous Settlement

1. This type is found on the flood plains of the Anambra-Niger, the Orashi Niger and the Delta. Its character is obscured by the statistics for Onitsha North, Onitsha South and Oguta countries where it forms only part of the total county areas, but may be noted in the figure for Ahoada, Ikwerre, Asa and Ndoki counties in the south. Population densities are low but the marshes constrict settlement to a new favoured area of high ground occurring at river terraces and interfluves along which they are linearly aligned. Although most of the settlements are small—*vide* the low median size for the counties named—there are several large settlements such as Oguta, Omuku, Omanelu, Elele and Igirita on the edge of the region. Most of these have been associated with trade and commerce between the riverain and inland peoples. The principal markets are located in them.

The seasonal flooding of the Niger floodplain imposes its rhythm on the space economy. Within the settlement and around it on firm ground is permanently cultivated compoundland. The farmland and commons are fragmented by the water channels into numerous strips some of which are very far from the settlement. Satellite

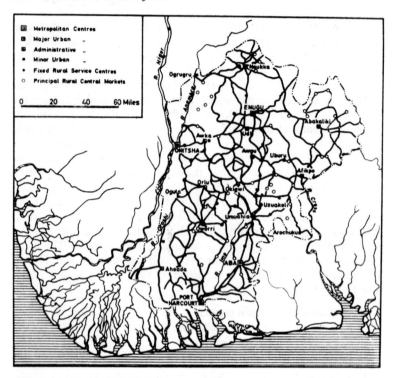

Fig. 17   The Ibo marketing landscape.

settlements—temporary huts on stilts usually—are erected here
for the agricultural season between the floods. But the main settlements remain the centre of economic life.

2.   There are three sub-regions. The first comprises the densely
populated northern plateau. The rolling landscape is broken up by
outcrop rings of ironstone into wide bowls two to three miles across
in which the many large settlements are located. There is a tradition
that the hills themselves were favoured in more unstable times
and a few hill settlements still remain, being relics of old defence
posts on these natural castles. The dwelling unit is the walled-in
family homestead. But the homesteads are close together, especially
in the more densely populated parts in Isi Uzo and Igbo Etiti
counties. The foothills region at the foot of the escarpment is a
region of low population density. Colonies from the plateau have
been established here in ribbons extending from the main gaps in
the plateau face. Several of these satellites bear the names of their

mother settlement, e.g., Obollo Eke, Opi, etc. — and their links are very strong.

Owing to close settlement within the village group areas there is usually only one outstanding market in each of them, and the smaller ones have tended to die away. There are distances of up to four miles between village groups, and the fragmented terrain makes direct communication with individual villages difficult. The marketing is dominated by a few very large markets—the Nkwo Ibagwa, the Eke Enugu Ezike, the Oye Orba, the Opi Afor and the Obollo Oye.

The other two areas of nucleated settlement are somewhat different. One is in the central eastern part of Iboland, corresponding rather closely to the hill and valley country in Northern Okigwi county and Afikpo and Bende Divisions. The other occupies most of the counties of Ohoba, Oratta and Ngor Okpala on the coastal plains. Here population densities are moderate to low, ranging from about 250 to 500 persons per square mile in 1953. The median size of settlement is between 1,000 and 3,000 for the various counties, i.e., medium, except for the border areas of Aro-Igbo and Ikwuano counties where it is small. The smallest unit of settlement is the compound. Individual homesteads are attached end-to-end in circular, oval or rectangular pattern. There is no outside wall, the outside ring of the inward-facing houses doing for it. The *ezi* or courtyard is shared by all the inhabitants of the compound who are usually of the same kindred. An outhouse meeting place—the *agbala*—is usually built at the entrance or on the path leading to the compound and is a further expression of the strong communal life. The compound of Amaukabi in Ugwueke illustrates the pattern.

The amount of compoundland around each compound and the distances between compounds are largely a function of population density. The general alignment of the compound units making up the village and of the village units constituting the village group also emphasise the strength of community links. Just as the home-steads focus on the courtyard, so the compounds focus on a village square with paths radiating from it to them. The senior village is usually near the centre of the group and is itself the hub of radiating paths to the various villages. The ideal spatial alignment is very much disturbed by local relief—on the Okigwi-Ahaba-Arochuku ridge for instance—but the intimate physical connection at various levels between the settlement units in a village group is the distinctive feature of the consolidated settlement pattern in these areas.

Jones has pointed out that the underlying principle of this kind of settlement is to give each village in the group room for expansion radially while maintaining group cohesion at the centre.[12] A parallel has been drawn between the land-use rings which result and the theoretical Thunen rings,[13] together with the land-use rings which Weber has described for medieval Germany.[14] The farm land may lie up to a mile or two from the settlement and may extend for a further couple of miles. From the point of view of agricultural production the village is a dormitory. The produce is not necessarily stored in the village but usually in barns out in the farms to which the peasants commute daily.

The Ibo rural market system here approximates its ideal form with a hierarchy of rural periodic markets, most of which are firmly attached to settlements.

3. We may recognise three sub-divisions: the remaining areas of Udi and Nsukka Divisions on both sides of the sandstone zone, i.e., (a) the foothills region and the Adaba basin, (b) the Aboine Basin, and (c) the Ngwa counties of Aba Division. The first area is characterised by moderate to low population densities but very large settlements; the second by low densities and small to very small settlements; and the third by moderate densities and small settlement units. These are, on the whole, regions of recent colonization and in the first two areas the process is being continued by migrant tenant farmers. Settlement in the northern areas conforms to the regional type of individual homestead units. The large size of village groups in Udi and Nsukka Divisions reflects the greater social cohesion of the units. The village group may spread over several square miles, a maze of paths and a recurring pattern of rings of compoundland woodland marking out its area from the surrounding savanna country. Some village groups such as Nike have small satellites far out in the farmland and bush area. In this area of sprawling village groups the periodic market system is well developed. The markets are usually established at nodal points between sectors or at the centre of the group. A few markets are outstanding, notably Iwolo Oghe, Nkwo Agu Umuneke and Eke Agbani.

The settlement pattern of the Aboine Basin is structurally the most immature. Migration waves were in full spate here when the Pax Britannica fixed settlement. Thus the Ezza people, now occupying an area of relatively high population density, were actively advancing eastwards up to the beginning of this century. Individual homesteads are dispersed in small groups of two or three over wide areas. The nature of the terrain—a low lying plain criss-crossed by shallow seasonal streams liable to flooding during the rains—lends itself to this kind of settlement. There are very few markets in the area. They tend to be located on the major routeways and are usually large.

Ngwaland marks the frontier of advance of Ibo pioneers into Annang and Ibibio country. The area constitutes a trough of relatively low population density between the Isuama country and the Annang heartland. The basic unit of settlement in Ngwaland is the nucleated compound, but the compounds are not well consolidated into villages and village groups. They tend to be distributed linearly along paths. Sub-regional divisions are recognised by the people—Nsulu, Ngwauku, etc.—but these are sociological categories and have little morphological significance. Large markets usually located at nodal centres are few and far between. There are numerous small markets, but because of the lack of cohesion between compound units, no marked pattern of group markets emerges.

4. The belt of continuous settlement and compoundland stretches from near Onitsha south-eastwards to the Imo river. The whole area lies on the central Ibo upland zone and is terminated in the north by the series of scarps, ridges and gorges separating it from the valleys of the Mamu and Imo headwaters. The distinctive character of the belt derives mainly from the very high population densities which are everywhere over 800 persons per square mile and rise to over 1,200 in the Orlu-Mbano area. In detail the belt falls into two types, the nucleated type and the dispersed homestead type, corresponding in structure to regions 2b/c and 3a from which they may be said to have degenerated under population pressure.

The southern type covers the counties of Etiti and Mbano in Okigwi Division, Mbaise, Mbaitoli and Ikeduru in Owerri, and the southern part of Orlu Division. Northwards it merges into the northern type which covers the rest of Orlu Division, the south-western part of Awka Division and the upland region in Onitsha Division east and south-east of the town of Onitsha. In the southern type the expansion of compoundland and village units and the establishment of new ones in the outer farmland and forest zone has turned the area into a continuous scatter of villages with scarcely any farmland left except the compoundland and palm trees. It is difficult to distinguish at ground level one village group from another since the distances between villages both within and between village groups are very small.

Basically the market pattern is the ideal central Ibo type, with the chief market attached to the senior village and a group of smaller markets located in other villages and rotating with it. But as settlements coalesce many of the smaller markets have died out. A few large markets are outstanding, and these by reason of their general location, but the high population densities enable numerous medium-size markets to exist. There is a marked tendency for markets to be held on days other than their official market days, usually in the evenings, and also for daily service centres to develop, sometimes but not always on the sites of existing markets.

In the northern type expansion has led to a continuous scatter of individual homesteads within the village group area and to the elimination of the fringing forest, gradual in some areas but almost complete along the main roads. Markets are typically located in nodal positions between the various sectors of the village.

Market Regions

The trends in market development which have been noted in the areas of continuous settlement are incipient in many areas. Briefly, we can identify four market-type regions:

1. areas of immature market development;
2. areas of mature market development with incipient central-place institutions;
3. areas of disintegration of the periodic market system and strong development of fixed central places;
4. areas of strong urban polarization.

Type 1 occurs in the Aboine Basin region of dispersed settlement.
Type 2 covers much of the area away from the major towns, in areas of consolidated settlement patterns. Here the periodic markets are still numerous and vigorous.
Type 3 corresponds to the area of continuous settlement, high population density and dense network of roads.
Type 4 includes the immediate hinterlands of Onitsha and Aba, the suburban area of Port Harcourt and, to a lesser extent, the immediate hinterland of Umuahia-Ibeku.

The Awka-Orlu uplands in Orlu's hinterland combine the development of fixed local centres with strong polarization to the metropolitan centre. This is the area of greatest change in the Ibo marketing landscape. In Aba's less densely populated hinterland with dispersed settlements, the pull of the metropolitan centre has had the effect of stultifying rural market development: the markets retain their periodicity but become less important as more producers and consumers travel to Aba directly. Port Harcourt's suburban population extends northwards along the Port Harcourt-Aba road as far as Umukoroshe, but owing to the specialised character of

Port Harcourt as a trade centre the city's influence on market development outside this ribbon is minimal. Similarly Enugu has had little effect on the evolution of rural markets in its hinterland. By contrast, the growth of Umuahia-Ibeku has led to the decline of many rural markets in Odida Anyanwu county.

The general tendency in Iboland is towards a strengthening of the central-place sub-system. The number of rural centres is increasing and these centres in some places attract local shifts of settlement. Some of the markets have become less periodic or have even developed daily sectors. These developments strike at the roots of the market-place sub-system; they belong to a continuing process of transformation in the marketing landscape.

NOTES

1. R. E. Dickinson, *The West European city*. London, 1951.
2. W. Christaller, Die Zentralen Orte in Suddeutschland', partially translated into English by C. W. Baskin, 'A critique and translation of Walter Christaller's Die Zentralen Orte in Suddeutschland.' Unpublished Ph.D. thesis (microfilmed), Virginia. 1957.
3. J. U. Marshall, 'Model and reality in central-place studies', *Professional Geographer*, Vol. 16, 1964.
   Although the rigorous mathematics of central-place theorists elude him, Marshall makes a strong methodological case against the various theories which usually assume or imply a reversal of the normal sequence of the evolution of central-place systems.
4. See B. J. L. Berry, 'Remarks on central-place studies conducted in the United States and Canada', *Urban Systems and Economic Development*, (ed.) F. R. Pitts. Also L. King, 'A multivariate analysis of the spacing of urban settlements in the United States', *Annals of the Association of American Geographers*, 1961.
5. Thus J. E. Brush and H. E. Bracey, 'Rural service centres in south-western Wisconsin and southern England', *Geographical Review*, 1955.
6. W. Christaller, op. cit.
7. P. J. Bohannan, 'Concepts of time among the Tiv of Nigeria', *S.W. Journal of Anthropology*, 1953.
8. D. Tait, 'On the growth of some Konkomba markets', *Report of the Annual Conference of the West African Institute of Social and Economic Research (Sociology Section)*, 1953.
9. R. Kluckhohm, 'The Konso economy of southern Ethiopia', in P. J. Bohannan, and G. Dalton, *Markets in Africa*. Evanston, 1962.
10. A. Allix, 'The Geography of fairs', *Geographical Review*, 1922.
11. A. Southall, *Social change in modern Africa*. London, 1961.
12. G. I. Jones, 'Agriculture and Ibo village planning', *Farm and Forest*, 1945.
13. M. Chisholm, *Rural settlement and land use*. London, 1962.
14. M. Weber, *General economic history* (translated by Frank H. Knight) Glencoe Free Press, 1950.

CHAPTER ELEVEN

Patterns of Trade

The Marketing Population

IT is commonly said that in West Africa almost everybody engages in trading and that most people do not regard it as a distinct occupation. The great concourse of persons at market places lends colourful support to this assertion, and in this study our analysis of several communities will show that virtually everyone goes to the market place several times during an eight-day period to buy or sell goods. But the people themselves make a clear distinction between *marketing*—the sale of produce or the purchase of utilities—and *trading*—buying or selling for profit. The former is *izu ahia*, the latter *igba ubiri*. Selling of local produce is considered as part of production and is related as much to the agricultural régime and market conditions as to the random incidence of personal needs. The bulk of the commercial exchanges associated with market places concerns producers and consumers directly, and from their point of view involves only a local movement from their place of residence to the market place or shop and back. The exchange history of the commodity—the chain of institutions and the places through which it has passed or will pass—involves them only indirectly. It is their activities which define the patterns of local orientation.

Trading activities are much more complex than marketing. There are many grades of traders operating at various levels. The degree of differentiation depends on the economic and technical requirements of the commodity in question. However, in general, we may distinguish the following grades of traders in Iboland:

1. Part-time traders—forestallers, peddlers, collectors and retailers;
2. Professional petty traders;
3. Transporters, including produce buying agents, who are engaged in long-distance trade and large-scale commodity transfers;
4. Exporters and Importers, small firms;
5. Exporters and Importers, large firms (mainly expatriate).

Most women traders are part-time traders and handle local produce. Owing to the low level of occupational specialization, many men in the rural areas—particularly in the densely populated areas—combine trading with other activities. There are also seasonal fluctuations in the number of traders, the proportion being lowest at the height of the farming season. Among nominally full-time professional traders, the turn over rate is considerable. Entry into trade is easy and cheap but the chances of failure are correspondingly high. Young men are liable to set up in proud independence as traders, having collected a few pounds from relations or saved up from the proceeds of more humble callings, only to run through their capital and revert—perhaps temporarily—to their former occupations. The higher up the ranks of traders, the more stable is the system and the more clean-cut the distinction between types of traders.

Entry into trade is not always impulsive and ill-considered. The most accepted way is to start at a very early age as an apprentice to an established trader. This continues a tradition which we have already noted in the historic Awka and Aro trade systems. The apprentice is usually from the trader's village group and often a kinsman and their relationship is personal and close. He is at once apprentice, ward and servant. As he learns the business he is given a little capital to buy goods on his own account and sell alongside his master's goods. The rate at which he builds up his capital is a test of his competence and usually determines the date of his independence, when his master sets him on his feet with a capital gift or loan. In the case of non-relations, a more formal arrangement may be made. The master is paid to teach the apprentice for a specified period. The apprenticeship system is largely responsible for domination of many lines of business by specific ethnic groups. The system is strongest in those lines of trade which require some specialised knowledge and skills—keeping up with fluctuating market prices, assessing quality of goods, anticipating public tastes. The long-distance trade in food commodities, the trade in tobacco and in textiles: these are good examples. For local trade in food produce and the trade in standardised goods of low value—domestic hardware, groceries—the initial special skills necessary are minimal and the threshold for entry low. These are the haunts of the part-time and the small independent trader.

Typically, the Ibo trading organisation is an independent one-man concern. A successful trader with a number of advanced apprentices is able to use them as agents operating at lower levels of business—retailing goods in the rural markets or buying produce there for

their principal; and the links forged during the period of apprenticeship may be informally continued afterwards, but otherwise there
are few structural links between individual traders. Goodwill,
however, is an all-important element in trade. A successful trader
has a hard core of devoted customers whose loyalty he cultivates
by economic inducements such as credits, advance information
and first options on 'fast' lines, as well as by gestures of personal
friendship. Formal links exist in the inter-regional trade with Lagos,
the Western Region and the Northern Region. Here traders in the
chief commercial centres in Iboland have correspondents or agents
in some of the main centres. Their distribution is suggested by the
local concentrations of Ibo-speaking peoples in these areas, the
most important being Lagos, Ibadan, Kano, Jos, Zaria, Lafia,
Maiduguri, Gusau, Minna, Kafanchan and Makurdi. The correspondents and agents at Lagos keep their Iboland contacts informed
of latest arrivals in Lagos and often buy and store goods for them
to come and collect. With the correspondents and agents in the
Northern and Western Regions the relationship is symbiotic. The
traders based in Iboland send off yams, palm oil, *gari* and second-
hand clothing and get in return kola nuts and Yoruba cloth from
the West or grains, fish, meat and onions from the North. Joint-stock
companies with limited liability are common in the produce-buying
business. In the retail trade in imported goods the few pioneers
are dealers in fashionable clothing and jewelry, and in bookshops—
Verity Stores, Collins Mba, Bachon's Bookshops, etc. But the
majority of shopkeepers, both urban and rural, are independent and
transact their business in much the same way as their market-place
counterparts. The most closely integrated regional organisations
are those of the large expatriate firms.

While casual or part-time traders operate from their homes and
are to be found in every settlement, professional traders are very
unevenly distributed. We have already noticed the existence of
specialist communities in traditional society. Today the old pattern
is reflected in two ways. Firstly, the new towns and commercial
centres drew their initial trading population largely from the traditional trading communities. Although the pattern is becoming
more diversified, through the apprenticeship system, several lines
of business are still dominated by these groups. Thus Item and
Abiriba traders, and through their influence traders from the
surrounding villages—Ugwueke, Alayi, Ohafia—control the textile
and clothing trade at Aba and Umuahia-Ibeku. Nkwerre and Orlu
traders reign in Port Harcourt, Awka and Nnewi in Onitsha.
Secondly, in the rural areas, there are wide differences in the regional

concentration of professional traders, and at the local level most of the traders live in a few leading settlements. Whether these traders are local people or immigrants often depends on the traditions of the area. The trade in the Ngwa railway town of Nbawsi is dominated by Igberre people, that at Omoba by Aros. The Nkwerre element at Igrita is strong enough to constitute an effective block in local politics. In Nsukka and Abakaliki Divisions the trading communities are also strangers' settlements—Orba, Eha Amufu, Ibagwa Ani, Enugu Ezike, Ezillo and Abba Omegge. Most of the Ibo traders come from Onitsha, Awka and Orlu Divisions. On the other hand the trading communities in the central Ibo uplands and in Bende Division are drawn mainly from the immediate hinterland.

On the regional scale the distribution of the trading population would appear to be related more to the main routes of trade than to any regional differences in population density. In most counties the proportion of traders is between 10 and 29 per thousand of total population, but along the riverain and delta areas and in the southern counties the proportion is much higher. Orlu Division, Aguata, Northern Okigwi, Odida Anyanwu and Elu Elu counties, traversed by some of the busiest roads in the region, also have high concentrations of traders. The more isolated areas—Isi Uzo, Izi and Owuwa counties, especially — have relatively few traders.

Trade in Agricultural Produce

Trade commodities may be classified into three broad groups; (a) local produce, including agricultural produce and local crafts: (b) export produce; and (c) imported and manufactured goods. Depending on the activities of masses of peasant producers and consumers as well as on traders of various kinds, the trade in agricultural produce generates the greatest number of marketing trips and determines the general pattern of movements to rural market places. Marketing of farm produce in Iboland is consistent and planned for. The wide areal differences in population density and soil fertility, in the magnitude of production and in the types and relative importance of crops cultivated, in pure stands or in combinations, give considerable scope for trade; a scope which is increasing as more people move from agriculture into other occupations—and into urban centres.

In Okigbo's admittedly conservative estimate, the distribution of local agricultural produce may be valued at 11 % of the National Gross Domestic Product or 19 % of the total value of the product of the agricultural sector.[1] Much of this is local and is carried on by marketers travelling on foot. Yet the internal trade in agricultural produce takes up some one-third of the motor lorry traffic; and the export trade another third.[2] It is also an important contributor to railway traffic, particularly the interregional trade with Northern Nigeria. Market places are the chief venues for marketing of agricultural produce. In the areas of large surpluses, such as Izi and Uzo Uwani counties, traders may have arrangements with farmers to buy their harvest crops on the farm. The development of market gardening since 1950 has introduced a new kind of producer and marketing organisation into the trade. At present this is confined to the neighbourhood of the four cities. Market gardeners aim at the higher-income market—senior civil servants and other professionals, businessmen and expatriates as well as institutions such as schools, hospitals and prisons to whom they sell directly. The bulk of their transactions thus lies outside normal trade channels.

The marketing of agricultural produce is an activity dominated by women, a common feature in West Africa.[3] With the differentiation of economic functions within the Ibo household, individual members retain to a large extent the personal control and rights of disposal of their produce. But it is usual, except after the main harvest, to delegate the selling of crops to the women of the house. In addition to this marketing function the women are also traders in their own right, buying and selling foodstuffs and sauce ingredients.[4]

On any market day groups of women may be observed busy at the outposts on the routes leading to the market places. Here they buy up produce from the producer-seller before she reaches the market. The main function of the *forestaller* is sorting and bulking. The typical producer going to market may carry a gallon-size calabash of oil, one or two yams, some maize, vegetables, plantains, a small basket of kernels and perhaps some snails and crabs. The forestallers recombine this medley into homogeneous and larger units for sale to visiting traders. This sort of business requires very little capital—a few shillings will do—and is attractive because of the very high profit margins. The forestaller who collects oranges at 6 for a penny can easily sell them at 3 for a penny to bigger traders or at 2 for a penny to consumers later in the day when the producers have all sold their stock.

Itinerant collectors operate on much the same scale as forestallers. They are usually rural traders who go the rounds of rural markets collecting produce for sale at their own rural central market or at an urban market. The itinerant collector has her dual in the *itinerant retailer* who is more common in food deficit areas. She buys her produce from the main rural central markets or urban centres to sell on the local round of markets. At this level of marketing, specialization is very low and the distinctions are between roles rather than persons. Most women marketers combine some or all the roles or switch between them at different times.

Full-time professional traders in agricultural produce are usually men. They are engaged in long-distance trade between ecological regions or between rural and urban markets. Like sellers of imported goods they have to be concentrated in the towns and in a few rural communities where they usually form part of stranger-settlements. They visit a very narrow range of markets, buying from producers and petty traders at the principal market in one area and sub-wholesaling at a market at the other end. Hence they are not a very prominent feature of the local rural marketing rounds. The principal means of transport is by lorry, but bicycles are still very important in Owerri, Ahoada and Aba Divisions. Interregional trade is dependent mainly on urban-based traders. We have already mentioned the reciprocal relationships between these traders and their correspondents or agents in the other regions. The trade in cattle is a special case, depending almost exclusively on Hausa and Fulani traders resident in Ibo centres.

In relation to the trade in agricultural produce we may distinguish three types of rural central markets: (a) Food Surplus markets; (b) Entrepôt or Border markets; and (c) Retail markets. The distinctions are a matter of degree and have to do with the relative importance of the various functions—bulking, transfer and distribution. During the peak of the harvest season the distinctions are blurred since most areas have enough local food supplies and long-distance trade tends to be confined to rural urban exchange. The proportion of long-distance traders is highest in entrepôt markets. Located between two ecological regions, an entrepôt market is a meeting place for two sets of traders: a distribution centre for traders from surplus food markets and a bulking centre for traders who will eventually return to retail markets. Quite often exchange between two traders would be a simple transfer involving no change in bulk. The roadside and the lorry park, where the lorries from the contrasting regions park, are very busy sections of the market.

Bulking being the dominant activity in food surplus markets, marketing activity can be concentrated in a small space and markets in food surplus areas tend to be smaller in size than markets of similar rank elsewhere. Even more than in the entrepôt markets the approach roads and the lorry park are the centres of trade. Retail markets are to be found in the heart of food-deficit areas. Here the area covered by the market is usually very large since the principal business of the market is to serve the consumer directly. Since the food deficit areas are the densely populated areas, the potential number of consumers is high. There are very few transfers or bulking transactions. The flow of goods is from the professional traders through one or two traders selling in smaller lots, or from the local producers, to the consumer.

As noted in Chapter Eight, Iboland is by no means self-sufficient in food. Food imports from other areas and from abroad constitute a vital part of Iboland's food supplies. The principal centres for interregional trade are the metropolitan markets of Onitsha and Aba, and the great food centre of Abakaliki. The principal railway centres —Port Harcourt, Aba, Umuahia-Ibeku, and Enugu—import grain and meat from the Northern Region. There are also smaller scale movements of food through the rural central markets in border areas—*gari* from Ibibioland into Iboland; *gari* and cassava from Ogoni Division into the central Ibo uplands through Obigbo and Igrita; Igala food-stuffs (yams, grain) through Nsukka markets to Enugu, Awka and Onitsha; rice, plantains, yams, maize and a variety of vegetables through north-eastern Ibo markets into the Ibo heartlands. From their point of entry these imports merge into the general flow of the trade in food produce and are sold by much the same traders who deal in local produce.

The Production and Marketing of Rice

The production and marketing of rice in Abakaliki Province illustrates a new development in the trade in agricultural produce in Iboland. It is of special interest because in some respects it gives a foretaste of trends in the more traditional crops which will become more evident as their production becomes more locally concentrated and more thoroughly commercialised.

The Abakaliki phenomenon is a rare example of the introduction of a new food crop into an area already more than self-sufficient in food. Rice is an insignificant part of the local diet and cash returns are the primary incentive to production. In this sense it is rather like an export crop. But unlike export crops, it is destined for an internal market, hence the orientation of the producer is not to ports as such but to the population centres. Secondly, the movement of rice depends almost exclusively on road transport, in contrast to the historical association between export crops, railroads and waterways. Thirdly, the crop has always been entirely in the hands of indigenous entrepreneurs, and its financial and administrative organisations are on different lines.

Certain varieties of rice, the wild rice and the red rice, have long been cultivated in Eastern Nigeria, but before the war the bulk of the rice consumed in the Region was imported, although some rice came from Northern and Western Nigeria. With the war came import restrictions, cutting off the external supplies and diverting the Northern and Western Region supplies partly to the war effort and partly to local consumption. The Government, exploring possibilities of local production in Eastern Nigeria, in 1942 experimented successfully on the water-logged bowls of the Abakaliki region. At first the yam-planting people did not take readily to the new crop. It was left mainly to the stranger tenant-farmers, who were generally more adventurous—*vide* their sojourn here—and less inhibited by local customs and traditions. It was fortunate that rice required land marginal to yam production, so that it was relatively easy to rent plots. Some of the local farmers have been converted to rice-farming and in areas like Afikpo Division where the crop was introduced after Abakaliki had proved successful, local farmers are in the majority. By 1960 an estimated 75,000 acres in Abakaliki and Ogoja Provinces were under rice. The estimated tonnage produced annually is 50,000 tons, equal to that of Sokoto Province, formerly the leading area for rice production.

In Abakaliki town itself, the importance of the rice business is reflected in the fact that in 1961, some 79% of the 1,045 members of the Abakaliki Anglican Church to which most of the immigrants belonged were engaged in it. The figure for the whole town is estimated to be over 70%.

Some indication of the distribution of the produce is given by the figures for the sales of the Rice Traders Company Limited, the principal rice exporting organisation in Abakaliki. Between March 1960 and February 1961, 23,810 tons of rice were exported as follows:

Table VIII

DISTRIBUTION OF ABAKALIKI RICE

Destination	Tonnage	Percentage of Total
Lagos	17,208	72
Aba	3,811	16
Onitsha	1,429	6
Port Harcourt	953	4

Calabar	239	1
Enugu	118	0.5
Umuahia-Ibeku	60	0.25

The figures for the Rice Traders Company rather overstate the importance of Lagos as a market for Abakaliki rice, since the large companies tend to concentrate on the longer hauls. Statistics for the smaller traders are not available, but the Eastern Nigerian towns would appear to be ranked in the order shown. In addition, local centres such as Orlu, Owerri, Amaraka and Orie Agu in the central upland area are important receivers. The degree of concentration in the trade is indicated by the fact that nearly 48 % of the estimated produce is marketed by members of this one organisation.

Although the pioneers of the rice trade were mostly former yam cultivators or dealers, who relied to some extent on the established chain of collection from the rural markets to the town, the organisation of this trade is much more complicated than that of yams. In the first place there are two intermediate processing stages—parboiling and milling—between the harvest of paddy and its marketing in usable form; and the opportunities for middleman intervention are correspondingly multiplied. In the second place, rice stores much better than yams. Threshed paddy can be stored in unprotected heaps for up to three months before milling,[5] and if properly stored can remain in good condition for years.[6] There is thus much leeway for manipulating the market, for speculative buying and for withholding stocks. In addition, old rice, with its lower water content, higher food value content per unit mass and better taste, is greatly preferred by consumers, so that at harvest time old rice is at a premium on the markets. With this consideration and the fear of a glut on the market, only a small proportion of rice harvested is processed immediately afterwards. In these circumstances, the grain store becomes a characteristic feature of the rice lands. It is estimated that at the beginning of a new crop year some 80 % of the previous year's produce is still in stocks.

Thus the marketing of rice is largely independent of its ecological calendar. The bulk of the rice harvest comes in the first two months after the rains. The broad pattern of marketing is shown by the average monthly tonnages marketed in the period 1958-59 to 1960-61 by the Co-operative Mill Society, the premier milling business in the town, which in 1960-61, with an output of 3,084 tons, handled over 6 % of the estimated total produce of the area. In spite of the fact that paddy harvesting is concentrated in two months, the relative variability of the mean monthly marketed tonnage is only 24.4 per cent of the annual average, with a range of from 65.2% in December to 38.3% in October.

The harvest period for rice overlaps with that for yams and encroaches on the land-clearing season for the next year's crop. The level of the rice cultivator's involvement in the trade depends on the degree of his specialisation. In Abakaliki Division where rice cultivation is still dominated by migrants, most planters are specialists. Elsewhere in Afikpo, Obudu, Ikom and Ogoja Divisions —all tributary to Abakaliki town—it is different. Most planters are natives and they cultivate both yams and rice, sometimes on the same plot. With the more traditional demands of the yam business pressing on them, these non-specialist producers tend to sell their produce soon after harvest. They sell to middlemen, visiting traders or their neighbouring specialist farmers, in the local markets, or take the produce direct into town for sale to the larger middlemen. The specialist producers commute between the farm and the town, storing their produce in either place until it is sold or parboiled.

The distinction between specialist farmers, middlemen and parboilers is to some extent an analytical one. Quite often one person combines some or all of the roles. With time the entrepreneur changes his balance of roles in accordance with changing economic conditions. Very little money is required for starting a rice farm. Von Blanckenburg puts the amount at £6 rent per acre and 13/- per acre for seed.[7] Of the labour costs estimated at £20. 7s. per acre, all but clearing, weeding and bird scaring—jobs for women and children and valued at £5. 10s. an acre—may be costed to the farmer's own labour. Thus a two-acre holding would require a capital of under £30. As the tenant farmer prospers, he may share his capital between expanding his production and speculating on the market. On the other hand a person may start from the paid labour ranks on the farms or at the mills and move to marketing. The parboilers are usually the bigger traders with enough money to speculate in rice on a large scale. They also finance both the farmers and the smaller traders.

From the point of view of commodity flow, husked rice has a short exchange history. There are at most two bulking stages before the speculative or parboiling stage. Speculative transactions are essentially horizontal adjustments of stocks between traders. Unlike other transactions, they do not necessarily achieve any economies of bulking or bulk-breaking. Secondly, they do not generally involve any significant spatial displacement, the commodity changing hands but remaining in the town. Thirdly, at this level the commodity rarely makes a physical appearance at the Abakaliki urban market, although the negotiations may take place there. Most of the produce of the migrant specialist producers by-passes the rural markets and goes straight to Abakaliki into their own stores, to established customers or co-operatives. For the rest the rural markets are the principal venues. The most important markets for rice are the Kpiripiri market, Okwo, Effium, Abba Omegge, Orie Egbe, Nwofe, Izuogu, Egberi and Igboji. The Ezza markets, although very large and important for other goods, particularly livestock, are principally retail markets for imported goods. The small-holder generally brings the unmilled rice to the market in small baskets, basins or calabashes. It is sold to women traders who bulk in baskets of one-quarter bag size, the cost of filling which in June 1962 varied between 15/- and 19/-. The basketfuls are then sold to urban traders who fill up bags in the market for resale, storage or parboiling.

Parboiling needs considerable expertise, and although in the early days most producers parboiled their own rice, the job is now left almost entirely to the specialists who either own mills themselves or take their parboiled rice to millers afterwards. However, a certain amount of parboiled rice may be obtained in the rural markets during the peak season for milling. In the first years of production, the grain was hulled in deep mortars with hand pestles. But as production rose the Government established an old mill at Abakaliki in 1946. In the next year four more mills were established, two stationary at Abakaliki and two mobile units. Following the success of these mills, private millers went into business from 1950 onwards, most of them at Abakaliki. In August 1961 the main centres for milling in Abakaliki Province were as follows:

Abakaliki	123 mills
Abba Omegge	4 „
Afikpo	23 „

There were a few others scattered in the main rice-growing area. Thus since the inception of rice, Abakaliki town has dominated its milling and hence its trade. The rice mills rather than the market place are the forum for dealings in the final product. Here buyers come into contact with the milled rice directly or even before it is ready for the market. There is a premium for shimmering, freshly milled rice, which depreciates by two to three shillings per bag after a week's storage.[8] Besides, the seller is saved the cost of storage, which amounts to 3d per bag per night at the Co-operative Rice Mill, or the cost of transportation back to his stores.

Rice mills are run largely on a co-operative basis, the members of the co-operative being usually persons from the same ethnic group.

Thus the Co-operative Rice Mill Society is dominated by persons from the Agulu-Awka area in Awka Division. Of its 165 members in 1961, 63 came from Adazi, 47 from Awka and 32 from Agulu. The organisation is also fairly typical. On payment of an entrance fee, two shillings when the Society started in 1955 but now two guineas, members may buy shares at a nominal value of 20/- per share, by which they are entitled to declared dividends. The minimum number of shares has been raised from 6 in 1955 to 8 in 1958. In addition to dividends, members are paid, at the end of the year, bonuses proportional to the amount of rice hulled by them. The bonus may be as much as 9/- per ton, as in 1959/60, and this is an incentive to centralised hulling. Besides, under clause 42 of the Society's constitution, there is a £5 a time penalty for disloyalty imposed on any member 'who has paddy rice and fails to bring it to the Society's mill for hulling'. In the smaller societies there is also an element of mutual aid. Members may obtain loans from the society at the very low rate of 6d in the pound per annum, and refund them in January.

In Abakaliki town the private mills were originally situated in the heart of the town near the central market. Owing to the nuisance caused by industrial fumes, effluents and chaff, as well as to the restrictions to expansion in the built-up area, an industrial estate was established in 1958 on the outskirts of the town. The majority of the mills have now moved there. The Co-operative Rice Mill retains its strategic position near the town centre. In the rural area, including Afikpo and Abba Omegge, the mills are situated near the market place. The régime of their operation is also attuned to that of the market; they are periodic, working on market days and on the evening before.

The Export Trade in Palm Produce

Three producing institutions are concerned with the trade in export crops in Iboland: the peasant farmers, the large-scale plantations, and the processing plants, notably the Pioneer Oil Mills. The principal crops — palm kernels, palm oil, rubber and cocoa—are exported and marketed externally through a statutory corporation, the Eastern Nigeria Produce Marketing Board, which has a monopoly of the trade.

Peasant production accounts for over 80% of the total value of export crops in Eastern Nigeria. From its very beginnings the trade in peasant produce has been characterised by a certain duality in organisation. The inland side of the trade has been in the hands of local traders relying mainly on the traditional routes and markets of internal trade for the collection of produce. At this level the movement of palm produce is similar to that of the staple food crops. The produce is then delivered to the agents and outposts of the exporting organisations, and from this point it moves to port through administrative channels. This pattern has remained fairly stable through changes in the control of ports and agencies, from the coastal city states and the European firms to the Produce Marketing Boards, and through changing patterns of spatial orientation. Owing to the deliberate policy of the Colonial Government discouraging large concessions to European enterprises, there are only about 63,000 acres of large-scale plantations in Eastern Nigeria, of which only 3,000 are in Iboland. These Ibo plantations, concentrated in Enugu, Port Harcourt and Umuahia Provinces, are owned mainly by a state organisation, the Eastern Nigeria Development Corporation. The Corporation processes its own produce for delivery direct to the Marketing Board.

The traditional methods of extracting palm oil from fruit are inefficient and wasteful. Much of the oil produced is of low quality, with high content of free fatty acid (up to 30%), and only about 50 to 60 per cent of the oil is extracted. The kernels are obtained by the slow and tedious process of crushing the nuts between stones and extracting them by hand. Hand presses were introduced into Nigeria in 1932 and rapidly became popular, the number purchased rising from 58 in that year to 834 in 1938.[9] With them it was possible to produce oil with low free fatty acid content—as low as 1.5% when the fruit is processed fresh—and to extract up to 65% of the oil. Hand presses did not very much alter the spatial pattern of the trade. They were small and served very small localities. The producer took her fruits to the hand press immediately after harvest, paid for the processing and took away her oil and kernels for sale. But sometimes the owner of the hand press traded on his own account, buying fruit for processing and sale and also bulking oil and kernels brought in by producers, thus making his premises a local centre for the trade. Large-scale oil mills were introduced after the war. After considerable local opposition they became established in the chief palm-producing areas in Eastern Nigeria. Today there are 59 of them in Iboland. The oil mills have hitherto been operated as agencies of the Eastern Nigeria Development Corporation. In pursuance of the Government's policy of encouraging local private enterprise, some of them are now being sold to private entrepreneurs, but the organisation remains the same. The oil mill buys fruits brought in by producers and traders, processes them and sends the palm oil and kernels to the E.N.D.C. depots at the various ports. The E.N.D.C., acting as a licenced produce buying agent, delivers the produce to the Marketing Board under the normal statutory conditions.

The Eastern Nigerian Produce Marketing Board at the apex of the organisation is a lineal descendant of the statutory export monopolies established by the British Government during the second world war. When the outbreak of war led to a partial closure of its traditional export markets and threatened a collapse of local cocoa prices, the British Government undertook to purchase all West African cocoa offered for sale at annually fixed prices. For this purpose it created a statutory export monopoly which was entrusted first to the Cocoa Control Board of the Ministry of Food, then transferred in 1940 to the newly established West Africa Cocoa Control Board. In 1942 the organisation was enlarged and renamed the West Africa Produce Control Board on taking over the monopoly marketing of groundnuts and oil palm produce. In 1947 there was some decentralisation, the various West African countries taking over the handling of exports and the responsibility for deciding future policy and prices for their own produce.[10] In Nigeria new boards were created for individual export crops—a Cocoa Marketing Board, a Groundnut Marketing Board, a Palm Produce Marketing Board, and so on. With the coming of the federal constitution in 1954, the structure was again reorganised. New regional all-purpose boards were created to inherit the regional assets and liabilities of the various Marketing Boards. Since then, each region fixes its own producer prices and the terms of operation of its appointed produce buying agents. Activities are co-ordinated at the federal level by the Nigerian Produce Marketing Board, which is responsible for checking standards and for external marketing.

The arrangements between the Board and its agents have remained substantially the same since the war. The Board undertakes to purchase through its licenced agents all the exportable export produce offered for sale at gazetted buying stations. Purchases are made by the Board on the basis of a fixed naked ex-scale port of shipment (or bulk oil plant, for palm oil) prices. The agents are responsible for getting the produce there. They are required to 'purchase at gazetted buying stations at not less than the minimum gazetted prices with reasonable regularity throughout the season' at least the quota assigned to each agent. Failure to do this, for any reason barring exceptionally low crops or accidents, may cost an agent his licence. Agents are also required to arrange for inspection of the produce by official produce inspectors, and to finance purchase

and provide suitable storage at buying stations and 'such intermediate stations as may be required' until the time of delivery.

The Board determines the port or depot to which each gazetted
buying station may evacuate its approved and graded purchases, and
pays the agent's transport differentials based on the officially
estimated cost of doing so by officially approved routes. The
producer prices, i.e., the minimum prices which the agents may offer
their suppliers, are the port of shipment prices less the transport
differentials. The agents are not obliged to evacuate their produce
by the approved routes but they 'will not be reimbursed any
additional expenses incurred through evacuation by a more expensive
route than that specified . . . unless the prior approval of the Board's
executive for the use of such abnormal route has been obtained'.[11]
In addition to the purchase price and transport differentials the
produce buying agents are paid a buying allowance per ton
purchased, which covers the buying commission and other necessities
such as insurance. In 1962/63 this allowance was £6. 12. 9d for
special grade palm oil and £2. 14. 0d for palm kernels.[12]

When the Marketing Board system was instituted the principal
buying agents were the large expatriate firms. Today there are 75
licenced buying agents. Only twelve of them are expatriate firms,
two are subsidiaries of the Eastern Nigerian Development Corporation, and the rest indigenous agents. Most of the indigenous trading
agents have been appointed since 1954. Unlike the older expatriate
firms they do not partake in the import trade. Their methods are
much the same—most of the traders served their apprenticeship as
commission agents of the expatriate firms—but their overheads in
plant and personnel are considerably lower and their organisation
more flexible. There is also public pressure for the Nigerianisation
of the export produce trade. As a result the expatriate companies
are tending to leave the produce trade, concentrating on the
distribution of imported goods.

Licenced buying agents usually operate from a number of stations,
with factors or commission agents buying produce through sub-
agents or free-lance traders. These smaller operators visit the urban
and rural central markets or set up posts just outside the licenced
buying stations to buy directly from producers and petty traders and
deliver to the licenced agent. The large expatriate firms generally
have several factors buying for them at each of their branches. Here
all produce is bulked and eventually sent directly to the ports. The
Nigerian buying agent, operating with little capital, usually acts as
his own factor at one of his stations while the others are run by
'factors'[13] trading more or less independently but under his name

and licence. At the ports the depots of the various buying agents receive all out-station produce for delivery.

For so regulated an activity one would expect the spatial patterns of the export trade to be clear-cut and stable. But this is not so. In a very useful discussion of the movements of export crops in Nigeria, White has pointed out that produce is not always moved along the officially designated routes.[14] There is an overall tendency for road haulage to supersede the traditional rail and river routes. The degree of divergence varies between the regions. It is greatest in the Eastern Region, where owing to the difficulties of obtaining data it is often underestimated. In the Northern Region the road system is well integrated with the railways. The railheads —Kano, Gusau, Zaria, Jos, Kafanchan—are also the centres of the road haulage traffic to the West so that the internal lines of movement are not altered significantly. Only the mode of evacuation is changing. The railway tariff, with tapered rates for long-distance haulage, succeeds in keeping much of the traffic loyal to the railway. In other southern regions where the distances to port are less, the road network much more dense and providing direct connection between the producing areas and the ports, the switch to road haulage is greater. In the Western Region the road has taken over almost completely and the road routes are recognised as the official evacuation routes. In the Eastern Region, however, the waterways flank and penetrate into the main producing area while the railway crosses the centre. The official routes are determined on the basis of transport costs. Given the differential rates on the three strongly competing transport systems, the cheapest routes are often a combination of all three. On the other hand the produce buying agent lays premium on speedy evacuation, which increases his turnover and hence his commission, rather than on crude transport cost per mile. Hence he tends increasingly to rely on motor transport. This being faster and more flexible, he can switch produce between ports according to need, diverting produce from Port Harcourt or Calabar to Abonnema if the former are congested. Port Harcourt, by far the best equipped Eastern Nigerian port, is very rapidly displacing the other ports in the export trade. Fig. 18 shows the official evacuation routes and the flow of palm kernels in what was reported to be a normal week in mid-season of 1963. Virtually the whole of the produce of the hinterland between the Niger, the Cross River and the coastal swamps, including all of Iboland, is now evacuated through Port Harcourt. The change is much more pronounced for palm oil, which deteriorates quickly and therefore needs more rapid evacuation than do palm kernels.

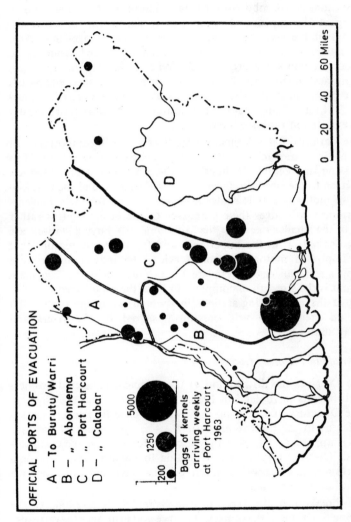

Fig. 18 *Official ports of evacuation of oil palm kernels.*

In sympathy with the changes in the routes and means of transport the relative importance of produce buying stations has also changed, the stations favourably located in relation to the road system gaining at the expense of those mainly dependent on either the railways or the waterways. In addition to the changes associated with modes of transport there has been a marked tendency to concentration in a few large centres. Whereas in 1946 the ten largest stations accounted for 51.2% of the palm kernels graded and 64.1% of the palm oil, in 1960/61 the comparable figures were 67.2% and 15.9%. In the latter period the stations were also more clearly differentiated in rank-size hierarchies.

The pattern of development reflects the growing importance of the major commercial centres. The concentration of the fast increasing marketing facilities at these centres increases their attraction to the rural producers and petty traders, and the development of motor transport routes makes it feasible for the sub-agents and traders to deliver their purchases to the larger centres rather than to the smaller ones. At the same time new buying stations are being opened up in the hinterland, and for the same reason: that with improved motor transport services the indigenous produce buying agent can easily evacuate his produce to port. The main restraint is the strength of competition from the established stations. Most of the new buying stations in Iboland are in the central Ibo area, an area which was previously served by the rivers and railway stations.

The Trade in Imported Goods

Table IX gives the distribution of the principal registered business establishments in Iboland in 1963. It is derived from the Nigerian Trade Directory and is by no means a complete list; nevertheless it enables us to see the overall pattern. The dominance of the four cities is apparent. Together they account for 96% of the establishments. Owerri, Oguta and Umuahia-Ibeku are also of some importance, but the other seven centres have only one or two establishments reported.

The breakdown into types of establishments is revealing of the differing functions of the centres. Finance and insurance, advertising, and the sale of transport machinery are concentrated in the four cities. Enugu leads for advertising and finance, Port Harcourt in most other lines, including exports and imports. Aba is generally more important than Onitsha, and Enugu ranks lowest on most of the merchandise items. Firms engaged in exporting and importing

Table IX

DISTRIBUTION OF REGISTERED BUSINESS ESTABLISHMENTS, 1962

Location	Type of Establishment					Total	
	Advertising, Publishing, Marketing Agencies, Finance & Insurance	Machinery, Office Equipment & Stationery	Chemicals	General Merchants, Exporters & Importers	Food, Drinks & Tobacco	No.	%
Port Harcourt	28	118	7	101	54	308	35.6
Aba	22	72	5	75	32	206	23.8
Enugu	24	71	1	42	26	164	19.0
Onitsha	11	54	6	53	31	155	17.9
Owerri	1	—	1	6	1	9	1.0
Umuahia Ibeku	1	1	—	5	2	9	1.0
Oguta	1	—	—	3	—	4	0.5
Awka	1	—	—	1	—	2	0.2
Abakaliki	—	1	—	—	1	2	0.2
Enugu Agidi	—	—	—	—	1	1	0.2
Ezinihite	—	—	—	—	1	1	0.2
Mbaise	—	—	—	—	1	1	0.2
Ogwe	—	—	—	1	—	1	0.2
Abiriba	—	—	—	1	—	1	0.2

(*Source:* Nigerian Trade Directory, 1962.)

are also represented in the urban centres of Owerri, Oguta and Umuahia-Ibeku, and at Awka and Ogwe. The firms operating in the smaller centres are concerned with general merchandise, particularly food, drink and tobacco.

Table X shows the pattern of formal links between the establishments. All the expatriate firms have their head offices in Lagos. These national enterprises are very strongly represented in Port Harcourt, which claims 46% of all the branches in Iboland. Aba, next in rank, has less than half this proportion. Onitsha has even fewer branches than Enugu, a feature which points to its position as an indigenous marketing centre. Only a few of the firms based in Iboland, which are mostly Nigerian-owned firms, have branches outside their base. Here Onitsha comes into its own. Every third firm registered at Onitsha has a branch elsewhere in Iboland; the figures for the other three cities are 21% for Port Harcourt, 17% for Aba and 13% for Enugu.

Table X

CONTROL OF BUSINESS ESTABLISHMENTS, 1962
(LOCATION OF HEAD OFFICE)

	Local	Elsewhere in Iboland					Lagos	North	West	Total
		Onitsha	Port H'ct	Aba	Enugu	Umuahia				
Port Harcourt	61	3	—	—	1	—	64	—	1	130
Aba	44	3	4	—	1	—	31	1	1	85
Enugu	23	3	2	1	—	—	22	—	—	51
Onitsha	33	—	1	2	1	—	19	1	1	58
Owerri	—	2	2	1	—	—	—	—	—	5
Umuahia-Ibeku	1	—	1	—	—	—	3	—	—	5
Oguta	—	—	1	—	—	—	3	—	—	4
Awka	—	—	—	2	—	—	—	—	—	2
Abakaliki	1	—	—	—	—	—	—	—	—	1
Enugu Agidi	1	—	—	—	—	—	—	—	—	1
Ezinihite	—	—	1	—	—	—	—	—	—	1
Mbaise	—	—	1	—	—	—	—	—	—	1
Ogwe	—	—	—	1	—	—	—	—	—	1
Abiriba	—	—	—	—	—	1	—	—	—	1
Total	164	11	13	7	3	1	142	2	3	346

(*Source:* Nigerian Trade Directory, 1962.)

Bower and Bauer have shown clearly the oligopolistic nature of West African trade in imported goods, arising from the dominant position of a few large expatriate firms.[15] These firms are usually vertically integrated organisations handling trade at various levels. Not all their imports reach consumers through subsequent stages of their own organisation. Some of it is sold to middlemen, wholesalers, sub-wholesalers and retailers, who compete with one another and with the large firms at the lower stages of distribution. The presence of a significant number of indigenous traders in the import trade is a special feature of West African trade. In other parts of Africa the trading organisation of the importing firms reaches down to the small village shop, restricting the scope for local enterprise. Notwithstanding the tradition of cooperation and interdependence between the large firms and the Nigerian traders, some of whom served their apprenticeship as servants or agents of the firms, it may be said that to some extent the development of local enterprise has been in spite of the large firms. Bauer documents the various ways both they and the colonial governments sought to restrict competition from new entrants into the import trade during the inter-war years.[16]

Since 1960 when effective political power passed into the hands of the local people, the trend in Nigeria has been towards a reduction in the dominance of these firms, largely through the entry of indigenous traders into the business of importing general consumer goods like textiles, stockfish, other non-branded staples and domestic hardware. The large firms have tended to concentrate on the importation of technical goods—electrical goods, machinery and heavy industrial goods—for which financially and technically they are much better equipped. Usually they provide not only the goods but also technical advice on their use as well as servicing facilities. To the extent that this is the sector with the highest potential for growth, the shift in emphasis partly offsets the decline in the other sectors.

The organisation of the older firms has passed through several successive stages, some of which have been considered in Chapter Nine. From the period of inland penetration to the beginning of the second world war the numerous inland stations were used for both the export and the import trade. After the war the retail trade in the smaller stations became more vulnerable to local competition and began to be abandoned even in places where the companies still retained some hold on the produce trade. The changing merchandise trade was concentrated in the large centres. Thus the U.A.C. now has branches only at Port Harcourt, Aba, Onitsha and Enugu, with smaller stations at Umuahia-Ibeku, Okigwi, Orlu and Owerri. In the two leading French firms, S.C.O.A. and C.F.A.O., the change has been even more drastic. Only Aba, Enugu and Onitsha are left in Iboland, with Imo river station remaining as a palm produce beach. The post-war firms, like the Swiss firm of U.T.C. and the Greek, A.G. Leventis, have not established branches outside the four cities.

The old firms began by the amalgamation of a number of small all-purpose firms. This was reflected in a cumbrous bureaucratic structure with a branch manager at each trading station in charge of all aspects of the business and responsible to a regional manager. In line with the trend towards specialisation they are being reorganised vertically, with departments for personnel, management, and various lines of business. The reorganisation is furthest in the U.A.C. where the various specialist sections—U.A.C. Motors, Kingsway Chemists, etc.—have been incorporated in their own rights and are run as subsidiaries of the parent organisation.

The departments selling specialised goods deal with the consumers directly. The staple commodities are distributed through the well established trade channels. Three types of commercial customers are recognised in the trade: commission agents, credit customers and cash customers. The commission agents, most of them former branch managers or assistants, are very intimately connected with the firms. They deal exclusively in the firm's goods and are paid commission on sales. Since many of them also occupy the abandoned premises of the firms, the functional links are very strong. But there are no formal organisational ties.

Credit customers usually do business with a number of firms, although where they are heavily committed to one financially they may be under pressure to buy from it exclusively. Credit buying is an old tradition of West African trade, reaching back to pre-penetration coastal trade.[17] It is now important only in the large centres of Port Harcourt, Aba and Onitsha. Credit customers serve a dual function: credit trading proper, and brokerage operations between the firms and the less knowledgeable or less well-connected traders, usually from up country. Some of the less efficient 'customers' depend entirely on the latter function. They do not have any store or market stall for the sale of merchandise but arrange for the third parties to collect their purchases direct from the firms. Credit customers also include local dealers in certain technical consumer goods—bicycles and radios in particular—who specialise in selling the merchandise of certain firms. The advantage from the point of view of the firm is that the arrangement relieves it of the final stages of distribution while there is some guarantee that the goods will be handled properly and the brand name protected.

Cash customers include the mass of small-scale traders who buy from the firms as well as from the bigger traders in the shops and in the markets. The possibilities of breaks in bulk and subdivision of units of commodities offered for sale in West African trade are so great that it is difficult to give any precise meaning to the formal distinction between wholesale and retail. Bauer has explained the senses in which the terms are used:

> ... wholesale transactions refer to direct importing and to sales by importers to resellers without breaking bulk of unit of shipment or individual containers. Transactions subsequent to this stage are frequently termed retail transactions, and they are almost invariably thus referred to officially, even though the transactions may be in substantial units, and the merchandise may have to pass through the hands of several resellers before reaching the consumers.[18]

It is in this context that the claim of one of the major firms at Port Harcourt, that the wholesale-retail ratio is 1:6, is to be understood.

Nigerian importers are concentrated in the four cities, with Port Harcourt pre-eminent and Enugu lagging a long way behind. They are mostly private companies run by members of the same family of persons from the same village group. The majority of them have risen from the ranks of petty traders. Mostly illiterate, some of them depend on the services of import agencies at the ports to transact their business with the overseas firms—letters, cablegrams and bank transfers—and on customs agencies to clear their goods from port. Nigerian importers are most firmly established in the stockfish, textiles and used-clothing trades, but are making inroads into the market for domestic hardware. The policy of successive Governments in restricting imports from Japan and other non-European countries—justified on the grounds of maintaining or restoring favourable bilateral balance of payments positions with these countries—has had the effect of restricting the scope for Nigerian importers. The expatriate firms have their buying strength and contacts in Western Europe and North America. Some of them are vertically integrated with important manufacturing enterprises in the metropolitan countries or have been granted the sole agencies for selling brands of goods which have established reputations. The chances of Nigerian firms breaking into the market are thus very slim. One would expect a more liberal official attitude to enable Nigerian traders to buy from the very pushful, competitive, and rapidly expanding Asian markets.

The rural local shop is a retail establishment selling a rather limited range of goods. An inventory of a typical shop would include imported groceries—tinned foods, pomade, sugar, mineral waters and soft drinks, kerosene, soap, exercise books and domestic appliances. The bigger ones would also sell some articles of clothing —shirts, singlets and blouses, drills and white shirting—but rarely cotton prints, since the customer demands a wider selection which only a cross section of sellers in the market place can give him. The rural shopkeeper trades on his own or on behalf of a principal who may be in business elsewhere. But the shop is a self-contained unit and has no structural organisational links with any other shops; there are no rural chain stores.

All ranks of markets are involved in the trade in imported goods and manufactured articles. Rural central markets become more important with increasing distance from the urban centres. There are no large markets within ten miles of any of the principal towns, the development of urban trade having led to the decline of such markets as the Oba market near Onitsha, the Eke Ndume market near Umuahia-Ibeku, and the Afor Osukwu market near Aba as centres for imported goods, although they still retain some of their importance for local produce. In areas where permanent centres are few and undeveloped, rural markets provide most of the imported goods bought by rural consumers.

Patterns of Commodity Flow

Imported goods reach Iboland through two main ports, Port Harcourt and Onitsha. Port Harcourt receives about £46 m. worth of goods annually. This is 95% of the total for Eastern Nigerian ports. The share of the other ports has fallen steadily, even more rapidly than their share of the export trade. In 1960 the figures for Calabar and Degema were 3.9% and 0.1% respectively as compared with 14.3% and 1.2% for 1950. As a distributing centre Port Harcourt specialises in the bulk transfer of goods and in the retail of higher order goods. The position of the firms is dominant and the role of the market place relatively unimportant. Its main market-place outlet is the Aba market, most of whose traders have contacts with Port Harcourt suppliers. Situated on the plains 40 miles north of Port Harcourt and with easy direct access by road from all directions, Aba is more strategically located than Port Harcourt in relation to competition with Onitsha for the trade of the hinterland, and so Aba, rather than Port Harcourt, is Onitsha's main rival for the custom of rural petty traders.

Onitsha draws its supplies mainly from the Delta ports and from Lagos. The river trade is dominated by two expatriate firms—U.A.C. and John Holt. Onitsha traders also travel by road to Burutu and Warri to buy goods, particularly textiles and crockery. Lagos is the chief supplier of staple commodities to Onitsha market traders, who travel there by lorry weekly or fortnightly to buy from the wholesale stores. They are able to retail these goods at prices low enough to attract petty traders from Lagos itself. Port Harcourt is becoming increasingly important as a source of supply. Enugu depends on Onitsha for most of its staple commodities. Its important as a trade centre is confined to higher order goods, which the shops supply directly to the relatively wealthy urban population.

An analysis was made of the destination of lorries leaving Onitsha and Aba lorry parks. The surveys on which it was based covered different periods. Inspection of lorries standing in both motor parks showed that most of them carried a wide range of imported goods in addition to local produce. Hawkins' earlier survey[19] suggests that about a third of lorry luggage space is occupied by imported goods. It therefore seems fair to regard the pattern emerging as an approximation to the pattern of commodity flow from the two cities. The divide between the Onitsha and Aba hinterlands lies along an ESE. to WNW. axis through Owerri, Okigwi and Afikpo, corresponding very closely to the locus of equidistance between the cities. But, of course, the divide is far from water-tight and many traders on each side cross it to the other centre. As the survey also shows, Aba and Onitsha are each other's best customers. A large part of the trade between the centres is made up of short-term adjustments to stocks, traders from one centre travelling to the other to buy goods as local stocks are depleted or local prices rise relative to those of the other. But there is also a more stable relationship. On the whole Onitsha is the more important centre. It is much more important than Aba as a market for hardware and general consumer goods, while Aba has developed the trade in textiles and clothing. In particular Aba is the national centre for the trade in imported used clothing, which has grown from the immediate post-war trade in used army outfits. It also has numerous small-scale dress-making enterprises making underwear, shirts, shorts and blouses, which find a ready market throughout Nigeria.

The survey illustrates another important distinction between Onitsha and Aba as centres. In addition to the long-range contacts, Onitsha has developed very close links by bus services with its immediate hinterland, which lies within a 24-mile radius. Most of Aba's lorry connections are with towns and rural centres in the middle distance—25 to 60 miles. The immediate hinterland is poorer and less densely populated than that of Onitsha; and in spite of the strong polarisation of the area to the city, the rural periodic markets are more vigorous than those of the Onitsha area. This would appear to be partly a function of the dispersed settlement pattern, which has the consequence that a large proportion of settlement units are not directly linked to the city by the arterial roads.

It will be observed that although the main urban centres receive more traffic from the two metropolitan centres than do the smaller towns and the rural centres, they are by no means dominant. The development of motor transport means that many rural traders can by-pass the towns and obtain their supplies direct from the metropolitan centres. It is the very small petty trader, making part of his living by substituting his own labour for transport costs—transporting his goods on his head or by bicycle—who depends on the nearby urban centre for his supplies. The urban centres serve their rural hinterland in other ways. Within about ten miles radius persons who wish to buy durable consumer goods or higher order goods will usually go to the urban centre directly. Beyond this the tendency is for urban petty traders to visit the rural central markets.

Urban-based traders have to compete in the rural markets with rural-based traders, some of whom also keep local shops. The rural-based traders tend to be concentrated in a few settlements in a given area. There is a wide range in the scale of their operations. At the lower end, the petty trader with a capital of less than about £30 may be found in most settlements. He tends to confine himself to the local markets, including the nearby rural central markets. He may be a part-time trader appearing in his local market on market days and following other pursuits on ordinary days. Near the towns rural traders also carry on business in the urban markets, particularly during the agricultural slack season. The bigger rural trader, with a capital of up to £200 and sometimes more, usually travels on bicycle and can therefore cover a much wider area than can the petty trader. He visits much the same markets as his urban-based rival—usually the most important ones in the locality—and his marketing ring may extend over several counties.

An attempt was made to illustrate the interlaced networks of spatial relationships resulting from activity at various levels. It was based on sample surveys of buyers in the Nkwo Ndielu, Umuahia-Ibeku and Aba markets as examples of a rural central market, an urban daily market and a metropolitan market respectively and gives some indication of the extent of the hinterland of each type of market. On the assumption that 90% of the sample of buyers in each market come from its normal hinterland, this hinterland lies within a radius of 19 miles for the rural central market, 30 miles for the urban central market and 75 miles for the metropolitan market. A high proportion of the buyers in each market come from the immediate vicinity, the percentage of buyers coming from within five miles being 59, 39 and 59 respectively. The hinterlands of the two higher order centres are futher extended by the activities of urban-based traders who visit rural markets and by the visits of rural traders to these centres.

NOTES

1. P. N. C. Okigbo, op. cit.
2. E. K. Hawkins, *Road transport in Nigeria*. London, 1958.
3. See F. J. Pedler, *Economic Geography of West Africa*. London, 1955, p. 139.
4. Sauce ingredients include a wide range of oils, spices, meat and fish preparations and vegetables used for seasoning 'soup', the sauce with which some of the staple foods — cassava, *gari* and pounded yam — are eaten. Other important items are palm oil (by the bottle, calabash or pot), smoked dried fish and crayfish, pepper, salt, melon, okra, and various dried seeds and fruits.
5. Sir H. Tempany and D. H. Grist, *An introduction to Tropical Agriculture*. London, 1961.
6. D. H. Grist, *Rice*. London, 1953.
7. Peter von Blanckenburg, *Rice farming in the Abakaliki area: a study of the process of introduction of a new crop*. Ibadan, NISER, 1962 MS.
8. F. I. Ekejiuba, *The production and marketing of rice in Abakaliki*. MS, 1961.
9. D. Forde, and Scott.
10. P. T. Bauer, 'Statistics of statutory marketing in West Africa, 1939-1951', *Journal of the Royal Statistical Society*, 1954.
11. *Eastern Nigeria Marketing Board Memorandum*, No. EN/63/PK.
12. *Eastern Nigeria Marketing Board Memoranda*, Nos EN/63/PO and EN/63/PK.
13. The competition among licenced buying agents for the adherence of these 'factors' without whom they might find it difficult to fulfil their buying quotas ensures that the factors receive very favourable terms. Thus in addition to supplying weighing scales, and other materials, one licenced buying agent paid his factors a buying commission of £5 a ton for oil in 1963 when the official rate was £6. 12. 9d.
14. H. P. White, 'The movement of export crops in Nigeria', *Tidjschrift voor Economische en Sociale Geografie*, 1963.
15. A. Bower, and others 'Mining, commerce and finance in Nigeria', Vol. II of *Economics of a Tropical Dependency*, edited by M. Perham. Faber and Faber; 1948; P. T. Bauer, 'Concentration in tropical trade', *Economica*, 1953.
16. P. T. Bauer, *West African Trade*. Cambridge, 1954, Chapter III.
17. See C. J. Gertzel, op. cit.
18. P. T. Bauer, *West African Trade*. Cambridge, 1954, p. 54.
19. E. K. Hawkins, op. cit.

CHAPTER TWELVE

Case Studies: Rural Markets

HAVING considered the economic roles of the various institutions and the general patterns of commodity flow, the study now turns to some regional case studies so as to take in various other related aspects of the marketing system. This section starts with two studies of rural communities, examining in some detail the rural economic landscape and the place of the various exchange-place institutions. In these studies the perspective, so to speak, is switched to looking at the marketing centres from the point of view of each community and examining the patterns of spatial orientation in which it is involved by the operation of the system as a whole.

I. UMUNAKANU

The village group of Umunakanu, with a population in 1953 of 8,741, belongs to the densely populated Isuama country on the south-eastern part of the central Ibo uplands. It is situated in the Mbano County, the most densely populated county in Iboland. The village group itself occupies some four square miles of territory. It is surrounded by related village groups, Umueze, Umuezeala, Abaja and Umukabia, with which it makes up the patrician of Ehime, now a local council administrative unit. Umunakanu's web of kinship has been extended by inter-marriage to include other neighbouring but unrelated groups. The closest links both by group kinship and by intermarriage are with Umuezeala, whose territories flank Umunakanu on the northern side. Politically the village group is oriented to Umuduru, the county headquarters; to Okigwi, the divisional headquarters; and to Owerri, the provincial headquarters. Economically these centres are of little account to it, the important centres being Umuahia-Ibeku, 24 miles to the east-south-east, and Aba, some fifty miles to the south-east.

Economically, Umunakanu is a poor community. The ecological environment is typical of the central Ibo upland region. Farms are small and fragmented and fallow has become non-existent as

200

settlement and compoundland have spread into farmland. Continuous farming has stripped the soil of most of its nourishment,
leaving it fit only for a stunted varieties of yams, used mainly as
seed yams, and for the tolerant cocoyam, cassava and vegetables.
For their cash earnings most farmers depend on palm produce—palm
kernels, palm oil, and palm wine as well as the weaving of baskets,
mats, twine, rope ladders and raffia bags. The community is far from
self-sufficient in food. It depends on the Isuochi-Ogu Ukwu area
north of the Imo and east of the Awgu-Okigwi ridge for yams,
cassava, plantains and vegetables; and on the Ikwerri and Oratta
areas for *gari* and cassava. The sex ratio of 915 men per 1,000 women
indicates a high rate of male emigration from the village group,
in line with the general pattern for the region. Some of the migration
is to urban centres, particularly Umuahia-Ibeku and Aba, but a
large number of the emigrants are seasonal migrant farmers. The
principal area is the Isuochi country beyond the Imo river,
particularly on land belonging to Otanchara people. Centres of
labour migration include the Oru and Ikwerre country, Benin and
Fernando Po. The oldest communication links are the maze of paths
linking the various sectors of Umunakanu to one another and to the
surrounding village groups, a maze which has become very complex
as settlement has spread. The principle is the central Ibo one of
radiating paths from the centre of the village or hamlet, which is
known locally as *Ogboto*, to other equivalent units. The paths
are still used for communications between settlements, since they
generally provide the shortest cut. But movements and activities
associated with long-distance relations are oriented to the main
roads. In addition to local paths, vestiges of the old paths to the
Imo river stations of the early European trade phase still remain.

Umunakanu is located in an area with a very dense motor road
network and near some of the busiest roads and junctions in Iboland.
The principal road passing through the village group is the Okigwi-
Umuahia road. From road junctions at Umuduru, three miles to the
north-west, roads go through Angara to Onitsha and Owerri. From
Ukwu Ugiri in Umunakanu an earth road links up farther south
with the Okigwi-Aba road, which takes off from the Okigwi-Umuahia
road a few hundred yards from the eastern boundary of Umunakanu.

All the principal markets in Mbano county are now on the main
roads. Most of those visited by Umunakanu people lie on the
Okigwi-Umuahia road. No lorry services originate from or terminate
at Umunakanu but the stretch of road carries traffic from three
main lines and is very busy. Lorries usually stop at Eke Umunakanu
and Ukwu Ugiri to pick up or drop passengers, and may stop

anywhere else on demand. It is possible to go to Okigwi or Umuahia at any time of the day from dawn to dusk and the fare, 1/- to 1/6 for 24 miles, is quite cheap. Transport to Aba is much less frequent, depending on traffic from Okigwi. Lorries for Onitsha can usually be caught only in the early hours between 5 and 7 a.m. as they pass through from Umuahia; the charge is usually 3/- for the 76 miles. On important market days lorries ply the chief roads in the county picking up passengers to and from the markets. The fare to Afor Ezuru (6 miles) or Orie Agu (4 miles) is only 4d to 6d; to Orie Amaraka (14 miles) is 6d to 1/-. Bicycle taxis are being driven out of the passenger business by low lorry fares and now tend to concentrate on carrying palm produce, which they can pick up more conveniently on site and on the minor roads.

Umunakanu is in an area of numerous markets. The transition from periodic to daily activity is very advanced in most of the larger markets and there are a number of rural service centres not attached to markets. Three rural periodic markets in Mbano county stand out clearly as rural central markets of a higher order. They are the Afor Ezuru market, the Orie Agu market and the Orie Amaraka market. In addition, each village group in the area has its own cycle of markets, some of which are of more than local significance.

1. Afor Ezuru is essentially a frontier market and entrepôt. Located on the Okigwi-Umuduru ridge which carries the Okigwi-Umuahia road across the Imo valley, it stands between the food-scarcity areas to the south and the food-surplus areas to the north and north-east. The main commodities which change hands here are yams, cassava and plantains. These are brought in by lorries from markets in the food-surplus areas, notably Oye Awgu, Nkwo Acha and Nkwo Akeze, and taken by traders in other lorries to the centres in the south. The principal termini for the out-going lorries in Mbano county are Orie Agu, Orie Amaraka and Umuezeala-Owerri-Aba junction, which is a specialised transport and service centre. Traders who come from areas outside the main roads take their purchases away by head porterage or bicycle. The market has large retail sectors for both foodstuffs and imported goods. There are a few permanent stores, the most important of which is a produce-buying depot. Afor Ezuru is still very much a periodic market. Outside the permanent stores little trade is done on days other than its market day, once in eight days.

2. Orie Agu market is the second largest market in Mbano county. It is in the middle of a densely populated area and is mainly a distributing centre. The market is fast developing into a central

place of the Western type, with permanent stores on the streets facing or leading into it, and with lock-up shops in the market itself. Several lorries are based in Umukagu, the village which owns the market, and these take local traders to the urban centres of Umuahia and Aba as well as the more important rural markets. There is daily activity in the market as well as in the shops. The busiest section of the market is usually the cassava section. Cassava comes mainly from Oye Awgu, Afor Ezuru, Nkwo Inyi, Nkwo Akeze, Obinagu and Uburu, and the cassava section of the market is busy daily as supplies are stored for market day. Subsidiary sources of supply are Bende Division—Elu Elu and Owuwu counties, and the Ikwerre-Etche areas. Ikwerre-Etche and Ngwaland are the principal sources of *gari*. Yams are also very important, the main sources being the great metropolitan markets of Aba and Onitsha and Abakaliki and Afikpo. Umukagu-based traders travel to these places. Orie Agu is also the distributing centre for interregional trade goods such as groundnuts, rice and beans as well as for imported and manufactured goods. Evidence of other activities in the service centre include carpentry shops, industrial establishments, produce buying agencies, petrol stations, advertising agencies and newspaper offices. In addition Umukagu is an important educational centre for the area.

3. Orie Amaraka is the largest rural market in Eastern Nigeria. Like Orie Agu it is situated in the heart of a very densely populated area and it is essentially a retail market. It draws food crops from both the food surplus areas north and south of the central Ibo uplands. In addition it is the great market for local crafts: iron-mongery from Nkwerre and the Awka area, mortars and pestles from the forested southern plains, pottery from the Imo valley. There are regular lorry services between Amaraka and the two metropolitan centres of Aba and Onitsha, the latter through Orlu. The chief speciality of Amaraka by way of imported goods is the sale of bicycles, bicycle parts and accessories, the bicycle being the chief means of transport in the Isuama country. Traditionally, Orie Amaraka is a periodic market but like Orie Agu it has acquired shopping streets and permanent service centres as well as large daily sectors in the market place itself.

Umunakanu markets are mainly of local importance. The chief traditional market of Umunakanu, the Afor Dim market, ceased to function during the war years. The second market to be established, the Eke Umunakanu, is still functioning but is less important than the Afor Mgba market which was founded about 1935 in the Umunakanu Owerri sector of the village group. The Afor Mgba is an important intergroup market in the area and is noted for palm produce and crafts from Umunakanu itself as well as livestock, particularly poultry, goats and tortoises from the Mbaise county area. The Eke Umunakanu is mainly a local retail market. Both markets have daily sectors but there are more shops adjoining the smaller Eke market, which lies on the main Okigwi-Umuahia road, than there are at Afor Mgba. There are two very small markets, the Nkwo Umunakanu, and the Orie Umugolo; but today they are falling into disuse, their users tending to prefer marketing in the daily sector of the Afor Mgba even on the traditional days. The Orie Umugolo market was actually started by the Ehime Local Council as a clan market and located at Ukwu Ugiri because this was supposed to be the geographical centre of the local council area. But Ehime is already well served by several markets much better located in relation to the main lines of movement, particularly by the Umuezeala Owerre centre whose market is held on the same day. The Orie Umunakanu seems to have been doomed to failure and now even the local users have lost interest in it. Umugolo, the sector of Umunakanu in which the market is located, vainly tries to keep it alive by various stratagems. On the eve of the market day the women of the sector meet and ceremonially clean the market. Singing and dancing, they call on patriots to support their 'child whom enemies have conspired to ruin', and on the gods to mete out due punishment to renegades. But the scheme is a very limited success; attendance at the market, buyers, sellers and all, rarely exceeds fifty.

As has been remarked, it is in this area that permanent rural service centres are most developed in Iboland. These service centres are usually at road junctions or attached to new settlements. Thus Angara is an important road junction where the Okigwi-Owerri road crosses the Umuahia-Onitsha road. Isinweke, the site of the administrative headquarters of the Etiti county, lies outside Mbano county but may be cited as a local example of the latter kind of development. The service centres nearest Umunakanu are at Umu-duru, the site of the headquarters of the Mbano county, and Umuezeala-Owerri-Aba junction where the road to Aba branches off from the Okigwi-Umuahia road. In Umunakanu itself there are service centres at the sites of the two principal markets and at the road junction at Ukwu Ugiri where the service centre preceded the small market. There is also an oil mill which serves the Ehime clan and part of Mbaise county.

Economic Transactions

The analysis which follows is based on a 12-day survey of exchange transactions in Umunakanu, from 18 August to 29 August 1963. Statistics are based on the activities of 56 informants for 8 days, August 22 to 28, this being a complete cycle in an area of 8-day markets. The pattern of market transactions is typically Ibo, with men and women dealing in different kinds of goods. The details of the economic transactions are given in Table XI. Men dominate in the purchase of imported goods, including tobacco which is usually sold by women. Although women also sell palm produce they deal in much smaller quantities than the men, the average amount realised per seller of palm kernels, palm oil and coconuts being 6/2d., 2/3d., 2/4d. for men and 1/6d., 2/7d., 1/5d., for women.

Table XI

FREQUENCY AND VALUE OF TRANSACTIONS BY UMUNAKANU
MARKETERS, AUGUST 1963
(COMMODITIES ACCOUNTING FOR 5% OR MORE OF TOTAL TRANSACTIONS)

Commodities	Percentage Frequency of Transactions				Average Value of Transactions			
	SALES		PURCHASES		SALES		PURCHASES	
	men	women	men	women	men	women	men	women
Major Staples								
yams	—	—	6	1	—	—	3/-	6d
gari	—	—	11	18	—	—	7d	5d
Palm Produce								
palm oil	24	16	—	—	2/3d	2/7d	—	—
palm kernels	38	25	7	—	26/5d	1/6d	29/7d	—
palm wine	—	—	12	—	—	—	5d	—
Vegetables								
vegetables	1	53	—	—	7/-	5d	—	—
Meat Fish & Spices								
stockfish	—	—	17	2	—	—	1/9d	1/2d
fish	—	—	5	6	—	—	1/2d	8d
condiments	—	—	3	21	—	—	7d	9d
salt	—	—	—	6	—	—	—	2d
Other								
tobacco	—	—	18	2	—	—	4d	3d

Other commodities show contrasting patterns too. Men buy more yams but less cassava, more meat and confectionery but less fruits, vegetables and sauce condiments than do women. The weekly market-visit cycle of the Umunakanu people may be briefly described.

Day 1. *Eke Ukwu* is the day of the traditional Eke Umunakanu market. More Umunakanu marketers on this day visit the market than visit any other (46% of the day's sample), with the daily sector of the Afor Mgba ranking second (30%). Purchases in both markets are confined to food crops and sauce ingredients, with some livestock, particularly poultry, in Eke Umunakanu. For higher order goods—imported durable consumer goods—the Eke Ikpa market, some 11 miles away in Etiti county, is the chief rural source. Both Eke Ego and Eke Mbeke are visited mainly by Umunakanu traders who deal in palm produce.

Day 2. *Orie Ukwu* is formally Orie Umunakanu day. But the greatest pull of marketers is the Orie Agu market, attendance at which reaches a secondary peak on this day. Afor Mgba comes next, followed by Orie Ehime, Orie Umunakanu's stronger rival in the neighbouring Umuezeala village group. A few persons visit other intergroup markets in the neighbourhood, in our sample the Orie Umuzu market and the Orie Ugiri market, mainly for foodstuffs.

Day 3. *Afor Ukwu* is Afor Ezuru market day. This great entrepôt is the most frequented market by Umunakanu consumers. Afor Ezuru market does not appear on the table. The day in the survey period happened to fall on a Sunday, a day on which, thanks to missionary influence, very few people in this area visit markets.

Day 4. *Nkwo Ukwu* The dominant market is the Nkwo Umuezeala, two miles away from Umunakanu, in the neighbouring village group. In our sample it accounted for 60% of all market visits on this day. The only other important market attended is the Afor Mgba, most of whose visitors had previously been to the Umuezeala market. In contrast to both Orie Agu and Afor Mgba markets, the Nkwo Umuezeala market is still strictly a periodic market held only on its traditional market day. As an intergroup market it is much larger than the Afor Mgba market and offers a wider range of commodities, both imported and locally produced.

Day 5. *Eke Nta* No important market is held within 10 miles of Umunakanu. There are fewer marketers on this day than on any other in the week (17.4% of the sample), most of whom visit the daily sectors of the Afor Mgba (6% of the visits for the day), the Orie Agu and the Eke Umunakanu. It may be noticed that although the nearby Eke Umuezeala market is held on this day, very few Umunakanu marketers visit it.

Day 6. *Orie Nta* is Orie Agu day. About 51% of marketers in the sample visited it. Afor Mgba came next with 31%, but purchases at Afor Mgba were confined to foodstuffs. The great Orie Amaraka market is held on this day and also draws Umunakanu marketers, particularly for imported goods. The two marketers in the sample who visited it bought bicycles and bicycle-parts in addition to palm kernels, yams and tobacco.

Day 7. *Afor Nta* is Afor Mgba day. Virtually no other market is visited by Umunakanu marketers on this day, a feature emphasising the dominance of the Afor Mgba in the village group's marketing. The number of market visits made to it on this day accounted for 36% of all the market visits by persons in the sample.

Day 8. *Nkwo Nta* There is no important market held in the neighbourhood. The Nkwo Umunakanu market is becoming insignificant with the growth of Afor Mgba's daily sector. Two inter-group markets in the neighbouring village groups, the Nkwo Umueleke and the Nkwo Onumiri, are the principal markets visited, but a few marketers visit more distant rural markets.

2. UGWUEKE NA EZEUKWU

Ugwueke na Ezeukwu is strictly a federation of two village groups (pop. 7,762 in 1953) and Ezeukwu (pop. 1,645). The former is made up of three villages: Ndielu, Amaokai and Amaba. The latter, though divided on the dual principle into Amaukwu and Amanta, is a closely knit unit and regards itself as a single village. The territories of the federation sprawl over 30 square miles, from the foothills of the Okigwi-Arochuku ridge northwards into the low-lying plains of the Eze Aku basin. The three Ugwueke villages are located linearly at intervals of 1 and 1½ miles on the western bank of the Eze Aku river. Ezeukwu lies on the western bank of its principal tributary, the Ogbukwu, some four miles to the west of Ugwueke. The adherence to water-courses is rather unusual for Iboland where settlements tend to avoid them.[1] Otherwise the settlement pattern is normal for the region. Each village is a compact nucleation of compound units. The settlement units of neighbouring village groups are four to six miles away from the nearest Ugwueke na Ezeukwu villages, and the federation is clearly marked out from them by a wide expanse of fringing farmland, orchard bush and forest. The federation is closely related to Alayi, Item, Ozuitem and Ozuabam village groups, of which Alayi is the closest both sociologically and geographically. Socially Ugwueke na Ezeukwu is a much more self-contained community than

Umunakanu. In contrast to the Umunakanu pattern, most of the marriages are within the federation. The few matrimonial links outside are chiefly with the related village groups of Alayi and Item, the other neighbouring but unrelated village groups—Akeze, Obilago, Acha and Isu—being very poorly represented. Politically, the federation is oriented to Ozuitem, the headquarters of the Elu Elu county and to Umuahia-Ibeku, the Bende Divisional and Umuahia Provincial headquarters.

Again in sharp contrast to Umunakanu, Ugwueke na Ezeukwu is isolated from the main lines of traffic in Iboland. The sole motor road connection is the road from Alayi to Akeze linking the Ahaba-Ohafia road to the Okigwi-Afikpo road. Yet the two main bridges on this short stretch of road, the Eze Aku bridge and the Ogbukwu bridge, located on either side of the federation, are chronically in disrepair. They cannot, in any case, bear heavy vehicles. Hence although the route shortens considerably the journey from the country east and south of the Imo to the Aboine basin, very little through traffic uses it. Owing to the importance of the federation as a food surplus area, lorries from the urban centres usually come in on the principal market days at Nkwo Ndielu. On these days the charges range from 2/- to 2/6d. by lorry to Umuahia-Ibeku, 27 miles away, a rate more than half as much again as that of Umunakanu. On other days the Ugwueke na Ezeukwu traveller has the choice of trekking to the trunk road at Alayi (5 - 9 miles) or to a railway station, unless he is lucky to catch the occasional chartered or transit lorry. The railway line passes two miles to the west of Ezeukwu and six miles to the west of Ugwueke, but the only connection with the station at Ozara is a bush track. Bush tracks are also the shortest links with most of the surrounding village groups.

A much higher proportion of the population is engaged in agriculture than at Umunakanu, and the range of occupations is smaller. There are few traders. Ugwueke na Ezeukwu has plenty of land; the amount of forest still remaining shows how little the pressure on land is. Cultivated land comes in three main types, giving rise to three marked patterns of land use. In the south the hill and valley country at the foot of the Okigwi-Arochuku ridge gives rise to soil catenas ranging from coarse sand on top of the hill to heavy loam at the valley bottom. Yellow yams are grown on the higher, coarser and better drained slopes; white yams on the loams of the intermediate slopes and gently rolling country; and water yams on the heavy soils of the valley bottom. The usual intercrops are planted. In the middle is a wide expanse of lateritic-capped plateau with a covering of coarse grass and shrubs. Formerly largely unexploited, it has, since the war, become important for the cultivation of cassava, making Ugwueke one of the chief sources of cassava and *gari* for Bende, Umuahia-Ibeku and environs. The basin of the Eze Aku river widens northwards to include over a quarter of the cultivated land of Amaba village. The environment is similar to that of the Aboine Basin. The traditional crop is the white yam, and the Amaba villagers are justifiably proud of their large, sugary and spongy *Avuvu* yams which fetch as high a price in the towns as the best Abakaliki yams. Following the success of rice cultivation in Abakaliki and Afikpo, Amaba people have in the last ten years paid increasing attention to the new crop, which they grow on the flood plain of the Eze Aku river.

Tree crops are important everywhere in Ugwueke na Ezeukwu. The most important are oranges and coconuts. The multi-purpose raffia palm is cultivated in groves on the river valley. There is a modern oil palm plantation owned by an enterprising native court clerk. But the area lies outside the main oil palm country and earnings from this source contribute only a small proportion of the people's income. A few specialist farmers grow cocoa and pineapples. Most peasants possess a goat or two and some poultry.

The picture is that of a community rich in resources, but the people are by no means rich in monetary terms. Owing to the relative isolation of the area these resources are very much under-exploited and the produce does not yield the best returns. Yet the people are now well aware of their opportunities and are beginning to make fuller use of them.

The distribution of exchange-place institutions conforms to the regional type. The traditional periodic market system persists near its ideal form and central-place development is weak. Ugwueke na Ezeukwu has six periodic markets, Akeze five, Item eight and Alayi three. Each village group has one or two markets but on a regional scale none of these is particularly outstanding. The most important rural central markets in the area are the Orie Ndu market at Ahaba, 9 miles to the south of Ugwueke and the semi-urban Eke Uzuakoli market, a further 6 miles away.

Like the Uzuakoli market the Orie Ndu market is of historical importance, being an old Aro trade market located at a strategic position on the Okigwi-Arochuku ridge. Today it has lost its traditional role and is important mainly as an entrepôt for the transfer of local produce from the surplus food producing areas in the Elu Elu and Owuwa counties into the southern part of Okigwi Division. The settlement of Ahaba is an important route centre and terminus for long distance traffic from the south, particularly from

Port Harcourt, Aba and Umuahia-Ibeku. There are a few permanent shops and service centres, but in spite of Ahaba's long history as a trade centre its central-place institutions are much less well developed than those of Orie Agu or Orie Amaraka in Mbano county. The Orie Ndu market is held every eight days. Attendance is particularly heavy every 24th day, a survival from the days of the Aro trade system when it was influenced by the Agbagwu Uzuakoli 24-day rhythm. The historical antecedents of the Uzuakoli market have already been discussed in some detail. A famous Aro trade fair, it was given a new lease of life by the establishment of European trading firms during the colonial consolidation phase. As in other old trading stations, the importance of the European-owned shops has declined. Uzuakoli, however, retains its semi-urban, central-place character. Situated at the node of communications from the dissected county of Elu Elu and Owuwa counties, it has become a major transportation centre for contact with the south. Until the massive road improvement programme of the late fifties, Uzuakoli was the effective limit of wet-season motor transport from the coast in this direction; the steep, muddy and slippery gradients of the ridge roads to the interior discouraging from further advance all but the most intrepid motorists. Regular lorry services from Umuahia-Ibeku, Aba and Oron usually terminated here. With the tarring of the main road from Umuahia-Ibeku through Uzuakoli to Arochuku, Uzuakoli has lost some of this advantage, but it has gained a new one. Regular taxi services now exist between the centre and Aba, Ikot Ekpene and Umuahia-Ibeku. There is a substantial agricultural population in the various institutions at Uzuakoli—a leprosy hospital, a secondary school, a teacher training college and several primary schools in the neighbourhood. These consumers and the transit travellers as well as the petty traders from the hinterland making purchases not valuable enough to warrant further travel, support daily trade at Uzuakoli. The market place has developed a small daily sector. Shopping districts are developing. These are, however, not opposite the market place but along street frontages in the residential areas. Another important daily activity at Uzuakoli is the timber and carpentry trade, which depends on timber from the wooded hinterland. It is carried on both in the market place and in various parts of the stranger settlements. In an area of relatively low population density, long distances between settlements and vigorous periodic markets, the rate at which Uzuakoli can develop as a daily market for the masses of consumers is rather limited, and the full potentialities of its location are not exploited.

The Eze Uzuakoli market is full every fourth day, in contrast to the eight-day periodicity usual in this area. This is because the present site of the market replaces the two traditional markets of Eke Ogboto and Eke Oba. It is thus in effect a pair of 8-day markets held on alternate Eke days. On normal Eke days the market draws traders and peasants from all over Bende Division. The great Agbagwu market is still held every 24th day, drawing traders from areas far beyond its normal service area. It now lasts for only one day instead of the former four, but the surrounding villages in the north and north-east still make an occasion of it.

In contrast to Umunakanu, the traditional markets of Ugwueke na Ezeukwu are all existing and vigorous, although their relative importance has altered. Nkwo Ndielu, the oldest and most important market in the federation, is reported to have been 'carried over' from Alayi when the ancestors left there in search of a new home. It was then located in the senior village of the new settlement. The site remains the social and ritual centre of Ugwueke na Ezeukwu community. In 1961 the market was moved to its present more spacious site only a few hundred yards away from the village centre on the Ozara tableland opposite the Ugwueke central school. Here there is space for a lorry park. A few permanent stalls have been built, but these are mainly for sellers of cooked foods who minister to the increasing number of visiting traders. The market remains a strictly 8-day affair. As a rural central market Nkwo Ndielu's function is mainly in the bulking of local produce. Yams are the traditional speciality, but the recent expansion of cassava cultivation on the Ozara orchard-bush county has made it one of the chief markets in Bende Division for cassava and *gari*.

An evening sauce market, serving village needs and attended only by Ndielu women, has developed on the old site of the Nkwo Ndielu.

By date of origin and social importance the next Ugwueke market is the Eke Amaba. But in the last ten years it has been overtaken in economic importance by the Afor Oputu market. The rise of the latter is closely associated with the development of rice cultivation in Amaba village, which was pioneered by people from Oputu and surrounding compounds. Small rice mills are located at the site of the market and a few shops are beginning to operate. Eke Oboo at Amaokai is the last of Ugwueke markets to be established. Located in the smallest Ugwueke village, it is also the smallest market, and the farthest from the main road. It is mainly a sauce market but it is also noted for palm wine, both locally produced and brought in from the neighbouring Item village of Okagwe.

Owing to differences in rival oral histories, it is not clear which is older, the Eke Amaba market in Ugwueke or the Eke Ezeukwu market. The Eke Ezeukwu market is held on the same day as the Eke Oboo Amaokai; it is even known by the same name of Eke Oboo. This reflects the traditional rivalry between Ugwueke and Emgukwu. The Eze Ezeukwu market is now a small local market. It is a periodic eight-day market but has a daily evening sector devoted almost entirely to sauce ingredients. The Afor Ukula market, which is a later arrival in Ezeukwu, has become much larger than the Eke Ezeukwu. It is the one visited by Ugwueke marketers, as well as by buyers from the nearby village groups, particularly Acha and Obilago.

Ugwueke na Ezeukwu conforms to the general pattern of balance of transactions in Iboland. The details reflect both its agricultural abundance and its relative isolation. The detailed analysis is based on two surveys. The first (Table XII) is an interview survey of a

Table XII

ECONOMIC TRANSACTIONS ON NKWO NDIELU MARKET DAY BY
MARKETERS FROM AN NDIELU COMPOUND (AUGUST 1962)

Commodities	Sales				Purchases			
	MEN		WOMEN		MEN		WOMEN	
	No.	Value	No.	Value	No.	Value	No.	Value
Tobacco	—	—	—	—	3	1/8d	—	—
Palm kernels	—	—	3	1/3d	—	—	—	—
Palm Wine	—	—	—	—	1	1/6d	—	—
Yams	1	10/-	—	—	—	—	—	—
Cassava	—	—	4	9/-	—	—	—	—
Gari	—	—	1	1/4d	—	—	—	—
Ugu vegetables	—	—	2	-/6d	—	—	—	—
Maize	—	—	—	—	—	—	1	-/6d
Melon	—	—	—	—	—	—	1	-/2d
Agbolo	—	—	—	—	—	—	3	-/6d
Cowich	—	—	—	—	—	—	1	-/1d
Okra	—	—	—	—	—	—	1	-/6d
Pepper	—	—	7	6/5d	—	—	—	—
Groundnuts	—	—	—	—	2	-/2½d	4	-/5½d
Kola-nuts	—	—	—	—	2	-/9d	—	—
Cooked foods	—	—	—	—	—	—	3	-/6½d
Coconut	—	—	—	—	—	—	1	-/3d
Stockfish	—	—	—	—	—	—	3	2/6d
Meat	—	—	—	—	2	3/-	1	1/-
Fish	—	—	—	—	—	—	9	5/2d
Crayfish	—	—	—	—	—	—	10	2/8d
Salt	—	—	—	—	—	—	4	-/9d
Bread	—	—	—	—	—	—	1	-/10d
Soap	—	—	—	—	1	2d	—	—

compound unit: Amaukabi, Emuoko in Ndielu, Ugwueke, on an Nkwo Ndielu market day, 3rd August 1962. This was at the beginning of the harvest season. The second (Table XIII) is a questionnaire survey of economic transactions of a sample of households between December 1963 and January 1964. It gives a more general picture of the pattern of sales and purchases in the federation. Table XIII may be compared with Umunakanu (Table XI), but with caution. Although the two are compiled in the same way they refer to different agricultural periods. In December and January the harvest season is well advanced. There are also a number of festivities associated with New Year celebrations and entertaining visiting sons from abroad, which involve more spending than usual.

Table XIII

FREQUENCY AND VALUE OF TRANSACTIONS BY UGWUEKE NA EZEUKWU
MARKETERS, DECEMBER 1963—JANUARY 1964

Commodities	Percentage Frequency of Transactions				Average Value of Transactions			
	SALES		PURCHASES		SALES		PURCHASES	
	men	women	men	women	men	women	men	women
Major Staples								
yams	34	1	1	—	11/4d	5/11d	9/11d	—
cassava	2	15	—	2	5/3d	3/9d	—	8d
cocoyams	1	6	1	—	1/3d	1/3d	6d	—
Palm Produce								
palm fruits	9	9	—	1	7/9d	12/6d	20/-	12/-
palm kernels	2	12	—	1	3/1	3/7	—	5/3d
palm wine	14	—	18	—	3/8d	—	2/8d	—
Vegetables	4	30	2	11	7d	8d	9d	3d
Meat, Fish & Spices								
dried fish	—	—	2	16	—	—	1/7d	1/-
crayfish	—	—	1	17	—	—	7d	3d
salt	—	—	2	8	—	—	4d	2d
Others								
kola-nuts	—	—	6	1	—	—	4d	6d
tobacco	—	—	15	1	—	—	5/11d	1/3d
mats	10	—	—	—	3/9d	—	—	—

Of the six heads of households interviewed, four visited the market but only one sold anything—yams (Table XII). The four spent 7/3d between them on the usual men's goods—tobacco, kola-nuts, meat, palm wine, soap and groundnuts. Of the twelve women in the compound, eleven went to the market that day and the twelfth was nursing a baby.[2] On the whole the women spent less than they realised, generally financing the purchases from their sales, and only four had deficits on the day's accounts. The value of transactions was very low, averaging 1/8d for sales and 1/3d for purchases.

Table XIII emphasises the very small scale of most marketing transactions already observed for Umunakanu. The details of the patterns of sales and purchases differ somewhat. The average value of produce sold per marketing trip by members of the survey sample was 8/5d for men and 3/11d for women. A wider range of produce is sold than at Umunakanu, another indication of an agriculturally richer envronment. The most important local produce sold by men was, in order of frequency, yams, palm wine, mats (made of raffia and palm fronds), palm fruits and rice. Yams and rice yielded most of the revenue, 45.4% and 17.3% respectively, and palm produce contributed 14.1%. For women the most important items sold were vegetables, cassava, palm kernels and palm fruits, in order of frequency of sales, but owing to the low value of vegetable sales per trip (8d.), palm produce was the most important source of revenue during the period.

The average value of purchases per trip was, as in the Amaukabi compound survey, rather lower than that of sales: 3/11d for men and 7d for women. The most frequently bought items were palm wine, tobacco, meat, kola-nuts and clothing for men. For women the order was dried fish, crayfish, vegetables and salt, differing from the Umunakanu pattern mainly in the relative infrequency of staple food purchases. Imported goods other than food items and clothing are bought usually at long intervals. Books and stationery, plates, lamps, knives, nails, padlocks and cosmetics together accounted for only 4.1% of the men's purchases and less than 1% of the women's. The normal marketing cycle of Ugwueke na Ezeukwu is as follows:

Day 1. *Eke Ukwu*   Eke Amaba is the dominant market for the federation's marketers. The Eke Igbere is an important rural central market in the county and attracts some marketers, particularly from Ndielu. The Eke Uzuakoli market is the chief venue for the sale of palm produce and cassava as well as the purchase of imported goods.

Day 2. *Orie Ukwu*   There is no local market held on this day. Most marketers, particularly from Ndielu and Ezeukwu, visit the Orie Ndu market.

Day 3. *Afor Ukwu*   The Afor Ukala market at Ezeukwu is the main attraction, but Amaokai marketers tend to favour the Afor

Amokwe market at Item, which is nearly the same distance from the village but much larger.

Day 4. *Akwo Ukwu* The Nkwo Adielu market is held and claims virtually all marketers on this day. On no other day is the market important.

Day 5. *Eke Nta* The two rival markets, the Eke Oboo Amaokai and the Eke Ezeukwu, attract marketers mainly from their own villages. Neither Amaba nor Ndielu people visit them much. Eke Alayi is the nearest central rural market in the neighbourhood. It is noted chiefly as a source of palm wine and livestock and as a market for Ugwueke yams. The Eke Abiriba market, nearly twenty miles away, is the chief source of commodities coming through the Cross River—contraband spirits and tobacco as well as stockfish, dried fish and crayfish. Some marketers visit the Uzuakoli market.

Day 6. *Orie Nta* is generally considered a day for farming, and very few people travel to markets. There is no large market held within ten miles of the federation.

Day 7. *Afor Nta* Most marketers visit the Afor Oputu market. The Afor Acha market, four miles from Ezeukwu, attracts a handful of visitors from that village.

Day 8. *Nkwo Nta* Three of the neighbouring village groups have large periodic markets on this day. Most Amaba marketers go to Akeze, Amaokayi and Ndielu to Okoko market in Item, and Ezeukwu to Isiagu. Nkwo Akeze is more important than the others as a source of imported goods.

Rural Market Visiting Patterns in Iboland

Several of the conclusions which may be drawn from an analysis of market visting patterns in the two communities studied apply more generally to Iboland. One common feature is the large number of markets visited by a rival community during the Ibo week. In the survey periods Umunakanu marketers visited 20 different markets and Ugwueke na Ezeakwu marketers 19. The average number of market visits per sample marketer was 4.2 for Umunakanu and 3.6 for Ugwueke na Ezeukwu. The results of a questionnaire survey of 56 rural communities indicate that these figures conform to a general pattern. The average number of markets visited by each marketer in the total sample population was 3.1. The average for various communities varied between two and five markets. There was a marked tendency for communities in the central Ibo uplands, where the periodic market system is most disrupted, to visit fewer markets, otherwise the variation does not show any consistent pattern. The actual number of markets visited by marketers from each community is usually between 10 and 25. The large number of market visits per person exaggerates the actual amount of time spent on marketing. Only the most important markets tend to be held for the greater part of the day, from about 10 a.m. to about 5 p.m. The smaller markets are usually held early in the morning (say 8 a.m. to 11 a.m.) or in the late afternnoon and evening (2 p.m. to 5 p.m.; 4 p.m. to 7 p.m.). The time spent by a peasant marketer in the market is usually less than three hours. Thus she can go to her farm before or after marketing. She can also visit more than one market on the same day. Indeed this is quite common when there is a local evening market or when an important outside market clashes with the local periodic market. The number of market visits varies considerably from day to day, depending on the importance of the various markets and their periodicity. There are contrasts also in the market visiting patterns of men and women. The discrimination is mostly a function of the difference in the marketing activities of the sexes, the choices thus reflecting the various opportunities offered by the markets. The bigger markets offer a wide range of opportunities and the local markets are very convenient to everyone, so that for these two groups the discrimination is not very marked. But the issue becomes critical with increasing distance from the community, the men concentrating on the markets important for imported goods and the women on the food markets.

   The contrasts in the market visiting patterns at Umunakanu and Ugwueke na Ezeukwu point to some of the trends in market development in Iboland. In Umunakanu the most frequently visited market, the local Afor Mgba, accounted for 44% of all visits recorded during the survey period. The next two markets in rank, Orie Agu (13%) and Nkwo Umuezeala (11%), are outside the village group. The second largest Umunakanu market, the Eke Umunakanu, comes next (10%). The four markets together accounted for 77% of the market attendances recorded during the survey period. With Afor Ezuru market, which normally comes fifth in the list, they are the principal markets for Umunakanu. Of the 16 remaining markets, only five are visited fairly frequently (5%), two of these in the village group and the other three within two miles of it.

   The most remarkable feature illuminated by the examination of the Umunakanu marketing sequence is the degree to which the neat periodicity of rural markets has been dislocated in this area. Only 40% of the market attendances at the Afor Mgba market during the period fell on the traditional Afor Mgba market day. The other 64% is spread rather evenly over the remaining days of the cycle. Afor Mgba remains the most frequented market on two of these days and comes second on the others. It is evident that the development of its daily sector is at the expense of the other rural markets to which it is offering such strong competition. The daily sector at Eke Umunakanu is not as well developed as that of Afor Mgba. On the other hand central-place development here is much more advanced, business in the shops and service centres which face or adjoin the market being the principal activity on non-traditional market days.

In view of our remarks about the development of daily marketing at Orie Agu, its relationship to Umunakanu marketing habits calls for some comment. Most Umunakanu visits to Orie Agu fall on the traditional Orie Agu day (57% of the sample) and on the secondary Orie day (38%). This feature points to the fact, implicit in the Afor Mgba and Eke Umunakanu patterns, that when periodic markets develop daily sectors these sectors do not perform the same functions as the markets do on the traditional days. They are more restricted in scope, serving a smaller hinterland and usually offering a narrower range and smaller aggregate of goods and services. In the case of Orie Agu, where the daily sector is very strongly developed, transactions differ more in volume than in kind. The shops and service centres attached to the market are involved in the traditional market rhythm to the extent that when important periodic markets are being held in the hinterland, business tends to be very slack at the centres. Some of the shopkeepers may leave their shops to the care of assistants and take goods to the markets. In the more rural Afor Mgba market, on the other hand, the pattern of transactions on the traditional market day is different from that on other days. The main activities of non-traditional market days being local trade in foodstuffs and sauce ingredients.

In contrast to Umunakanu, the greater self-sufficiency and relative isolation of Ugwueke na Ezeukwu are reflected in the fact that a higher proportion of the marketing visits take place within the federation, 73% as compared with 56% for Umunakanu. Secondly, there is a greater balance between the principal markets visited. The first-ranking Nkwo Ndielu market accounted for only 27.2 of all market visits during the survey period, while the least important Ugwueke na Ezeukwu markets each accounted for 5.2%. The two markets most frequently visited outside the federation, the Orie Ndu and the Nkwo Akeze, were ranked fifth and sixth, each recording only 7.4% of the visits. In this area the traditional periodicity of the markets is still very vigorous. Ugwueke na Ezeukwu people visit outside the federation only on the traditional days, the only exception

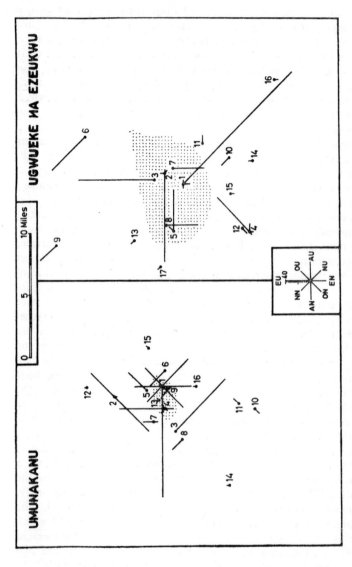

Fig. 19   Distances travelled to market at Umunakanu and Ugwueke na Ezeukwu

during the survey period being the Orie Ndu market which was visited on ordinary days by marketers en route to or from other markets. The market visiting patterns for the various villages differ to some extent, particularly on the days when no markets are held in the federation, when each village tends to visit the outside markets nearer it. All the Ugwueke na Ezeukwu markets are dominant on their own market days and marketing is largely confined to these days. The occasional transactions on other days are mainly in sauce ingredients. There are small evening markets for this purpose on the sites of the Nkwo Ndielu and the Afor Oputu markets as well as on the village squares of Ezeukwu and Ameze in Ndielu.

The analysis has shown that Umunakanu marketers travel rather shorter distances to markets than do Ugwueke na Ezeukwu marketers (Fig. 19), although in both cases most of the visits are to markets within five miles of the village group. Examination of the data from the questionnaire survey of the 56 communities throws further light on the question of distances travelled to markets, revealing certain uniformities as well as patterns of variation. Of the crude total of all market-visiting journeys recorded in the survey,

Table XIV

DISTANCES TRAVELLED TO MARKETS: TERMINATION OF MEDIAN
AND 90TH CENTILE JOURNEYS, 1963

	DISTANCE IN MILES	Under 5	5-9.9	10-14.9	15-19.9	Totals	Cumula-tive Totals
	Under 5	7.1	—	—	—	7.1	7.1
	5-9.9	26.8	1.8	—	—	28.6	35.7
90th	10-14.9	8.9	10.7	—	—	19.6	55.3
Centile	15-19.9	5.3	1.8	1.8	1.8	10.7	66.0
Journey	20-29.9	8.9	5.3	1.8	—	16.0	82.0
	30-39.9	3.6	1.8	—	—	5.4	87.4
	40-49.9	3.6	3.6	3.6	—	10.8	98.2
	50 *and over*	—	1.8	—	—	1.8	100
	Totals	64.2	26.8	7.2	1.8	100	
	Cumulative Total	64.2	91.0	98.2	100		

(*Source:* Sample Survey of Village Communities, 1963.)

50% ended within 3 miles of the village-group of origin, 90% within 15 miles and 95% within 24 miles. The pattern varied considerably between communities, but the importance of local markets was emphasised by the fact that in 90% of the communities the proportion of visits ending within 5 miles was 50% or more. In no community did the median distance exceed 20 miles. The outer limit of frequent marketing visits, as defined empirically by the 90th centile journey, was more variable. The spread was indicated by the first quartile, median, third quartile and 90th centile values of 7, 14, 25, and 42 miles respectively (Table XIV). An attempt has been made to relate the limits of the 90th centile journeys in the various communities to three environmental variables: population density; distance to the nearest urban centre; and density of the road network (Table XV). The most important of these appears to be the population density; the communities in areas of higher population density consistently travel shorter distances. Thus for 70% of the communities in areas of very high population density (800 or more

Table XV

Factors Associated with Distances Travelled to Markets: Cumulative Percentage of Communities in which the 90th Centile Journey ended within Specific Distances

Factors	5 miles	10 miles	15 miles	20 miles	30 miles	40 miles	50 miles	501 miles
Population Density								
800 and over	10	70	80	90	100	—	—	—
400—799	16	58	74	84	89	94	94	100
under 400	0	7	33	44	70	77	100	—
Distance in miles to nearest Urban Centre								
Under 10	10	50	60	70	80	80	100	—
10—19.9	0	32	68	86	100	—	—	—
20—29.9	9	37	53	57	74	84	100	—
30 and over	0	0	0	0	40	60	80	100
Density of Motor Road network mls/100m²								
600 and over	10	70	80	80	100	—	—	—
400—599	8	34	65	83	96	96	100	—
under 400	4	22	26	36	59	73	95	100

(*Source:* Sample Survey of Village Communities, 1963.)

persons per square mile in 1953), the 90th centile journey terminated within 5 miles as contrasted with 58% for areas of medium density (400-799) and only 7% for areas of low density (under 400). At 30 miles the proportions were 100%, 89% and 70% respectively. The relationship to the density of the road network showed a similar but less consistent pattern. The correlation with distances to urban centres was far less simple. Although it was clear that communities far from urban centres (more than 30 miles) tended to travel longer distances, the communities nearer the urban centres still visited distant rural markets, other things being equal.

The information of market visiting patterns for all the communities is summarised in Table XVI. In order to examine the pattern over Iboland more systematically, an attempt has been made to simplify and randomise the data. In general the number of market visits shrank very rapidly with distance from the community. The regression line of best fit appeared to be a log-log curve such that

$$p = a + b \log (\log x)$$

where p is the proportion of market visits; a is a constant; and x is distance. Restricting the analysis to visits within 100 miles, we obtained for each community a *mean distance travelled to market*, calculated by the formula:

$$\log \log x = \frac{\leqq p_j \log \log x_j}{100}$$

where j specified the market visited, p_j the proportion visiting it and x_j its distance. The values for the various communities are given in Table XVI. The statistical surface for mean distances travelled to market (Fig. 20) was derived by interpolation.

The unweighted average of mean distances for the communities recorded was 6.5 miles. The regional pattern suggested by our examination of 90th centile journeys was again apparent. Mean distances were lowest in the cental Ibo uplands and on the crest of the Nsukka-Udi plateau where the values were generally under 4 miles, falling to under 2 miles in the Nnewi District, Orlu Division, Mbano and Mbaise counties and the area near Enugu. The higher values were in the peripheries, in the areas of low population density, thin road network and greatest distance from urban centres, culminating in values of over 16 miles in the upper Anambra valley.

Table XVI

RURAL MARKETING PATTERNS:
DISTANCES TRAVELLED TO MARKETS FROM SAMPLE VILLAGE GROUPS

Village Groups	Cumulative Percentages of visits within specified distances (in miles):*								Mean Distance Travelled	Av. No. of markets visited
	5	10	15	20	30	40	50	750		
1. Abala	31	86	94	97	97	100	—	—	6.2	3.6
2. Abia Ohafia	46	71	71	71	82	89	96	100	12.3	2.5
3. Afikpo	56	84	87	94	97	97	100	—	7.0	3.2
4. Agulu	80	88	88	93	100	—	—	—	3.2	2.9
5. Akeze	72	78	83	90	90	90	95	100	8.5	3.0
6. Akoli	66	81	100	—	—	—	—	—	3.4	2.9
7. Akpo	100	—	—	—	—	—	—	—	0.2	1.3
8. Alayi	57	93	98	98	100	—	—	—	3.6	3.9
9. Amakama	61	91	91	93	98	100	—	—	4.2	3.7
10. Amazu	41	59	89	89	100	—	—	—	6.0	2.7
11. Anam	5	50	100	—	—	—	—	—	9.0	2.0
12. Ariam Usaka	52	88	88	95	95	100	—	—	5.3	4.2
13. Eberi	43	84	92	92	95	97	100	—	6.1	3.7
14. Edda	33	65	70	72	85	91	100	—	12.6	4.7
15. Eha Amufu	23	81	97	100	—	—	—	—	6.7	3.1
16. Ekenobizi	68	100	—	—	—	—	—	—	2.2	3.1
17. Ibere	64	84	96	100	—	—	—	—	3.6	2.5
18. Idembia	38	42	81	81	81	85	96	100	14.2	2.6
19. Ifite	22	48	52	52	98	99	99	100	17.4	6.5
20. Ihie	95	100	—	—	—	—	—	—	0.5	2.1
21. Mbidi	100	—	—	—	—	—	—	—	0.2	1.4
22. Nbawsi	46	95	97	97	100	—	—	—	4.2	3.7
23. Ndioji Abam	44	79	81	81	93	93	93	100	10.1	4.3
24. Ndiwo Itu	41	81	81	97	100	—	—	—	6.2	3.2
25. Ngbo	24	43	86	100	—	—	—	—	12.2	2.1
26. Nike	89	100	—	—	—	—	—	—	0.9	2.8
27. Nkalagu	70	70	70	70	100	—	—	—	6.8	1.6
28. Nkporo	59	72	87	97	100	—	—	—	6.0	4.0
29. Nri	58	100	—	—	—	—	—	—	2.9	3.0
30. Obegu	52	83	100	—	—	—	—	—	4.1	4.2
31. Obibi	89	100	—	—	—	—	—	—	0.9	2.6
32. Obigbo	43	67	81	81	91	91	91	100	12.2	2.9
33. Obinagu	62	97	100	—	—	—	—	—	2.8	2.4
34. Ogidi	73	100	—	—	—	—	—	—	1.9	2.9
35. Oguta	44	74	74	74	83	87	100	—	11.3	2.3
36. Ogwe	21	21	50	75	79	88	100	—	17.3	3.0
37. Okagwe Ohafia	60	90	90	93	98	98	100	—	5.0	4.0
38. Okoko Hem	73	96	98	98	98	98	98	100	3.4	4.5
39. Okpala	55	100	—	—	—	—	—	—	3.1	2.2
40. Okporo enyi	34	74	100	—	—	—	—	—	5.9	3.2
41. Okposi	68	92	92	92	92	92	92	100	7.3	3.3
42. Omanelu	56	61	61	67	72	95	95	100	14.2	2.3
43. Omoku	55	70	70	85	85	85	90	100	9.4	1.9
44. Orba	40	87	93	93	93	93	93	100	3.9	3.8
45. Osu	100	—	—	—	—	—	—	—	0.2	2.0
46. Owo	54	100	—	—	—	—	—	—	3.1	4.6

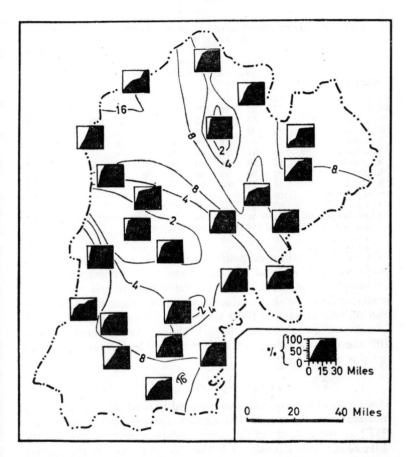

Fig. 20 *Distances travelled to market in selected areas of Iboland,* 1962.

Table XVI Continued

Village Groups	Commulative Percentages of visits within specified distances (in miles):*								Mean Distance Travelled	Av. No. of markets visited
	5	10	15	20	30	40	50	750		
47. Ozuitem	66	89	89	100	—	—	—	—	3.6	2.9
48. Ozuzu	27	59	95	100	—	—	—	—	7.4	4.6
49. Uburu	63	67	73	80	83	**93**	93	100	11.7	3.0
50. Umuaka	**90**	100	—	—	—	—	—	—	2.3	2.1
51. Umuda	70	85	87	**98**	100	—	—	—	3.8	4.2
52. Umuhu	42	84	84	84	**100**	—	—	—	2.8	4.2
53. Unwana	42	**90**	90	90	90	90	93	100	7.6	4.8
54. Umuapu	70	**90**	90	90	90	100	—	—	4.9	1.6
55. Umuduru	67	**91**	94	97	100	—	—	—	2.8	3.6
56. Umuobom	88	**100**	—	—	—	—	—	—	0.9	2.1

*The distance intervals in which the median and 90th centile journeys occur are given in italics and bold types respectively.

In order to test the areal pattern of variation, an attempt was made to eliminate the regional bias introduced by the uneven scatter of the sample communities. An equilateral triangular grid was placed at random over the statistical surface and the values at the 25 nodes read off (the average of these values was 6.0 miles, compared with 6.5 miles for the sample population). The new values were correlated with the relevant values for the three variables already mentioned and was of the form:

$$\log y = a + b_1 x_1 + b_2 \log x_2 + b_3 x_3 + b_4 x_4$$

where y was the mean distance travelled to market; a, an empirical constant; x_1, the population density (persons per square mile, 1953); x_2, the distance to the nearest urban centre; x_3, the density of the road network (miles per 100 sq. mls 1958); and x_4, the relative relief (feet per 15' i.e. approx. 16 ml. square).

The multiple correlation coefficient was 0.79; thus the equation satisfied statistically some 61% of the variance. The residuals of actual from predicted values, computed from the formula:

$$\frac{(y^1 - y^0)}{y^1}$$

are shown on Fig. 21. The predicted statistical surface was within 25% of the actual surface over 61% of the area. Nowhere did positive residuals exceed 50% nor negative residuals 125%. On the whole the tendency of the equation was to overestimate the distances travelled to market. The largest area of overstatement was the

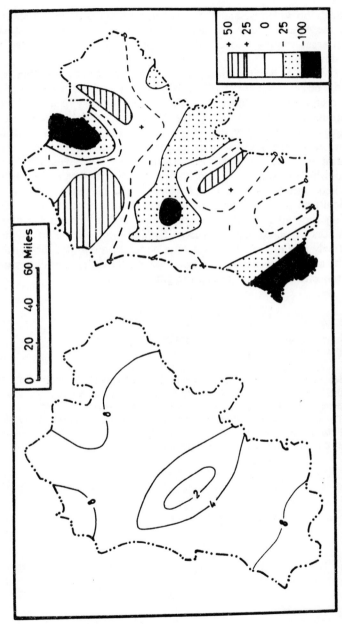

Fig. 21   Iboland: mean distances travelled to market.

central Ibo uplands, and the only large region of underestimation was the Adada-Upper Anambra area in the isolated north-west. In both areas the poor coverage of samples may have contributed to the deviation.

In view of the limitations of the data the derived equation can hardly be regarded as definitive. However, it lends strong support to the premise that distances travelled to market vary in a consistent fashion. At the local level, the friction of social distance—the degree of social affinity, cooperation or, on the other hand, hostility between village groups—may distort the pattern, but, with the continuing breakdown of traditional group attitudes, this is a diminishing factor. More significantly, the distribution and ranks of markets and the differences in price levels, particularly those of agricultural produce, affect the local choice of markets visited. Yet taking Iboland as a whole we may state that in general the mean distances of marketing visits from rural communities tend to vary inversely and exponentially with the population density, the density of the road network and, to a lesser extent, the difficulties of terrain. Distance to urban centres is a marginal factor.

NOTES

1. See R. K. Udo, 'Rural Settlements in Eastern Nigeria.' Unpublished Ph.D. thesis, London, 1963; and W. B. Morgan, 'Farming practice, settlement pattern and population density in south-eastern Nigeria', *G.J.*, 1957.
2. The market place is taboo to a nursing mother until a month after childbirth, when the child is taken ceremonially to the market. The custom has died out in many parts of Iboland but lingers on in places.

CHAPTER THIRTEEN

Case Studies: Urban Centres and Marketing Institutions

THE role of urban centres in the organisation of trade and the flow of goods has already been discussed. In the studies which follow the emphasis is on the evolution, location and morphology of urban exchange-places. Urban market places vary in size and level of activity. They are only part of the total complex of institutions which comprise the central business districts of urban centres. The studies demonstrate very clearly the general long-term trend towards a strengthening of the institutions in the central-place sub-system relative to market places; and the differing rates of development in the various urban centres underline some of the main factors and processes of change.

Umuahia-Ibeku

The rapidly growing urban settlement of Umuahia-Ibeku lies some 60 miles from the coast. It is situated on a small triangular tableland about 600 feet above sea level, at the tongue of a wedge of relatively flat country which pushes into the dissected south-east hill and valley region from the coastal plain sands. North of the town the head-waters of the Imo and Cross Rivers are within 100 yards of each other and a low watershed (in places less than 350 feet above sea level) carries the railway line from Port Harcourt northwards along the zig-zag course. Spurs projecting from the Umuahia-Ibeku tableland into the valleys provide routeways into the dissected country and across the Imo river into the central Ibo uplands. Southwards two important roads lead to the coast, one through Ikot Ekpene to Opobo, Eket and Oron, the other through Aba to Port Harcourt. The town is thus one of the major transportation nodes of Eastern Nigeria.

Umuahia-Ibeku is one of Nigeria's new towns. Founded when the railway crossed this marginal farmland of the Ibeku people in 1917, it attracted trading firms and soon became more important than the old Umuahia station, established two years earlier in Olokoro country some three miles to the south, and outstripped the old trade centre of Uzuakoli. After the Second World War it took over from Bende as the administrative headquarters of Bende Division and also became the provincial headquarters of a re-constituted Owerri Province and, in 1959, of the new Umuahia Province (Aba and Bende Divisions). With a concentration of schools, training institutions, hospitals and other public utilities, it is, like the other principal towns, a social and cultural centre. The establishment of a number of industries in the town during the last five years—a brewery, a ceramics industry, and a paints factory—as well as several Government agricultural projects in the neighbour-hood, continue to enhance its importance.

The present-day commerce of Umuahia-Ibeku is dominated by its main market, a general-purpose market at which a wide range of imported goods and local produce may be obtained. The export trade takes place largely outside the market place, in the depots and buying stations of the produce-buying agents and their sub-agents. Shopping facilities are underdeveloped. The expatriate firms used to sell general merchandise on their premises, but as these shops faced the railway sidings and there was no through motor road along their frontages, they were, to the bulk of the marketers, less accessible than the main market and were unable to compete effectively with traders there for the retail trade. They depended rather on the custom of the petty traders who bought goods for retail in the market, and on the few higher-income consumers (Europeans and senior civil servants). With the general country-wide decline of the share of expatriate firms in the retail trade, and the development of new shops facing the market and on some of the principal streets in the town, the expatriate firms have relinquished this side of their business. The old shops are now managed by their commission agents or credit customers.

The present picture (Fig. 22) is largely a post-war development. Indigenous produce buyers have occupied the area between the market and the old mercantile firms, extended the produce-buying area southwards, and created new ones along Onitsha road and Aba road. The market itself has extended northwards, taking in the open space formerly lying between it and the main residential area, and covering in all 18.7 acres. Both the administrative and residential areas have expanded and new areas have been developed to take the overflow as well as the industries and social services.

The railway runs more or less parallel to the western edge of the tableland, which is terminated by a series of scarps and gullies

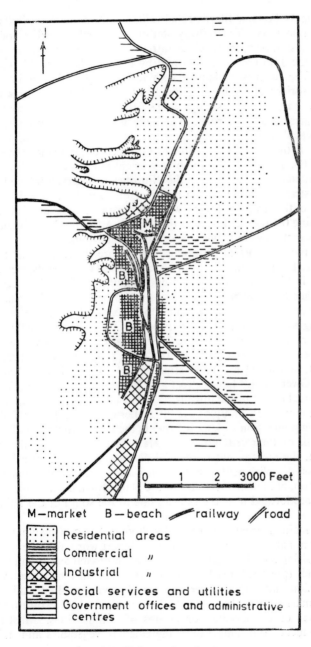

Fig. 22   Umuahia-Ibeku: urban land use.

marking the heads of the dissected valleys of the numerous tributaries of the Imo river. The railway station was sited in the line of the principal spur from the tabeland into the Imo valley, an old routeway across the Imo river and followed by the Onitsha-Umuahia motor road. The town was planned with the railway station as its hub. The factories and produce-buying depots of the European firms were established on railway sidings west of the railway line and south of the Onitsha-Umuahia road. This area is still popularly known as the 'Beach', a name reminiscent of the Oil Rivers beach trade. Behind it the land swells to an oval-shaped dome higher than the rest of the area. Here on the breeze-swept land to the windward of the settlement were located the 'European Reservation' and the administrative offices; on the north of the Onitsha-Umuahia road, opposite the trading firms, was the market; and beyond this, straddling the railway line, was the 'Native Allocation'. Between the various sectors were playing fields and open grounds.

The most important shopping districts are those adjacent to or opposite the market. The shops are retail establishments, but deal mainly in higher-order imported and manufactured goods — cement and other building materials, radios and other electrical goods and appliances, light machinery, and 'fancy goods' (high value textiles, clothing and jewelry). The other shops in the town are mostly small local or neighbourhood stores selling groceries. They are concentrated in the older parts of the main residential area, near the market, and along five main streets—Old Uzuakoli road, Kaduna street, Owerri road, Lagos street and Umuwaya road. Owing to the small areal extent of the town there is not much scope for expansion of neighbourhood shopping facilities. Besides, more than half of the working population seek their living in the market and naturally buy the bulk of their requirements there. Certain streets in the New Layout, the most recent residential district, have been set aside for business establishments, but so far only one establishment, a bookshop, has taken advantage of the plan. The industrial establishments are located near the railway line to the south of the built-up area.

The main market, is generally known as the Ogwumabiri, a common name derived from the Kalabari word for market and emphasising the historical analogy between coastal and urban trade. The old (pre-1947) market lay to the south of the railway yard. Expansion into the upper market (known as Ime Ahia, i.e. inner market) was by a gradual process of selective transference of sellers of commodities or groups of commodities. Most food items—meat, fish and sauce ingredients, vegetables and minor agricultural produce—are in the new section. Most of the sellers of cooked foods have also moved here, as have minor crafts-men—barbers, tinkers, cobblers and carpenters. On the other hand, bicycle repairers and sellers of the high value staples—yams, *gari* and rice—remain in the core. Low value staples—cocoyams and cassava—are in the upper market. Textiles and 'articles' are duplicated in both sections, but the bigger traders remain in the core while the smaller traders, whose business is almost entirely last-stage retail in the smallest units — cloth by the yard and sugar by the cube—operate in the upper market.

Thus there are two poles of market development: the movement of higher order activities into shops or central-place types of institutions; and the relegation of lower order activities into a subsidiary section of the market. The pattern is even more obvious in the metropolitan centres where the lower order functions have been siphoned off into subsidiary neighbourhood or special-purpose markets.

With every other working man in Umuahia-Ibeku a market trader, the principal role of the market is as a central market for the region. As such it has taken over the role of several formerly important markets in the area, and there is now no large rural market within ten miles of it. Before 1916 the most important rural market in the area was the Eke Ndume market, 4 miles away, a market associated with the Arochuku trade and much more important than the Nkwo Ndoro market, 7 miles farther to the south-east. Today the Eke Ndume is reduced to the status of a rural local market. Its former importance is today reflected only in the Ibeku village-group rituals and market ceremonies which still take place on the site, and in the traditional trade in livestock—notably goats—which has survived. The Afor Ibeji market in the neighbouring Olokoro village group and the Nkwo market in Ohuhu have suffered a similar decline while the rural markets nearer the town either exist as evening markets for sauce ingredients or have completely disappeared.

The rural communities around Umuahia-Ibeku do not merely use the urban market as a source of imported goods or as a market for their produce. Some of them operate as urban market traders, commuting every day from the village. Many of these are part-time farmers, so that their number in the market fluctuates with the season. During the planting or harvesting season many market stalls are empty, to be occupied by their owners when the season is over.

The growth of Umuahia-Ibeku as a commercial centre is inhibited by the proximity of Aba. With the improvement of the communication network, there is an increasing tendency for traders from the rural areas to by-pass the market for the larger and cheaper markets. The number of lorries from Aba to rural centres in the Umuahia-Ibeku hinterland is evidence of this trend. On the other hand the town is now the centre of fast taxi and bus services linking it with the hinterland within a radius of 12 miles, the termini being Orie Agu on the Onitsha road, Uzuakoli on the Arochuku road and Ndoro on the Ikot Ekpene road. There are also express taxi services to Ikot Ekpene and Aba. This development means that villagers can bring their produce into Umuahia-Ibeku easily and quickly and buy their requirements there directly. To that extent the bulking functions and last-stage retail functions of Umuahia-Ibeku are being enhanced. The development of an industrial population in Umuahia-Ibeku and the growth of professional classes and other tertiary activities would mean more retail trade in the market, but would also accelerate the pace at which shopping districts develop away from the main market.

Onitsha: A Metropolitan Centre (Fig. 23)

Onitsha, with a population of 76,921 in 1953, owes its rise as a commercial centre principally to its location on the river Niger, 172 miles inland from the Burutu estuary. Here the lower Niger, emerging from the alluvial flats of the Anambra area, is confined to a narrow course cut through the Bende-Ameki sandstones with banks rising to heights of 500 to 800 feet, or some 300 to 600 feet above the river in flood.[1] Below Onitsha the Niger enters the alluvial marshes of its delta. Above it the river valley widens again into the alluvial flats on the Anambra tributary. The area offers the best access on firm ground from the lower Niger valley to the eastern mainland. The concentration of the population of the eastern mainland in a belt running eastwards from the Onitsha area was a further locational advantage. A bridge has now been built here, the first practicable point on the Niger and will certainly further enhance the town's importance as a trading centre.

From the navigational point of view the site of Onitsha is also well favoured. It is the limit of all-year navigation for river steamers and barges. The Niger and Benue river system is seasonal, and during the low water season, from November to June, shipping reaches Baro and Makurdi only infrequently. From May to April it generally stops at Onitsha, very rarely going as far north as Idah. Onitsha is a half-way house between the seasonal ports and the coast, as well as the chief inland port during low water. For sail and paddle canoes,

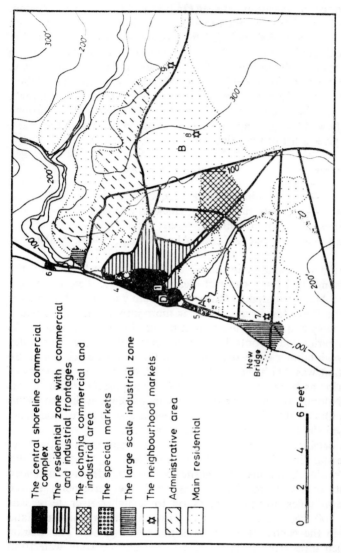

The central shoreline commercial complex

The residential zone with commercial and industrial frontages

The ochanja commercial and industrial area

The special markets

The large scale industrial zone

The neighbourhood markets

Administrative area

Main residential

Fig. 23 Onitsha: urban land use.

of course, the river system is open all the year round and there is
constant communication between Onitsha and the Northern Region.

Onitsha's origins are not Ibo. The town is reputed to have been
founded between 1600 and 1630 by a Benin war leader who, during
the great Benin wars, led his men eastwards from the crumbling
outposts of the Benin Empire, founding new settlements on the way,
among them Obio, Iseleuku, Aniocha Otu, and Onicha Ugbo.[2]
This was part of a general movement of peoples from Iboland, Igala
and Benin into the commercially strategic Niger valley through
which flowed the growing trade with European traders on the coast.
Dike[3] gives a list of the principal towns so founded:

Founders		*Towns Founded*
Ibo	—	Atani, Ogwu, Osuche, Umunakwo
Igala	—	Ossomari, Okoh, Odekpe, Umuolu
Benin	—	Aboh, Onitsha, Assay, Uchi, Onya
Mixed	—	Utoke, Adawai, Akrai, Okpai, Ndoni, Asaba

Onitsha's ascendancy in the Niger valley did not begin until the
establishment of European factories there in 1857. Before then the
town of Aboh, situated 50 miles to the south and 147 miles up river
from the Forcados estuary, was far more important. Aboh had a
strong navy and with its location at the head of the principal creeks
and estuaries could control the trade up and down the river valley
while maintaining trade relations with the various creek ports. So
important was Aboh that its king was known by the Europeans of
the period as King of the Ibos. The other important trading towns
were Ndoni, Ossomari, Atani, and Umunankwo, while the towns
of the Orashi distributary, notably Oguta and Omoku, competed
with Onitsha for the eastern mainland market.

The original Onitsha settlement was at Ndende, on a low river
terrace standing 30 feet above river-flood level or 100 to 115 feet
above sea level. But this exposed site could not be effectively defended
against attack from rival towns, and the settlement moved
some two miles north-eastwards on to a higher river terrace at
about 100 feet, creating what is now known as Onitsha Inland
Town in the centre of which was the *Obi's* palace. The market
was then transferred from Ndende to the Otu Okwodu waterfront
opposite the new settlement, where it remained with occasional
interruptions until 1913.

When in 1857 the ships *Dayspring* and *George* landed at Onitsha,
bringing European traders and Christian missionaries, they found

a flourishing market around which they set up their stations. According to Rev. Adjai Crowther:

> The shore at Onitsha offered a curious sight; the river was full of native canoes, and on the shore was a great crowd, motley and busy, coming, going, talking and gesticulating, and sometimes appearing greatly excited . . . It was market day and the canoes had brought men belonging to the neighbouring tribes to Onitsha to exchange their products for European wares which the black traders sell either on their own account or on that of the factors they represent . . . Standing or sitting, the women were exhibiting their wares; at one place calicoes, at another beads, here jugs or bottles of gin or rum, and everywhere large calabashes of salt. The men walked about among the groups, making exchanges with palm oil or ivory for the merchandise they wanted; or soldiers made their purchases with cowries . . . The traveller is everywhere struck with the diversity of the races.[4]

Among the diverse races mentioned were Ngwa and Ndoki men, from over a hundred miles to the south-east. The development of this great trade was in spite of great external insecurity. According to the same report,

> they [the Onitsha people] are at war with all the neighbours, but especially with the people of Aboh, who shut them out from the road to the coast. Besides this they are at enmity with the native of Asaba . . . as well as with the Orba on the eastern frontiers, the Nkure, the Obanikes, the Nsugbes and the Ogidis.[5]

For some time the European traders continued the tradition, bombarding Onitsha in 1879 and capturing the Obi (King) in 1898.[6] But by the end of the century Onitsha was already ahead of its rivals for the expanding trade. The development of road links from Asaba to Lagos and a network of roads from Onitsha to the eastern mainland confirmed its lead.

The commerce of Onitsha centred on the market and European factories. By 1916 the Otu Okwodu site, surrounded by the factories, and the Christian missions could no longer contain the rapidly expanding market, and a move was made to the new site some 250 yards down the river. Until 1928 the market consisted of canoe-side trading sites and private stalls strewn haphazardly on the banks of the Niger.[7] In this year the Native Authority built permanent market stalls and let them to traders, thus bringing a semblance of order into the market scene. By 1939 plans were being made to rebuild the market but these had to be shelved when the world war broke out. After the war the matter was again taken up. In 1950 the Chief Commissioner of the Eastern Provinces approved in principle an application by the Onitsha Native Authority for a loan from government funds and a firm of consulting engineers was retained to plan the reconstruction.

By this time the trade of Onitsha had grown in volume and complexity, mainly as a result of the post-war boom conditions in Nigeria, the great and continuing improvement in road communications between Onitsha and the hinterland, and the wider use of motor vehicles. Records show that the journey from Awgu to Onitsha in 1927 took the greater part of two days, and old traders in Bende Division report that it took three days from there.[8] With motor transport this was cut down to between three and five hours, and no part of the Eastern Provinces was more than ten hours away, the rather slow speed—20 to 30 m.p.h.— and frequent stoppages of the vehicles notwithstanding.

For long-distance trade in foodstuffs the advantages of Onitsha were further enhanced by road transport development, which brought it closer to the inland surplus food producing areas such as the Asaba, Aboh and Ishan Divisions of the Western Region, the Middle Belt, Abakaliki and Ogoja Provinces. For imported goods it improved its competitive position in relation to Port Harcourt and Aba for the hinterland trade.

With increasing trade the wholesale functions of Onitsha became dominant. Traders began to deal in specialist lines and in large quantities. The typical pre-war Onitsha trader was the man selling 'articles', from pomade and hurricane lanterns to pep pills and paper napkins—all on one display table. He began to give way to the dealer in singlets, lantern wicks or bicycle tyres. The tradition of open marketing is not particularly suited to large-scale or permanent wholesale trade. The bigger and more specialist traders began to move out of the market place into the surrounding residential areas where they could get permanent lock-up stores and large business premises. Meanwhile several business premises had also developed on the outskirts of the town—for the timber and carpentry trade, for motor parts and motor repairing services, and for crafts and small-scale industries.

The reconstruction of the market meant the erection of new buildings and stalls. It carried further the trend towards the creation of specialised business districts of which the main market itself was only one. The 'temporary' markets built to accommodate traders during the reconstruction became firmly established and stimulated the development of new business districts around them.

Today we may distinguish the following business districts:

(a) the central shoreline commercial complex,
(b) the residential zone with commercial and industrial frontages,
(c) the Ochanja commercial and industrial area,
(d) the special markets outside (a) and (b),
(e) the neighbourhood markets,
(f) the large-scale industrial zone.

Schematically the districts would appear to fit into the conventional concentric sector pattern noted for urban centres.[9] The major nucleus is region (a); and the Ochanja region forms a secondary nucleus. The large-scale industrial zone is displaced to the outskirts of the business district. For the purposes of this study, however, only the first five districts, which are the main commercial districts, will be discussed.

(a) This is by far the most important area and may be regarded as the central business district. Here the main market is hemmed in by an irregular horseshoe of old mercantile shops and shopping streets. The Ose Okwodu motor park and market, on the site of the original market, extend the complex which is terminated in the north by the premises of the old mercantile firm of John Holt.

Fig. 24 shows the breakdown of the central business district by type of commodity sold or service. It will be noted that functionally the markets are differentiated from the rest of the CBD only by the narrower range of merchandise and services offered. The most widely sold commodities in the main market—textiles, clothing, provisions and domestic hardware—are also the most important commodities in the shopping districts contiguous to it — districts which may indeed be regarded simply as an overflow of the market. The commodities not usually offered in the market place tend to be displaced towards the edge of the CBD where it merges into the outer zone of mixed residential, commercial and industrial establishments. The old mercantile firms sell a wide range of goods, from tractors to textiles, and supply both the market and the shopping streets with trade goods.

The Onitsha market[10] was completed in 1955 at a cost of half a million pounds and covers an area of 15.8 acres. It contains 3,264 market-stalls, each of which yields the council a rental of £2 per month. The number of stall users, however, is much higher. The market comprises two main sectors, an open section typical of Nigerian markets and a covered section, sub-divided as follows:

Open	open stalls	—	1,642 stalls
Section	meat tables	—	116
	lock-up stores	—	24
Covered		—	1,482
Section			

In the open stalls foodstuffs are the principal commodities. Most of the users are small-scale women traders, two or three of whom share a stall so that the number of users is nearer 4,000. Similarly there are about two users per table in the meat section and in the covered section. Thus the number of principals trading in the market stalls is over 7,000. Over 500 traders carry on business in the open spaces, on the waterfront, in Johnson Road and on the Bright Street frontage. The number of sellers in the Onitsha main market is thus, at a conservative estimate, 8,000. Most principals have between one and three assistants or relatives in the stalls so that the number of persons actively engaged in selling in the market is nearer 25,000.

Fig. 25 is a detailed map of the market showing the zoning pattern. The food section marches on the waterfront, where the canoes moor up, bringing in the bulk of the fish as well as grains from up river. Only the high value staples are sold in the main market. Yams, cassava, *gari*, plantains and other foodstuffs are sold in the subsidiary markets. In the general merchandise section, which deals mainly with imported goods, the range of commodities sold is very restricted. Textiles and clothing cover nearly half the stall frontage. Domestic hardware, tinned provisions, drugs and cosmetics come next. The largest group of services are barbers and dress makers but there are numerous shoemakers as well. Of engineering goods and machinery only parts and accessories are sold in the market. Thus several lines in the market are given to bicycle parts, but bicycles are sold in the shopping streets.

It will be noted that the section given to 'articles' is very small. Because Onitsha traders are mainly concerned with breaking bulk rather than with last-stage retail, they tend to specialise in narrow lines. In the section for bicycle parts some specialise in tubes and tyres, others in frames or light fittings. Textiles and clothing are subdivided by fabric and type of garment as well as by whether they are locally made or imported.

By and large the goods sold within the Onitsha market are lower order goods—those which enter into the rural market-place system. Technical consumer goods like bicycles, radio sets and electrical apparatus are sold outside in the shopping streets, although their accessories may be sold within. Similarly, heavy goods like cement and construction material are not sold within the main market. This neat division, which is not so well marked in the other metropolitan market centre of Aba, was made possible by the market reconstruction and by the council's decision, on the advice of the traders themselves, to allocate stalls only to those lines which most needed to be in the market. As a rule the bigger traders stayed out

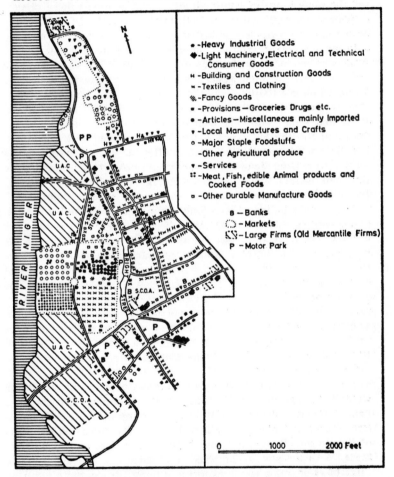

Fig. 24 Onitsha: the central shoreline commercial complex.

of the reconstructed market, preferring to carry on business in the shops. Those of them that retained their market stalls for their own use employed them mainly as display boxes for samples of their wares and to maintain contact with the smaller traders. The trade of the shopping districts is physically an overflow of the market. But it covers a rather wider range of goods, and the units of business are usually larger.

There is marked zoning in the shopping district, though this is less strict than in the market. The streets contiguous with the market sell the same range of commodities as well as high value technical consumer goods. Farther away from the markets the more bulky or specialised goods—e.g. industrial goods and construction material —become more important. These goods require a great deal of display space and here the pressure on space is not so high. There are a few craftsmen and general goods stores alongside the traders.

The wholesale shopping district occupies an area bounded on one side by the main market and on the other by Affar Street, Okwei Road and Bida Road. The overflow of the market into the streets began in the thirties, when a few streets opened in Bright Street, but did not become significant until after the war. Now practically all the street frontage of the district is given over to shops and more than half the total space behind it is storage space. The block between Nottidge Street, Okwei Street and the market is solidly commercial.

The Onitsha indigene has a long commercial tradition behind him and, contrary to what might have been expected otherwise, there has not been much property transfer. The outmoving landlords have preferred to let their houses to traders at competitive prices. Recently, increasing commercial pressure has been forcing vertical expansion on the district and since 1960 a lend-lease scheme has gained popularity. The trader advances money to the landlord to develop his site by putting up a two or three-storey building. The trader occupies some ground floor shops rent free and pays fixed nominal rents on the other rooms for a period varying between 10 and 40 years, after which unencumbered possession reverts to the landlord.[11]

The major expatriate firms retain their beaches on the Niger waterfront, and also have shops in the shopping districts. The United Africa Company (U.A.C.) and the firm of John Holt maintain river fleets plying regularly between the town and the ports of Burutu and Warri and using Onitsha as a base for the up-river trade. With the shift of emphasis to road traffic and a fall in the share of river traffic in the export and import trade, the role of the old mercantile firms in supplying the traders in the market and shopping districts is declining. In line with the general trend the firms are concentrating more on technical and industrial goods which they sell from specialised departments in the shopping districts.

Two of the traditional lines of business—crockery and the standardised textiles such as shirting and drills—are still important, since these are relatively stable lines of business and the goods can be brought in by the cheaper if slower river route without the risk of losing the market. The mercantile firms that do not possess river fleets depend on Port Harcourt and sometimes Lagos for their supplies of imported goods as do both the U.A.C. and John Holt for the fast moving lines. Goods coming to Onitsha through Port Harcourt or Lagos are mainly for retail or sub-wholesale distribution to up-country visitors and smaller traders. The bigger Onitsha traders who have trading arrangements with the mercantile firms usually obtain their supplies from the ports.

(b) The residential zone with commercial and industrial frontages —a zone which forms a horseshoe about the central business district—may be further subdivided into three parts. The first part is near the old market site of Ose Okwodu, between it and Old Market Road. Here there is a concentration of minor industries, arts and crafts—goldsmiths, blacksmiths, tinkers, barbers, carpenters, raffia and basket weavers—associated with the old market. The concentration at the other end of the horseshoe, south of the new market site, is also one of minor industries, arts and crafts. This is associated with the Hausa settlement which grew up near the firms and the market in the first decade of the century. Goldsmiths, tailors making traditional robes, and leather workers are dominant. In both sub-districts between 40% and 60% of the street frontage is occupied by business, but the rest of the area is mainly low-cost residential. The central part, between Iweka Road and Old Market Road is partly an extension of the central shopping district. What gives it character is the concentration of more modern crafts and industrial establishments—painters and commercial artists, carpenters, lorry-body builders, mechanics, panel beaters, battery chargers and tyre retreaders. These activities have a great potential for growth. The first lorry bodies were built in Onitsha in 1948. Today Onitsha is the centre of the industry in Nigeria. From the traditional wooden frames of the well-known 'mammy wagons' the craftsmen now build bus coaches modified from imported prototypes and constructed with tin, corrugated or scrap metal sheets, with locally made leather seats. The furniture industries build cabinets for radiograms as well as chairs and wardrobes. Metal workers make beds (often marketed successfully under prestigious foreign brand names), ornamental gates, construction material, agricultural and household implements. Most of the entrepreneurs struggle on with very little capital but a great deal of native common sense. With a little official encouragement, capital and training, these activities could be made the basis of small-scale industralisation in Eastern Nigeria. At present they are important enough to attract clients from all over Nigeria, persons who would not otherwise have come to the Onitsha market. On the whole the character of this area is more open than that of the shopping districts. Only about 50% to 75% of the street frontage is taken up by shops and service centres, but the larger industries such as motor mechanics, tend to occupy whole allotments.

(c) The Ochanja Commercial and Industrial area is situated on the outskirts of the town, on the Onitsha-Owerri road. It consists of the market and motor park at the centre surrounded by dealers in timber and scrap metal, carpenters and motor mechanics. The timber dealers were the first to establish business here, a site with plenty of room and away from the congested CBD, and so ideal for the creation of both the motor park and the market. The Ochanja market is relatively unimportant in Onitsha's role as a regional market. It caters mainly for the neighbourhood and for the personal needs of travellers. The scrap metal dump is the basis of much of the metal industry of the town. Industrial spare parts derived from them serve a wider market.

(d) Of the special markets, the Ose Okwodu market is complementary to the main market. It is mainly a food market and is divided into a wholesale and retail section. The former is concerned with the major staples—yams, cocoyams, *gari* and cassava as well as plantains—the latter with the whole range of local foodstuffs and condiments. There are also a few stalls for arts and crafts and for general imported goods.

The food market is supplemented by a market on the waterfront for produce brought in by canoe by producers and middlemen. On a busy day fifty to sixty canoes are moored up at the beach, in addition to the regular shuttle of launches and canoes between Asaba and Onitsha.

In addition to the Ose Okwodu waterfront there are two other special markets, both also on the waterfront. One is the small and not very important fish market north of the Nkisi stream. Here fishermen sell their catch and there are a few huts for smoking and selling fish. The other is the wood market on the Ndende terrace behind the Otumoye lake. Much of Onitsha's wood fuel comes by river from the Anambra area, Otu Ocha Aguleri being the principal suppliers.

(*e*) There are three neighbourhood markets, one in the heart of the inland town, the second at Fegge near the waterfront and the third on

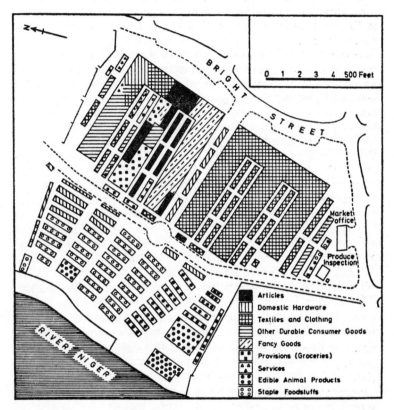

Fig. 25   Area specialisation by goods in Onitsha main market.

the outskirts of the town on the Onitsha-Awka road. The first two are small sauce markets held in the evenings. The Awka road market attracts rural producers from the neighbouring village groups who bring in fruits and vegetables for Onitsha urban consumers and are often confronted here by forestallers, early in the morning.

OTHER METROPOLITAN CENTRES

Aba

The history of Aba, Eastern Nigeria's second largest marketing centre, is not nearly as long as Onitsha's. As a town it dates from the establishment of a Government post here in 1902. As we have seen, the Ngwa people have a tradition of large central markets not attached to any settlements. There was a central market for the Aba na Ohazu clan, the Eke Oha, located on the right bank of the Asa river. The importance of the Eke Oha as a rural market derived partly from the fact that the site was near the head of canoe navigation on the Asa river, which is a tributary of the Imo river. It thus had easy access to the great markets of Azumini and Akwette and the coast. An old Bonny trade settlement on the left bank of the Asa river opposite the Eke Oha where the traders transacted much of their business, has survived to this day. The Eke Oha market was not, however, the chief centre of Ngwa trade. That honour belonged to the Aro-dominated Obegu market, twelve miles to the south. The sack of Obegu paved the way for Eke Oha's dominance. When a Government post was established opposite the Eke Oha market, Aba was set to become a major commercial centre. With the railway came the usual complement of European firms, and road development favoured it even further. More than any other centre in Iboland, Aba owes its eminence to its centrality. It is right in the heart of the coastal plain sands, on flat country, accessible from all sides, and was from the first on one of the major roads of the road network. It may be observed that the location is in an area of relatively low population density between the two high-density nuclei of Eastern Nigeria—the central Ibo uplands and the Annang-Ibibio heartland. From this point of view it is also a border town, a centre of interaction between the two ethnic groups.

As for Aba's urban land use the modern nucleus is the usual complex of railway station, expatriate mercantile firms, administrative offices and market. These firms and administrative offices were aligned between the railway and the Eke Oha market, along the main west-east route through Aba from the Owerri area to Ibibioland. In 1924 the Eke Oha market moved to its present site on Asa Road, the road leading southwards to Port Harcourt. Since then a business district has developed along Asa Road and some of the main streets, so that the CBD extends from the old mercantile firms and along Asa Road down to the townships boundaries. There is the usual segregation between the European Quarters (now Government Residential Area) and the main residential areas. The industrial establishments are located north of the rest of the town, on the banks of the Asa river, or on railway sidings.

Until the second world war the Eke Oha market was the only important market in Aba. With urban expansion, a small rural market at Eziukwu village has become incorporated in the town and now serves as a neighbourhood sauce market. As at Onitsha, post war expansion forced the Eke Oha market to become decentralised. In 1949 a new market was established on the northern outskirts of the town and the food trade was moved there, together with scrap iron, metal empties, bags, and such bulky low-value wares. A separate market was created for bicycle and bicycle parts. Unlike at Onitsha there was no total overhaul of the stall arrangements in the main market. The commodities which were not evacuated from the market have tended to remain in the same general area, with traders in similar goods being attracted to the new stalls.

The movement into the streets adjoining the market has been more selective than at Onitsha, where the pressure on market space was much greater and the reorganisation of the market more complete. Only the larger traders, whose business is mainly sub-wholesaling and who deal in the more specialised lines of trade or seek a status-conscious market (such as fancy stores), have moved onto the streets. Business premises take up some 50% to 80% of the street frontages within one residential block of the main market, beyond which the ratio falls to 30% or less, and the establishments are mainly provision stores, carpenters' sheds and motor mechanics' workshops. Asa Road has the widest variety of shops, from groceries to agricultural machinery, at both wholesale and retail levels. It also has a number of banks, insurance and clearing houses, and advertising, importing and exporting agencies. But the main concentration of these institutions is in Milverton Avenue near the motor park and the old mercantile firms. Wholesale sewing establishments, making dresses, mosquito nets and furniture fittings for sale in the main market and for long-distance trade, are concentrated in the residential blocks east of the market.

Although the reorganisation of the main market was less drastic than that of Onitsha, we may notice some interesting differences between the compositions of the present market and the previous one (Table XVII). Partly because of the movement of certain lines

Table XVII

COMMODITIES SOLD IN ABA MAIN MARKET 1946 AND 1963

Type of Commodities	Percentage of stall Frontage occupied by Sellers		Percentage Change 1963
	1946	1963	
Building and construction	6.0	—	− 6.0
Light machinery	2.9	1.6	− 1.3
Durable manufactured consumer goods	21.0	14.5	− 6.5
Textiles and clothing	32.7	59.0	+26.3
(including second-hand clothing)	(1.0)	(26.6)	(+25.6)
Provisions	2.7	13.0	+10.3
Miscellaneous (mainly imported articles)	19.3	12.5	− 6.8
Agricultural food products	9.1	0.8	− 8.3
Meat, fish, animal products, livestock, cooked foods and condiments	15.2	6.7	− 6.5
Services	9.6	4.4	− 5.2

(The 1946 figures are based on a contemporary map of the market made available by Mr. G. I. Jones; the 1963 figures, on market surveys)

to new markets—the bulk of the foodstuffs, scrap iron, timber and carpentry, bicycle parts and repairs—the range of goods offered in the Eke Oha market is much narrower than in 1946. Textiles, clothing and fabrics alone occupy 59% of the stall frontage, while hardware and imported foods account for another 30%. Thus imported goods take up 89% of the stall frontage as against 73% in 1946. Personal services, arts and crafts are down to 4% from 9% in 1946. The composition of the various sub-groups is also significant, particularly in showing the trend towards specialisation already noted for Umuahia-Ibeku and Onitsha. Thus for clothing, textiles and fabrics, the 1946 map shows only 3 subgroups—textiles and fabrics (20.2%); new clothing, including shoes (12.2%); and a small used-clothing section (0.4%). In 1963 the overall increase in the sector was accounted for by a decline in the general textiles and fabrics section (16.4%); a split between sellers of clothing (9.8%) and shoes (3.5%), their combined share remaining much the same; a new section for jewelry (1.2%); and, most significantly, a phenomenal increase in the used-clothing sector (26.6%). Similarly, for other general consumer goods the provisions section (13%) is more clearly marked out from the miscellaneous section (12.5%) in 1963 than in 1946 when the proportions were 3% and 19% respectively.

Port Harcourt

If Onitsha and Aba are market towns, Port Harcourt is pre-eminently a transportation centre, important for its port and wholesale functions. It has risen very rapidly from its establishment in 1917 to become the second port of Nigeria, outstripping Calabar as the premier port of Eastern Nigeria and gaining a share of the Northern Nigerian traffic. Today the town is the fastest growing urban settlement in Nigeria, a growth which it owes to the numerous industries attracted to the port since the fifties. Much of the increasing population is absorbed by dormitories and suburbs extending northwards along the Port Harcourt-Aba road from Diobu to Obigbo, 12 miles away.

Turning now to the urban land-use pattern of the municipal area of Port Harcourt, there are three large markets: the main market, as usual in the central business district comprising the transportation terminals and the shopping districts; the Diobu market at the north western boundary, which serves the suburban area around it; and a 'new market', built in 1950 in the heart of the main residential area. In addition there are small markets on the creeks: waterside markets for trade with the Kalabari communities and known after their principal users as Okrika, Bonny and Abonema waterside markets.

Both the main market and the Diobu market show in the wider range of commodities offered the unspecialised nature of their business, which is mainly last-stage retail. Diobu market is of special importance for its scrap metal and building materials section. New market is a specialised food market, the most important section of which is the dried fish section at which there are wholesale transactions in dried fish brought in by fishermen and traders from the creeks, and bought by inland traders. The waterfront markets are mainly for small-scale trade—purchases of fish and fuel (mangrove wood) brought in by Kalabari people, and sale of vegetables and sauce ingredients.

Services are not important in any of the markets. Rather, barbers, goldsmiths, cobblers, tailors, bicycle repairers and the like are to be found in the major streets of the main residential areas, which also have numerous small shops selling provisions. Minor industries, arts and crafts are concentrated in the Diobu suburb lending support to the municipal areas proud claim to being a 'garden city'.

For the long-distance wholesale or sub-wholesale trade in imported goods the markets of Port Harcourt are relatively unimportant.

Most of the business takes place in the warehouses of the large expatriate firms, concentrated in Kingsway Road, as well as in those of the newer indigenous firms concentrated in factory and industry roads, west of the main market, and in Aggrey Club, Potts-Johnson and Hospital Roads in the main residential area. The actual area occupied by business is small relative to the volume of business transacted. This is largely because many of the businessmen are importers and brokers dealing with traders from up-country—Onitsha, Aba, Jos and smaller centres. They operate from their offices and frequently negotiate for direct clearance of foods from port or warehouses by their clients, and keep only a minimum of stock on premises—as samples and for sub-wholesale or retail trade.

Enugu

As the political capital of Eastern Nigeria, Enugu has become the regional centre of financial and business administration. The concentration of highly paid civil servants, contractors, politicians and other professionals has created a rich market for high value consumer goods. Thus there is a large number of salesrooms for motor vehicles and other technical consumer goods, department stores, bookshops, fashion houses and various services.

As a regional centre for trade the town is of secondary importance. For the trade in general imported consumer goods, the area west of Enugu, on the Nsukka-Awgu plateau, is oriented more to Onitsha than to Enugu. The sparsely populated country to the east does not generate much trade and, in any case, the bigger traders from here by-pass Enugu to the principal source at Onitsha, a tendency which is encouraged by the excellent road connection between Enugu and Onitsha. The town provides an important market for the produce of the surrounding countryside, mainly cassava and vegetables. But for the high value staples, yams, *gari* and rice, it depends on Onitsha, even for some produced in the east. Thus yams and rice bulked at Abakaliki and by-passing Enugu, are sold at Onitsha, and are often bought there by Enugu traders for retail distribution. Similarly, much of the produce brought by rail to Enugu from the Northern Region—rice, fish and onions—is sent direct to Onitsha. For the export trade Enugu is a minor centre, ranking with nearby Agbani station in the amount of palm produce graded by the Marketing Board.

As for the urban land-use pattern of Enugu, the nucleus of the central business district comprises the trilogy of railway station, old mercantile firms and market, to which have been added since the war the new finance houses and business establishments. There is an overflow of these establishments into Ogui road. A number of streets in the main residential area have shopping frontages. The main market is a general-purpose market like that of Port Harcourt. It is now being reconstructed. The old market had 2,960 stalls, including 79 timber stalls, 36 meat stalls and a chaotic juxtaposition of stalls for various goods. One of the aims of the reconstruction is to introduce rational zoning.

There are five other markets in the main residential area. Two of them are special markets at Ogbette, a wood fuel market and an industrial market for mechanics, metalworkers, tradesmen, motor parts and metal scrap. The other three are neighbourhood markets in the older parts of the residential area, at Asata, Ogui and Ogui-urban districts. It is interesting to observe that two attempts to establish a neighbourhood market in the new residential area of Uwani, inhabited mainly by young, white-collar workers, many of them unmarried, have been unsuccessful. These workers tend to buy their foodstuffs from the main market or from women peddlers who hawk their wares from door to door.

The importance of shopping in Enugu highlights a feature which may be observed by the more varied character of the other three cities: the effect of income levels and social distinctions on the use of various exchange institutions. The market place has the advantage over a business street in offering a wide variety of goods at relatively low prices. Its appeal is to a mass market. Functionally, it is the equivalent of a supermarket, but it is run by thousands of competing managers. Market conditions approach the classical ideal, the open interplay of demand and supply, buyers and sellers bargaining publicly in the hearing of competitors and passers-by. While the housewife may take particular pleasure in pitting her wits against the wily trader and the poor man may find that the marginal penny makes a great difference, the white-collar worker is often prepared to discount the lower prices for the savings in time and nerves as well as the greater prestige of 'buying from Collins'. Secondly, in the market place the range of choice within a commodity group is narrow, restricted to the popular brands and standard items. The more stylish, more expensive goods are generally to be found in the shops. As the shopping district develops, more and more of the higher-priced goods move into it. Heavy industrial goods and some delicate instruments such as tape recorders rarely enter the market place to start with. In a town where traders constitute a large part of the population, such as Onitsha, Aba or Umuahia-Ibeku, the centre of gravity for marketing is within or near the main market and the development of neighbourhood shopping districts is retarded. The extensive shopping districts of Onitsha are geared more to the central marketing functions of the city than to serving the urban population.

*   *   *

To summarise on metropolitan centres, the four cities discussed here show marked contrasts in the development and patterns of trade and marketing. In Onitsha and Aba the main markets play a vital part in the roles of the cities as trading centres. In Port Harcourt and Enugu this part is played mainly by modern-type central-place institutions, while urban retail functions are dominant in the markets. At Enugu the balance has shifted away from the market place to the shopping districts, even for the retail trade. The growth of the non-commercial sector of the urban population (i.e. the proportional increase in the industrial and professional population) is likely to accelerate the trend towards more shopping here, as in other towns.

NOTES

1. Netherlands Engineering Consultants (NEDCO), *River studies and recommendations on improvement of Niger and Benue.* Amsterdam, 1959.
2. N. Ogo Ibeziako, *Some aspects of ancient civilization: the founder and some Celebrities of Onitsha.* Onitsha, 1937.
3. K. O. Dike, *Trade and politics in the Niger Delta,* 1830-1885. Oxford, 1956.
4. Rev. Adjai Crowther, in *Church Missionary Intelligencer,* 1857.
5. Ibid.
6. N. Ogo Ibeziako, op. cit.
7. O. Nzekwu, 'West Africa's largest market: Onitsha', *Nigeria,* No. 65, 1960.
8. M. Macgregor, *Intelligence Report* on Awgu Division, 1927, ref. 11/20681 in Ibadan Archives.
9. H. Hoyt, *The structure and growth of residential neighbourhoods in American cities.* Washington, 1939.

Additional Bibliography

Apart from the books, articles and unpublished materials referred to in the notes at the end of each chapter, mention must also be made of the following:

C. S. Belshaw, *Traditional markets and modern exchange*, New York, 1965.

B. J. L. Berry, *Geography of market centres and retail distribution*, New York, 1967.

B. J. L. Berry and A. Pred, *Central place studies*, Philadelphia, 1965.

T. L. V. Blair, *Marketing in Africa*, London, 1965.

A. Cohen, 'The social organization of credit in a West African Cattle Market', *Africa*, 35, 1965.

A. Cohen, 'The politics of the Kola Trade', *Africa*, 36, 1966.

C. Geertz, *Pedlers and Princes*, Chicago, 1963.

Polly Hill, 'Markets in Africa', *Journal of Modern African Studies*, 1, 1963.

Polly Hill, 'Notes on traditional market authority and market periodicity in West Africa', *Journal of African History*, 7, 1966.

Polly Hill, 'Landlords and brokers: a West African trading system', *Cashiers d'Etudes Africaines*, 6, 1966.

A. L. Mabogunje, 'The evolution and analysis of the retail structure of Lagos, Nigeria', *Economic Geography*, 40, 1964.

H. W. Ord *et alia* (eds.), *Markets and marketing in West Africa*, Edinburgh, 1966.

Index

Aba, 130, 145-7, 170, 175, 178, 190-1, 227-32, 244-6
Age specialization, 76-7
Areal specialization, 72, 77-9, 84
Arochuku system, 132-6, 139, 142, 209
Awka system, 131-2, 174

Badagry, 18, 25, 27-8, 34-6, 40-1, 43-4, 46, 52, 55, 64, 79
Barter, 44
Beans, 71, 105
Bulking, 58, 77-8, 80, 86, 179

Central-place theory, ix-x, 63, 80, 152-8, 160-3
Christianity, 24, 52-3
Cocoa, 15-16, 18, 42-3, 71, 90
Commodity structure, 29, 78-9, 242
Cowrie, 44-6, 143

Dahomey, 4-11, 19, 26, 28, 36, 63, 106
Daily markets, x, 59, 67-8, 80-4, 85-7, 97-103
Diet, 82, 103
Distances travelled to market, 62-3, 73, 215-26

Economic sense, 91-3
Enugu, 145, 160, 176, 190, 248-50
European impact, x, 33-47, 83-4, 139-45

Fairs, 30, 96, 135-8
Fetish, 52
Forestalling, 76, 80, 83, 177, 180

Frequency of market visits, 73-4, 92, 216-26

Guilds, 55-6

Hausa communities, 9, 38, 78, 81, 99, 102, 144-5

Ibadan, x, 7, 11-14, 28, 30, 34, 37-40, 55, 61, 66, 73, 80, 94-109, 175
Iboland, definition of, 113
    ecological regions, 119-21
    economic life, 118-24
    natural environment, 113-6
    population distribution, 116-8
    settlement pattern, 118 126-7, 146-7, 160-6
    social units, 126-7
Industries, craft, 16-17, 46, 71, 73, 82, 84, 87, 95-6, 119, 121-2
    factory, 17, 122-3, 185
Insecurity, 24-5, 33, 41, 52
Islam, 52-3
Itinerant trading, 71-3, 76-7, 173, 183

Kano, 71, 110, 175
Kola, 16, 38, 43, 71, 77, 79, 81, 99, 102, 132

Lagos, 4, 9, 13, 34, 41, 50, 59, 67, 85, 91, 103, 180, 192, 196

Market, definition of, ix, 19
    distribution, 61-7, 168-71
    origins, ix-x, 24-31, 64-6
    regions, 170-1
    ring (cycle or circuit), 66-7, 71-6, 94, 206-7, 214-5

253

typology, 58-9, 68, 94
Marketing Boards, 19, 182-5
Measures, 88, 91
Medieval Europe, x, xii, 30-1, 54-5, 60, 62-3, 77, 85, 89
Money economy, 33, 44-7, 143
Morning markets, 67-8, 80, 86, 97-9

Niger River, 3, 9, 28, 38, 113, 139-41, 165, 232-43
Night markets, 59, 68, 81-2, 102-3

Onitsha, 118, 122, 130, 160-1, 170, 191, 194, 196-7, 232-43
Organization of markets, 55-6, 89-91

Palm produce, 15, 42, 71, 97, 119, 139-40, 185-90, 205
Periodic markets, x, 59-67, 71-9, 82, 85-7, 94-7, 129, 155-60, 210-1, 216-26
Port Harcourt, 144, 160-1, 179, 190-4, 196, 247-8
Prices, 44, 72, 76, 88-91, 103, 157, 186-90

Rice   179-84

Scale markets, 43-4
Shops, retail, x, 84-5, 106-8, 195, 202

Slaving, 9, 25-7, 46, 136-9

Social and political elements, 50-6, 66, 87, 89, 123, 126-7, 173-6, 193
Storage facilities, 74, 90, 101

Tiv, 51, 58, 113, 143
Togo, 7, 9, 76
Trade, long-distance, 27-31, 76, 83, 132-6, 155
    local, 17, 19-21
Transport, headloading, 25-6, 35, 74-5, 84
    roads, 35-8, 40-1, 75, 84, 94, 188-90, 201-202, 210, 211
    railways, 38-40, 83, 149, 227-10
    water, 35, 38, 75

Ugwueke na Eweukwu, 157, 207-15
Umuahia-Ibeku, 118, 195, 227-32
Umunakanu, 200-7
Urbanism, 12-13, 54-5, 58-9, 67-8, 106-8, 152-5, 164-5, 227-50

Women, place of, 17, 24, 50-2, 73, 76, 174

Yorubaland, definition of, 3, 7
    economic life, 15-20
    natural environment, 3-7
    people of, 7-14, 61-2
    population distribution, 11-14
    urbanism, 12-13